AN INTRODUCTION

TO THE

STUDY OF THE CONSTITUTION

A Study showing the play of Physical and Social Factors in the Creation of Institutional Law

BY MORRIS M. COHN
Attorney-at-Law

THE LAWBOOK EXCHANGE, LTD.

UNION, NEW JERSEY

2000

ISBN 1-58477-032-5

Printed in the United States of America
On Acid-Free Paper

The Lawbook Exchange, Ltd.
965 Jefferson Avenue
Union, New Jersey 07083-8605

Please see catalogue at rear of this volume
or our website http://www.lawbookexchange.com
for a selection of our other reprints.

Library of Congress Cataloging-in-Publication Data

Cohn, Morris M., 1952-1922.
An introduction to the study of the constitution : a study showing the play of physical and social factors in the creation of institutional law / by Morris M. Cohn.
p. cm.
Originally published: Baltimore : Johns Hopkins Press, 1892, in series: Johns Hopkins University studies in historical and political science. Extra volumes : 12.
Includes bibliographical references and index.
ISBN 1-58477-032-5 (acid-free paper)
1. Constitutional law—United States. 2. Constitutional history--United States. I. Title.
KF4550.C56 1999
342.73'02—dc21 99-38730
CIP

AN INTRODUCTION

TO THE

STUDY OF THE CONSTITUTION

A Study showing the play of Physical and Social Factors in the Creation of Institutional Law

By MORRIS M. COHN
Attorney-at-Law

BALTIMORE
The Johns Hopkins Press
1892

THE FRIEDENWALD CO., PRINTERS,
BALTIMORE.

PREFACE.

In submitting the following work to the public a few words of explanation may not be out of place. It was written for the purpose of bringing before the student and reader of our American constitutional system a mass of information which at present lies scattered among the productions of many different writers, inquirers and thinkers. While it is not as serviceable a work to the active legal practitioner as so-called practical books may be, yet I believe it may lay claim to being of some use.

The scope of the present work embraces the presentation of what may tend to produce a better understanding of all that is implied in the existence of the Government of the United States of North America. It aims to trace the play of physical and social factors in the production of law in general, including constitutional law. A preliminary chapter indicates the faulty definitions of law which have been prevalent; under no one of which constitutional law can be fairly embraced. The play of physical and social factors as regards inorganic and organic conditions (as exemplified in the individual and in the aggregations of human beings, and as illustrated in the law of property, domestic relations, including the laws of succession, the law of obligations, the law of procedure and constitutional law, and in the formation of the Constitution of the United States), forms the burden of this work.

The reflections thus given are the outcome of years of close study and thought. The belief early formed in my legal studies, that the Constitution of the United States was one out of many; and could have no existence save in connection with well settled and somewhat diversely governed communities which preceded it, has grown into an unalterable conviction. Repeated expressions of federal tribunals bear it out.[1]

In this connection I desire to extend my sincerest thanks to Dr. Herbert B. Adams, of Johns Hopkins University, for valuable suggestions relating to this work, for kind words of encouragement, and other services.

---

[1] Texas *v.* White, 7 Wall., p. 700.

TABLE OF CONTENTS.

CHAPTER I.

LAW AND SOVEREIGNTY.

CHAPTER II.

PHYSICAL AND SOCIAL FACTORS OF LAW.

CHAPTER IV.

THE EVIDENCES OF PHYSICAL AND SOCIAL FACTORS IN CONSTITUTIONAL LAW.

CHAPTER V.

EVIDENCES OF PHYSICAL AND SOCIAL GROWTH IN THE CONSTITUTION OF THE UNITED STATES.

AN INTRODUCTION TO THE STUDY OF THE CONSTITUTION.

CHAPTER I.

LAW AND SOVEREIGNTY.

Much depends upon the mode in which one approaches the subject of law, in determining what signification is to be given to the term. As the notion of "sovereignty" has been found inadequate to account for all rules which may be embraced under the general designation of law,[1] it has become needful to reform the current definition in so far as it implies sovereignty at all times. As laws in their earliest forms found expression through priests or in the enforcement of possessions or in some practical mode of action without the aid of a sovereign body, and before any definite political organisms had yet grown up, sovereignty could not well be predicated of them.[2] Sovereignty itself is not represented by a word finding its use in ancient tongues; it is a word of feudal origin.[3] Its implications—the correlations it involves—testify to its dependence on certain elements, chief among which is the series of observances and customs giving charac-

[1] Bliss, Sovereignty, Chap. I.; Clark, Practical Jurisprudence, 154, 155; Maine, Early History of Institutions, Lectures XII., XIII.; Post, Bausteine für eine allgemeine Rechtswissenschaft, Vol. II., §103 *seq.*

[2] Clark, *loc. cit.*; Maine, Early History of Institutions, Lectures XII., XIII.; Fustel de Coulanges, Ancient City, Book III., Chap. XI.; Spencer, Principles of Sociology, Vol. II., Part V., Chaps. XIII. and XIV.

[3] Bliss, Sovereignty, Chap. I., par. 2. See opinion of Wilson, J., in Chisolm v. Georgia, 2 Dallas, 419; Bluntschli, Theory of the State, 463.

ter to the agent that in certain essentials claims to exercise it. Sovereignty depends upon law.[1] Anarchy is a condition implying absence of government, in which, as during the French Revolution, no one can be claimed to be sovereign; that is, a condition of lawlessness which inherently contradicts the possibility of a controlling agency.

Though it is claimed that in the United States, and in democracies, the people are sovereign, they are still not the legislators who *consciously* enact laws, nor are they in fact sovereign in any absolute sense.[2] They yield to the customs they have inherited, they do not ordinarily govern in any revolutionary way; their leading spirits control them; they build upon the family relationships which antedated them, upon the results of larger social experiences they have received from their ancestors and which they have experienced themselves. Some system of order, and with it a general consciousness of self-interest which is promoted by this system, lies at the base of every political organism. A man is sovereign over himself, but not over others, and if he aims to discharge his social obligations he must needs conform his activity, his will, and his intellect to the restraints these put upon him, and these restraints are the product of association, taking on different forms at different stages or under diverse circumstances, as amenable to the modifications of social development and physical environment as languages and religions and aptitudes are. Sovereignty is a growth, and it can be only applied relatively. In the United States

---

[1] Smith, Right and Law, §502. See Maine, Popular Government, Index "Sovereignty"; Burgess, Polit. Sc. and Cons. Law, Part II., Chap. II. Mr. Burgess, it seems to me, has left little in his notion of sovereignty, except an empty illusion.

[2] Bliss, Sovereignty, p. 15 *seq.*; Smith, Right and Law, Chap. V.; Woolsey, Political Science, Vol. I., §§72, 73; Maine, Popular Government, Essay I., pp. 7, 8; Lieber, Civil Liberty and Self-Government, 152, also Chap. XXV. *seq.*; Bluntschli, Theory of the State, Book II.; Bryce, American Commonwealth, Vol. I., 408 *seq.*; Wharton, American Law, §596; Clark, Practical Jurisprudence, Chap. XIV.

it does not reside in the people by virtue of any antecedent development nor by governmental recognition. The people have not reserved the power to annihilate the government. They can make changes in the Federal Constitution only in the mode prescribed by that constitution.[1] The Federal Government is not absolute sovereign, for it cannot annihilate the States.[2] The States are not so because within the grant of its power the Federal Government is superior to them.[3]

The idea of sovereignty being *inherently* implied in law is therefore not borne out by the facts of history or experience. It presumes the anterior existence of laws or their equivalents.[4] And it grows, in a later stage of development, with the expansion of jurisprudence. It is a somewhat vague term, for it assumes the existence of absolute power—which, however justifiable in theory, does not exist in fact—in communities where relative rights, powers and functions, conditionating one another, must, in order to the existence of a political body, exist.[5]

Laws may be enacted by legislative bodies; so may words be coined by learned scientists and scholars, and thought may be directed in certain channels by such minds as Moses, Lycurgus, Solon; but the great mass of law, the great bodies of usages and customs, whether crystallized by the formulations of legislative or judicial bodies, pass current because they symbolize the necessities, the feelings, the energies of mankind, in the course of a continuous social life; usages and customs which may involve the rise and fall of many social aggregates, a continuous social life which is not bounded by decades, generations or centuries.

---

[1] Constitution of the United States, Art. V. *Compare* Articles of Confederation, Art. XIII.

[2] *Ibid.*, Article IV., Secs. 3 and 4; also, Art. V.

[3] Art. VI., Sec. 2.

[4] See Wharton, Commentaries on American Law, §63, also p. 131.

[5] Wharton, *ubi supra*, Chap. III.; Smith, Right and Law, §502.

Law has been variously accounted for—internal desire to do right, consensus of the will of the members of the political aggregate, development of the aggregate from the family, divine inspiration, the need of protecting the weak against the strong, social contract, benevolent feelings, selfishness, utility, evolution of social forms and needs, national conscience, have each been credited with the principal part in its origination. Sometimes more than one of these views is utilized to account for it.[1]

We can obtain a better idea of the producing causes of law if we bear in mind that invention has played its largest part in the production of law in the latest development of statehood. Now the state is itself an entity of growth. The term represents political bodies as widely separated in character as the municipal sway of ancient Greek cities and modern nations.[2] Aristotle viewed it, with the best lights he had before him, in its component parts, and among its fundamental elements he found the *οἶκος* (family), which he ascribed to the animal impulse of cohabitation, to propagate species and give mutual support. From thence the natural course of extension and growth was, in his view, through the *κώμη* (village community) to the formation of village connections and an organic whole compounded of many village communities. This he called *πόλις* (the city-state). He regarded the state as a work of nature; and man he regarded not only as a social, but also as a political animal. A government complete in itself, in his judgment, constituted the best result of human development and existence.[3] Aristotle's knowledge, however acute his powers of observa-

[1] Holtzendorf, Encyclopædia, Systematischer Theil, Art. I., by Dr. A. Geyer; Wharton, Commentaries on American Law, Chap. II.; Woolsey, Political Science, Part II., Chap. I.; Clark, Practical Jurisprudence, Part I., Chap. VIII.

[2] The Indian tribes have been treated as equivalent to States by the Supreme Court of the United States. See 117 U. S. Rep. 288; 17 Wall. 211.

[3] Politics, Book I., Chaps. I. and II. See Chap. IV., *post*.

tion, did not extend beyond the ancient city-state and amphictyonic leagues of cities; leagues based on religious motives, though serving larger and more extended cohesive purposes. In his day no doubt *θέμιστες* (injunctions, judgments, prescribed rules) were known;[1] yet the general body of what we embrace under the head of law was customs and usages (*νόμοι*). Outside of what came from the gods through the Themis—and these ordinances were largely copied after the observances of the people—the usages and customs of the people in their relation to herding of cattle, or husbandry, or navigation, or commerce, or in relation to their changing governors who rose to greater power as the cities grew and extended, constituted the body of the law (*νόμος*). The history of these terms bears out this contention.[2] In Roman law *jus* antedated *lex*; for while the former related to that which was orderly, fitting, customary,[3] the latter came into use as a method of legislation or codification of usages,[4] or of enactments not depending upon usages.

That usages and customs, such as prevail among savage races to-day, were the current expressions in ancient times, no longer admits of doubt.[5] They never fully ceased to represent the whole sum of rules until political aggregates, having a capacity for permanent territory, a settled abode, and some

---

[1] *θέμις* in early Greek history and *fas* in early Italian history disclose the early influence of priests in the creation of injunctions. *Cf.* Leist, Graeco-Ital. Rechtsg., 205 *seq.*, §36, 533 *seq.* For similar phenomena among early Semites see Wellhausen, Hist. of Israel, 394, 395.

[2] Clark, Practical Jurisprudence, Part I., Chap. IV. See Coulanges, Ancient City, Book III., Chap. XI.; *cf.* Leist, Graeco-Ital. Rechtsg., 533 *seq.*, and compare Schrader, Sprachv. u. Urg., 201; same, Handelsg. u. Warenk., 8.

[3] Clark, *supra*, Part I., Chap. II.; also Part I., Chap. VII.

[4] *Ibid.*, Part I., Chap. III.

[5] Spencer, Principles of Sociology, Vol. II., Part V., Chap. XIV.; Post, Ursprung des Rechts, Introduction *seq.*; same, Bausteine für eine allgemeine Rechtswissenschaft, Chap. I.; Maine, Early Law and Custom. The earliest communities of India, Greece and Italy, we are now assured, had no law. *Cf.* Schrader, Sprachvergleichung u. Urgeschichte, 355.

form of governmental administration, came into vogue. Even then they were not superseded. The laws peculiar to statehood built upon them depended upon them; courts enforced them; legislatures only fragmentarily superseded them.[1] The largest dissolving and disintegrating factors which ever destroyed them were new social impulses, producing new needs, new customs, new observances. The forms of organization of earliest or most primitive peoples preclude the thought of sovereignty or laws; they admit of no conception going beyond the habits which spontaneously grow up.[2] Professor Clark says that "in the unconscious definitions of law furnished by [the] early names for it . . . different conceptions of law present themselves, not only in different nations, but in the same. The nearest approximation to a uniform or pervading idea is certainly not so much that of *enactment, position* and *command,* as of *antiquity, general approval* and *usage*: where an original notion of *ordinance* does appear, it is not human, but divine."[3]

From this plane of observation of Aristotle, some of the most modern of our writers upon the history of society, politics and law have not materially departed.[4] But the family organization from which these start is not the modern family. It is a growth depending upon association of individuals that had its beginning in cohabitation and carnal intercourse, but which grew by adoption or natural increase

---

[1] *Cf.* authorities in preceding note; also Bastian, Rechtsverhältnisse.

[2] Post, Bausteine, etc., I., §§ 1 to 16; same, Ursprung des Rechts, *passim*; Schrader, Sprachvergleichung u. Urgeschichte, 568 *seq.* See for a description of legal development, which attaches, however, too much importance to sacred factors, Leist, Graeco-Ital. Rechtsg., Book III.

[3] Clark, Practical Jurisprudence, Part I., Chap. VII., 90; Post, Bausteine, etc., Vol. I., §16 *seq.*; Leist, Graeco-Ital. R. G., Book III., Part II.; but see *Ibid.* §81 and Anmerkung 32, p. 760 *seq.* See *infra.*

[4] See Maine, Ancient Law, 128, 250; same, Village Communities; Early History of Institutions, Lec. III.; Early Law and Custom, Chap. III. *seq.*; Hearn, Aryan Household; Woolsey, Political Science, Part III., §138 *seq.* See especially Spencer, Principles of Sociology, Vol. II., Part V., Chap. V.

and depended originally upon ties of consanguinity.[1] Consanguinity became the sole test when priestly influence, co-operating with the dissolution of the tribe and village community, occasioned by their merging into the state organism, destroyed the integrity of the early group.[2]

In Roman law, evidences of the growth of law from early conditions are still extant. Take that system of law in its first stages of self-conscious expression, when the rules of action were made known and realized through procedure—the *actio sacramenti*. This brings before us in its symbolic forms the early combat, settlement of rights by recourse to arms (of which the wager of battle known to early English law, and also the grand assize, which comprised an assembly of knights in arms, as in the days when justice and war went together, were relics), and the voluntary recourse, generally of the weaker *injured* party, to the deposit of a wager and the arbitrament of the tribe.[3] This action lay not in earliest

---

[1] Starcke, Primitive Family (Int. Sc. Series), Sec. II., Chap. VIII.; Spencer, Principles of Sociology, Part III., Chap. III.; W. Robertson Smith, The Religion of the Semites, 260; same, Kinship in Arabia; Maine, Ancient Law, Chap. V., 128; same, Early Law and Custom, 200, 201; Hearn, Aryan Household, Chaps. III. and VII.; Woolsey, Political Science, Vol. I., §42 *seq.*; Amos, Science of Law, 120; McLennan, Primitive Marriage; Bachofen, Das Mutterrecht. See *post*, Chapter II., Sec. 2 and Chap. IV. No better illustrations of the growth from the matriarchal to the patriarchal state have been given, so far as my researches have disclosed, than in Dr. Smith's Kinship in Arabia.

[2] See Hearn, Aryan Household, 473 *seq.*; Starcke, Primitive Family, Sec. II., Chap. VIII. It required both a dissolution of the household group produced by *vis major*, and a conception of blood relationship according to formal classifications, based on natural ties of affection, which priestly classes were principally competent to accomplish, to produce the change. See for laws of early family life growing out of prevailing customs after the church had acted upon them, Essays in Anglo-Saxon Law, 121 *seq.*

[3] Siegel has given a history of the early procedure of the Germanic tribes: Siegel, Des deutschen Gerichtsverfahrens, especially §§1 to 6 inclusive. The action referred to emanated from the Pontifical College, and hence, as early expressions of law in formal modes in all cases, was the formulation devised by priests. Ihering, Geist des römischen Rechts, Vol. I., 298 *seq.*, 307 *seq.* See *post*, Chap. III., Sec. 4. For the still earlier procedure, see Leist, Graeco-Ital. R. G., Book II., Part III.; Book III., Part II.

tribal days, but when the community had developed a sufficiently organized political unit to give and enforce a means of redress. No consciousness of damages beyond the thing itself is observed in the earlier form of action. It has analogies in the early tribal life of other peoples and in the English remedy of distress and replevin.[1] The thing being brought before the magistrate (*in jure*), the claimant appeared; each touched it with a rod (*vindicta* or *festuca*); each person laid claim to the thing, seized hold of the thing claimed; the magistrate then interposed his rod (*vindicatio*).[2] When the thing could not be brought into court, something was brought in to represent it, as a piece of turf, a twig, a brick, one sheep, etc.[3] There is an obliviousness to anything which is not tangible, seizable, within the capacity of the senses to lay hold of. The idea of right to compensation for a mere damage without reference to a return of a thing *in specie* seems not yet to have been thought of. And so, too, is the early procedure of the Anglo-Saxon.[4]

Another relic of early life is to be found in the Roman law of possession. Early possession formed the criterion of property.[5]

---

[1] See Maine, Early History of Institutions, Lecture IX. See *post*, Chap. III., Sec. 4.

[2] The judge was merely selected to deliver his opinion regarding the title to the thing in dispute. He could not cite them to appear, or compel appearance: Ihering, Geist des röm. Rechts, Vol. I., 172. And he was selected from among the priests: *Ibid.*, Vol. I., 298. Of the use of the spear in Roman law, as a symbol of the early militant life, and for other evidences of that life, see Ihering, Geist, etc., Vol. I., 113 *seq.* The symbol of ownership was the spear (*Ibid.*). The growth of the *vindicta* from the spear and as a relic of early combat is shown by the same excellent authority (*Ibid.*, Vol. I., 163). The *actio sacramenti* was not a condemnation of self-help or revenge, but a substitute therefor. See Siegel, *supra.* For further illustrations of similar development upon an extensive scale, see Spencer's Principles of Sociology, Vol. II., Part V., Chap. XIII.; also Maine, Early History of Institutions, Lecture IX.

[3] See introduction to Sanders' Justinian, 50.

[4] Essays in Anglo-Saxon Law, 241; Maine, *loc. cit.*

[5] Essays in Anglo-Saxon Law, 241; Amos, Systematic View of the Science of Jurisprudence, pp. 153 *seq.*; Ihering, Besitzwille, pp. 326 *seq.*

Ownership, in so far as it came to exist outside of mere possession, was a later development, and took the shape in law of other forms—a facilitation of proof of such a title.[1] Possession found its first departure in Roman law, in the feeling that the household serf's possession was that of the master; because the serf's identity was lost in that of the master.[2] It further expanded to embrace landed property held under the master by persons holding it for stipulated services or rents, from which the master could oust them as he could the serf.[3] In German and English law, when the serf came to receive some recognition on his own account—which he did as the city life dissolved the elements of the household group and became the medium of independent rights—the notion of representative holding still further expanded. The commercial world still further expanded it in the shape of bailments.[4] The first form of holding was a product of *status*, the later was a form of *contract;* the former represents the early savage, barbarian, or tribal condition, and the absence of commerce and commercial forms of contract; the later ignored the ties and sentiment going with *status*, in the interest of traffic.[5] How leasehold developed on the Continent with the growth of cities is shown by Arnold.[6] Possession, in the absence of countervailing evidence, is still sufficient evidence of ownership in English and American jurisprudence.[7]

---

[1] Ihering, Grund des Besitzes.

[2] Ihering, Besitzwille, Chapters VII., VIII.

[3] *Ibid.*, Chap. VIII.

[4] For a history of bailment in English law, see Holmes, Common Law, Lecture V. Agents are an expansion of the law of master and servant: *Ibid.*, Lecture VI., p. 228.

[5] For a more extended notice of the difference between status and contract, and the greater antiquity of the former, see Maine, Ancient Law, Chap. V., 164, 165; Spencer, Principles of Sociology, Vol. II., Part V., Chaps. XVII., XVIII. Ihering affirms that the household is the basis of important and far-reaching legal classifications: Besitzwille, 103 *seq.*

[6] Arnold, Geschichte des Eigenthums in D. S., Chaps. IV., V., VI.

[7] 2 Wharton, Evidence, §§1331, 1332; 1 Taylor, Evidence, §123.

The *status*[1] of marriage in Roman law was attained by *coemptio*, a fictitious sale;[2] by *confarreatio*, in which none but those to whom the *jus sacrum* was open could take part; and by *usus*, that is, by cohabitation with the intention of forming a marriage.[3] It might be a sale, and as such a relic of transfer by barter—a substitute for capture—prevalent among somewhat developed tribes; it might be a mutual living together to form a legal family, which also constituted marriage at common law;[4] or it was a sacred ceremony, initiated by the pontifical (the priestly) class, as has become recognized in modern jurisprudence.[5]

In fact, law has come up in the body of habits, customs and observances of a given people;[6] but as courts and, later, legislatures came to give these form and new expression, came to expand the formal code, the great movement of the community in its ceaseless activity was lost sight of by the exponents and students of the letter of the law, who devoted a too exclusive attention to its form rather than the history of its existence.

---

[1] It is still a *status*. See Bishop, Married Women; Wharton, Commentaries on American Law, §271.

[2] There are relics of a similar condition among many people, including Anglo-Saxons. See Essays in Anglo-Saxon Law, p. 163; Post, Ursprung des Rechts, 54; same, Bausteine, §§30, 33; Engel, Ursprung der Familie, 32; Spencer, Principles of Sociology, Part III., Chap. X.; Schrader, Sprachv. u. Urg., 550.

[3] Sanders' Justinian, Lib. I., Tit. X., Note 93.

[4] James Schouler, Law of Husband and Wife, §§31, 32, 33.

[5] *Ibid.*, §34.

[6] Savigny, Heutigen römischen Rechts, Vol. I., §7; Holtzendorf, Encyclopædia, Syst. Theil, pp. 101–105, §§1, 2; Puchta, Institutionen, Vol. I., §§12, 13; Spencer, Principles of Sociology, Vol. II., §529 *seq.* Fustel de Coulanges (Ancient City, Book II., Chap. VIII.), who bases the growth of civil institutions upon family groupings organized for the purpose of remembering and worshiping dead chiefs, and who accords the largest effect to religious feeling, contends that "ancient law was not the work of a legislator; it was, on the contrary, imposed on the legislator. It had its birth in the family. It *sprang up spontaneously* from ancient principles which gave it root." To the same effect, *Ibid.*, Book III., Chap. XI. *Cf.* also, Leist, Graeco-Ital. R. G., Book III., Part II.

The causes tending to produce this are traceable to the casuistical mode of reasoning by which the written law is built up by the reasoning of courts and lawyers, a mode of treatment inaugurated by the early exponents of law, the priestcraft. One distinguished writer on the growth of society has contended that, in addition to the customs of every-day life, there occurred in archaic times, among primitive people, that accumulation of injunctions left by the ghosts of the dead and proclaimed by the priests, which led to the rise of the first unwritten codes; of which traces are found among such savage tribes as the Veddahs, among Scandinavian barbarians, early Hebrews, ancient Egyptians, East Indian tribes, the oracles of the Greek diviners, and the omens of the Roman *aruspices*.[1] The Pontifical College was an outcome, and the influence of the priestcraft in the declaration of prevailing duty as measured by existing usage on the Continent of Europe and in Britain, is another of the consequences of this fact. Thus the habit of obedience based on reverential fear gave a start to a stable body of superstitions and also useful rules. When they came into vogue, courts were likewise legislative bodies in a sense, that is, both would be within the province of the tribe, but controlled by the priests or scribes. These courts were first open-air meetings, and from them came the *Witenagemot*, which, as we shall see, divided its functions as England developed, to become an executive, legislative and a judicial body, separate and independent of each other.[2] The method of procedure of the priests, after they obtained corporate efficiency and stability, was to carefully preserve the traditions and pro-

[1] See Spencer, Principles of Sociology, Vol. II., § 529 *seq.*; Curtius, Hist. of Greece, Vol. II., p. 23 *seq.*; Waitz, Deutsche Verf. Geschichte, Vol. I., Chap. IX., pp. 326, 335, 336, also Chap. VII., p. 258; Fustel de Coulanges, Ancient City, *passim*. See especially *Ibid.*, Book III., Chap. XI. See also *ante* regarding *Themis* and *Fas*.

[2] See Chap. IV. *post*. See also Spencer, Principles of Sociology, Vol. II., Part V., Chaps. XIII., XIV.; Maine, Early Law and Custom, Chap. XI., p. 380 *seq*. *Cf.* Leist, Graeco-Ital. R. G., Book II., Part I., §33 *seq.*; also Book III., Part II.

cedure of their body.[1] Writing of the Delphic priesthood, Curtius pertinently says: "If we consider how, besides extensive knowledge of the world and men, in the circle of the priestly families there was handed down from one generation to another a peculiar wisdom, a safe tact in the judgment of difficult relations (for a series of similar cases already existed to serve for purposes of comparison with each case submitted for an opinion; and thus a practice came to form itself with continually increasing definiteness for answers and counsel of every kind); if we consider this, it is not difficult to understand how, even after the equalization of the original difference in culture formerly prevailing between the Apolline missions and the country people around, the oracle institutions could preserve their authority unimpaired for the good of the people."[2] The earliest English jurists were priests; and their knowledge of Roman law has made itself felt to this day in English jurisprudence. They devised the English Court of Chancery and they were the first Chancellors. The knowledge of reading and writing was spread by them, and therefore to them is due the first written codes.

---

[1] *Cf.* Leist, Graeco-Ital. R. G., Books II. and III.

[2] Curtius, History of Greece, Vol. II., p. 18. *Cf.* Leist, Graeco-Ital. R. G., Book II., Part I., p. 198; also Book II., Part II. "The verb from which Torah is derived signifies in its earliest usage to give direction, decision. The participle signifies giver of oracles in the two examples GIBEATH MOREH and ALLON MOREH. The latter expression is explained by another, which alternates with it, 'oak of the soothsayers.' Now we know that the priests in the days of Saul and David gave divine oracles by the *Ephod* and the *lots* connected with it, which answered one way or the other to a question put in the alternative form. Their Torah no doubt grew out of this practice. . . . But it continued to be an oral decision and direction. . . . There is no Torah as a ready-made product, as a system existing independently of its originator and accessible to every one; it becomes actual only in the various utterances, which naturally form by degrees the basis of a fixed tradition. . . . The Torah of the priests appears to have had primarily a legal character. . . . In proportion as the executive gained strength under the monarchy, *jus*—civil justice—necessarily grew up into a separate existence from the older sacred *fas*." —Wellhausen, Hist. of Israel, 394, 395.

To them is chargeable some of the peculiarities of our administration laws.[1]

To them is attributable the form which our doctrine of precedent obtained, which tended, when pursued, to crystallize into more and more rigid classifications and rules and methods. Precedent never obtained the same place in any other system of jurisprudence that it could claim in ours. Roman jurisprudence offers the nearest parallel to it.[2] But in so far as they tended to introduce into the continental systems of Britain their borrowed doctrines and their casuistical adherence to precedent at the expense of those pastoral, agricultural and commercial habits, usages and customs which laboriously grew up with the expansion of the community; in so far as they lost sight of those household and social relations which all communities implicate, the formal methods of the priest were bound to yield. By means of priestly initiative, invention and intellectual devices changed the law and anticipated the growth of the community, as well in the formation of codes and preparation of commentaries as in the field of legislation. Priestly activity as judge and legislator has ceased in civilized countries. Priestly sophistry and casuistry live only in the methods of the votaries of the law, and are being superseded by the material demands of humanity. One writer has said, "The current of decision sometimes varies like tides,"[3]—a consequence of the conflict between material interests and formalistic processes of reasoning. Formalistic processes must change, must vary with the change of material interests; the difficulty is of adapting language to needs.[4]

---

[1] See *post*, Chap. III., Sec. 2. See Fustel de Coulanges, Ancient City, Book II., Chap. VII. *Cf.* Leist *loc. cit.*

[2] Hammond's Introduction to Sanders' Justinian, xii. to xxiv.; Bishop, Non-Contract Law, Chap. LX., §1313; Clark, Practical Jurisprudence, Part II., Chap. III.; Leist, Graeco-Ital. R. G., Book III., Part II.

[3] Hare, American Constitutional Law, Vol. II., p. 670.

[4] *Cf.* Leist, Graeco-Ital. R. G., Book III., Part II., where is shown the gradual abatement of sacred initiative in the production of law, and its supersedure by material rules, in ancient Greece and Rome.

But the doctrine of precedent still continues in vigor.[1] It represents a mode of thought which forms its very basis. The doctrine of agreement and difference in inductive logic—whereby we make our estimate of the new from the plane of view of the old,—the very primitive conjoining of sentient experiences which forms the first sentient generalizations of savage and infant minds,[2] represent a similar process; the latter inaugurating the formation of language.[3] The doctrine of precedent plays a most important function in the creation and application of law, though it has frequently obtained an extravagant application in the English and American system.[4] One writer tells us that "what is called the English Constitution consists of the fundamentals of the British polity, laid down in custom, *precedent,* decision and statutes; and the common law (as given in custom and precedent)[5] in it is a far greater portion than the statute law. The English Constitution is chiefly a common law constitution; and this reflex of a continuous society in a continuous law is more truly philosophical than the theoretic and systematic constitution of recent France."[6] Yet, notwithstanding this eulogium, he was forced elsewhere to admit that precedent "may be sadly misapplied."[7] Another writer whose esteem for precedent is of the most exalted kind still finds much to criticise about its application.[8] It has operated as a conservative element in the preservation of order and method, but it has likewise been productive of grave abuse, and has operated not only to

---

[1] See Lieber, Civil Liberty and Self-Government, 208 *seq.*; same, Hermeneutics (3d ed., Notes by Wm. G. Hammond), Chap. VII. and Note n; Wells, Res Adjudicata and Stare Decisis, Chap. XL. *seq.*; Cooley, Constitutional Limitations, *50, *51; Pollock, Essays in Jurisprudence and Ethics, Chap. IX.

[2] Romanes, Mental Evolution in Man, Chaps. I. to IX., inclusive.

[3] *Ibid.*

[4] See Lieber, Hermeneutics, *supra.*

[5] Precedent embraces decisions. See *infra.*

[6] Lieber, Civil Liberty and Self-Government, *loc. cit.*

[7] Hermeneutics, 191.

[8] Joel Prentiss Bishop, Non-Contract Law, Chap. LX., Subd. III.

delay the progress of mankind, but it has bred confusion by ignoring the signs of that progress. To use it correctly always, even in the view of an English or American lawyer, involves an amount of intelligence and care which no judge or lawyer can lay claim to. When it comes to applying precedent in law, logic yields to experience and social sentiments, and the compass of language is being constantly abridged or extended by modifications and qualifications that are aimed to conform to social needs. The Supreme Court of the United States was supposed by the legal profession for many years to intend to follow State decisions on all questions relating to State law, except perhaps commercial law.[1] Yet in later years it has greatly qualified this doctrine,[2] and it has even gone so far as to ignore the decisions of State courts under State legislation.[3] As it stands now, the doctrine, however appropriate to a preservation of the limits of Federal control, may have no application where the Federal court has preceded the State court in its decision of a given point, or where the decisions of the State court conflict and non-residents of States are interested, or where to permit the application of later State decisions will impair contracts as understood under the earlier State decisions. One difficulty in applying precedent is to know how much of the language of the opinion to lay stress upon; too much or too little may change the construction to a noteworthy extent. Moreover, we ought to ascertain whether the judge who delivered it was prejudiced or ignorant, for such things have been. To confine the opinion to the case in which it was delivered is almost to deprive it of any effect as a precedent. To give the same weight to the language as to a legislative enactment is, of course, to be extravagant. But the greatest evil implied in

---

[1] Conflict between Federal and State Decisions: by Wm. B. Hornblower, Am. Law Review [N. S.], Vol. I., p. 211; by J. B. Heiskell, *ibid.*, Vol. XVI, p. 743.

[2] Burgess *v.* Seligman, 107 U. S. Reports, pp. 20, 33, 34, and authorities there cited.

[3] Mohr *v.* Maniere, 101 U. S., p. 421 *seq.*

its too extravagant use is the narrowness, the unelasticity which it gives to the law, and the reasoning on words, the casuistry, it produces. It is thus a legitimate child of its originators, a formal product of priestly creators. Nevertheless, if it can be made free of extravagances, it may be instrumental in giving a scientific turn to the law.[1]

In the process of its expansion not only has the domain of law been widened by the current of habit and custom, and by the activity of intellectual factors such as are implied in the judicial and legislative activity of the community, but it has likewise been irresistibly affected by the play of physical environment; physical environment not confined to the mere geographical, topographical and climatic conditions by which human beings are surrounded. In that play of physical factors is to be comprehended the cohesive forming of social aggregates in the slow course of social integration; the physical and neural character and development of human beings which betray themselves in ordinances against witchcraft, in rules favoring sacrifice even of human beings, in rules preservative of animals; the effect of connecting groups of the same social aggregates and diverse social aggregates by ties of consanguinity or by *nerves* such as are implied in channels of communication by footpath, wagon road, turnpike, river, railroad, lake or ocean, telegraph, etc.; likewise are to be included therein *ganglia* of industrial and political life such as municipal centers, and that less *organized*, yet not less important *tract*, the pastoral and agricultural non-urban sections of the country. The elaboration of this subject has been relegated to the succeeding chapters of the present work.[2]

---

[1] See Pollock, Essays in Jurisprudence and Ethics, Chap. IX., "The Science of Case Law."

[2] See Montesquieu, Esprit de Lois, Vol. I., Book XIV.; Ihering, Zweck im Recht; Spencer, Data of Ethics; Amos, Science of Law; Hosmer, Physics and Politics; Fowler, Progressive Morality and Principles of Morality; Holtzendorf, Encyclopædia, Systematischer Theil, p. 51 *seq.*; Maine, Early History of Institutions, and Early Law and Custom.

Let us remember that, as little as any single individual invention could create or change a language, so equally does it lie out of the range of individual power to change the legal current of a nation's life. And the laws which have come and gone, leaving only relics in the form of unconscious yet potential sentiment for right, have not died out through individual effort, as little as they could be kept alive or breathed into life again by such effort. The following illustrations from modern jurisprudence show how laws are *forced* into as well as out of existence. The corporate creations of Palestine and Greece were less definite and less numerous than those of Rome, and in all of that rich mine of judicial information which Roman jurisprudence has left to us we find nothing to resemble our stock companies. Even in England there is nothing to compare with the development which corporate life has gone through in the United States.[1] One English writer[2] and one American writer[3] have drawn and emphasized the distinction between the law of partnership and that of corporations, and though at present the courts have seemed to hold against the right of corporations to go into partnership, the day may come when, driven by the necessity of providing against a ruinous competition destructive of railways and channels of communication and transportation, the formation of partnerships among railroads may be measurably countenanced. The governmental prerogative of eminent domain has descended upon corporations who maintain railroads, telegraphs and (sometimes) gristmills.[4] And no good reason seems to exist why individuals should not enjoy the same right, where they are engaged in furthering similar enterprises. The tests of partnership have

---

[1] In Smith, Mercantile Law, a chapter on Corporations takes up less space than almost any other chapter in the book and is disposed of in a few pages.

[2] Judge Lindley, Law of Partnership.

[3] Mr. Morawetz, Law of Corporations. Mr. Morawetz has probably derived some of his inspiration from Judge Lindley's work.

[4] See Lewis, Eminent Domain.

been forced to yield to the demands of trade,[1] and so has the law of libel in relation to commercial agencies.[2] The law of evidence has yielded to the development of married women's rights so as to put an extraordinary burden of proof upon them in certain cases.[3] Now a man may not buy a stock of goods of an insolvent without taking extra precautions, that he do not pay money in addition to his debt, and that he pay no money which may be used by the insolvent to evade payment of debts.[4] There was no such law relating to fraudulent conveyances in the days of Elizabeth, or even in England in a much later day.[5] How the capacity of courts to enforce judgments may be completely thwarted by the adverse sentiment of the people, even though the incapacity involves a grave breach of contract rights under the constitution of the United States, is illustrated by the case of Meriwether *v.* Garrett,[6] decided by the Supreme Court of the United States. There, by the taking away of the existence of the political organization of the city of Memphis, the courts were disabled from enforcing a large obligation against the city, although the territory and property of the corporation still continued in existence as before. Mr. Hare, speaking of such cases, says that they are instances of the "often verified truth that the tribunals are powerless where the great body of a community are resolutely bent on frustrating the laws."[7] Evidence of the same truth is now accumulating in the Southern States, under the constitutional amendment which has invested the negro with the franchise.[8] The law

---

[1] Clement Bates, Law of Partnership, Chaps. I. and II.

[2] Errant, Law of Mercantile Agencies.

[3] Seitz *v.* Mitchell, 94 U. S. Reports, pp. 583, 584.

[4] See Clements *v.* Moore, 6 Wallace (U. S. Sup. Ct.), p. 299; Openheimer *v.* Halff, 68 Texas, p. 404; Brown *v.* Vaughn, 70 *ibid.*, pp. 49, 50; Leinkauff *v.* Frenkel, 80 Ala., pp. 136, 139; Christian *v.* Greenwood, 23 Ark., pp. 258, 265; Dyer *v.* Taylor, 50 Ark., p. 314.

[5] See May, Fraudulent Conveyances, 2d Eng. ed., edited by S. W. Worthington.

[6] 102 U. S. 472.

[7] Hare, American Constitutional Law, Vol. I., p. 648.

[8] Fifteenth Amendment.

of the United States relative to assignments for the benefit of creditors is a departure from the law of trusts, many legal trusts being bad assignments.[1] The creation of stock certificates has produced stock exchanges and the laws of stock exchanges.[2] The development of warehouses has produced warehouse receipts, which form a large part of the securities of large cities, and incidentally the law of warehouse receipts is expanding.[3] The municipal corporations have grown so fast and have changed so much that they not only have given rise to a law *sui generis*, but incidentally they have tended to enlarge the domain of commercial paper in the shape of warrants and negotiable bonds.

No mind can become intelligent without the pabulum which daily life produces from contact with the environing physical conditions, be those conditions phenomena of organic or of inorganic nature, social or anti-social in form; and it receives no small proportion of its character by inheritance. The mind is the abstract denomination for many elements which bodily contact with environing physical conditions produces, such as the five senses, together with such states as health, pain, fear, fatigue, etc., showing, with what precedes, that two factors are observable in the creation of laws, the one of which is traceable to a physical source, the other to an intellectual source. And the discussion likewise shows that the intellectual factors by no means preponderate; a fact very rarely, if ever, heretofore referred to.

One eminent German writer, whose pursuit of the study of law has taken the widest range, and who contends that the ethnic-morphologic mode is the only thorough way in which to approach the study of jurisprudence, has emphasized the play of physical and intellectual factors, by contending that custom and law are the forms in which the mechanical aspects of social and industrial activity present themselves,

---

[1] Compare Burrell, Assignments, with Perry, Trusts.

[2] Dos Passos, Law of Stock Exchange.

[3] See Tiedeman, Commercial Paper, §499.

they dealing solely with the acts of mankind.[1] But a better view is that which makes customs and laws a product of those evolving incidents of social growth which mark the growth and decay of groups and states and peoples.[2]

The outlines contained in this chapter, it seems to me, reveal a much grander and nobler place for jurisprudence, and what jurisprudence implies, in the world of human creations, than has heretofore been generally accorded to it.

Laws trace their earliest beginnings, the seeds, germs, or rudiments from which they grew, to a period antedating the rise of an alphabet.[3] From the savage's life and customs up to our day the spread of jurisprudence has gone on, constituting, with the lapse of centuries, one of the bodily elements with which social organization has been able to assume a continually better form. The basis, the very matrix of law is so imbedded, integrated, in the social organization, that the latter can as little be thought of without it as can the human body without lungs to breathe with.

Of this, the accepted definitions of law give us no inkling. Still more they lose sight of the heterogeneous character of our codes, bearing upon all manner of subjects, and embracing interpretative or declaratory provisions, directory and not mandatory provisions, optional provisions, and provisions which, like provisions in limitation acts and "statutes of fraud," depend upon how the parties have conducted themselves and whether they wish to invoke them. They lose sight of the many rules of construction which constitute the burden of works on construction and interpretation; rules[4] which contain no command nor strictly a rule of action, but rather a rule of interpretation—a form of definition or explanation.

---

[1] Post, Ursprung des Rechts, Chap. XV.; same, Bausteine, etc., Chap. I.

[2] *Cf.* Spencer, Principles of Sociology, Political Institutions.

[3] See Taylor, The Alphabet; Post, Bausteine, etc., Chap. I.; same, Ursprung des Rechts.

[4] See Endlich, On Interpretation; Lieber, Hermeneutics; Sedgwick, Statutory and Constitutional Law, Potter's Dwarris, etc.

Constitutional law, as that term is understood in the United States, and as it is largely understood in other countries, does not seem to be covered by the ordinary definitions of law.[1] Relating to organic political existence, and dealing with the structure and powers of the government, it defines as much the sovereignty as it does the tributary powers. It deals largely with grants of power and definitions of power previously existing.[2] And those powers represent a fundamental functional activity, whose coming into fruition was the growth of ages. We shall have abundant reason for saying, as we pursue the summary study of legal growth, that the law has a growth outside of constitutional growth, yet that both are the inevitable outcome of social development upon the scale of cosmical development.[3]

---

[1] See George H. Smith, Right and Law, Chap. III., §433, Chap. V., §505.

[2] See the last two chapters of this work.

[3] Dicey attributes a large constitutional influence to "the rule of law." Law of the Constitution, Part II.

CHAPTER II.

PHYSICAL AND SOCIAL FACTORS OF LAW.

SECTION I.—INORGANIC AND ORGANIC PHYSICAL FACTORS.

The elements with which the human being started upon his tremendous career, outside of his bodily organism, his associates and animals, comprised those physical elements by which we are still surrounded. They played a part in conditionating his development from lower to higher conditions, and discoveries point with yearly increasing frequency to the fact that they conspired to bring him into existence. A poisonous atmosphere will annihilate life to such an extent that, in the deserts of southern Arabia, human life seems impossible. Too cold an atmosphere, as in hyperborean regions or on the top of lofty mountains, produces the same results. And if life be possible, its possibilities in countries subjected to extreme cold will be so limited that bodily and mental growth, and the development of customs and institutions, will be stunted and meager. Man must have a climate which will give him some opportunity to do something beyond keeping alive, before he can develop any extraordinary characteristics. That is clearly shown by the history—if one may speak of history in that connection—of the peoples inhabiting the northernmost inhabitable regions of both hemispheres, and by the not less noteworthy fact that civilization and politics, including jurisprudence, are the outcome of people who lived in more congenial regions.[1]

[1] Montesquieu, Spirit of Laws, Vol. I., Book XIV., has dwelt upon the influence of physical factors on people and their legal institutions. Many of his conclusions would not now be accepted. Dr. Woolsey, Political Science, Vol. II., 515, 516, has referred to the influence of physical factors

"Where the temperature which man's vital functions require can be maintained with difficulty, social evolution is not possible. There can neither be a sufficient surplus-power in each individual nor a sufficient number of individuals. Not only are the energies of the Esquimaux expended mainly in defending himself against loss of heat, and in laying up stores by which he may continue to do this during the arctic night, but his physical processes are greatly modified to the same end. Without fuel, and, indeed, unable to burn within his snow-hut anything more than an oil-lamp lest the walls should melt, he has to keep up that bodily warmth which even his thick fur-dress fails to retain, by devouring vast quantities of blubber and oil; and his digestive system, heavily taxed in providing the wherewith to meet excessive loss by radiation, supplies less material for other vital purposes. This great physiological cost of individual life, indirectly checking the multiplication of individuals, arrests social evolution."[1] The Voguls of Asiatic Siberia, during their short summers, live in isolated families, each pursuing the forest game, while in winter they pitch their tents or build their huts at considerable distances one from the other, being nowhere grouped into villages. The family spirit among them seems but slightly developed. The Tunguses, in the same quarter of the globe, are still in a hunting state,

---

in politics. See also Bluntschli, Theory of the State, Book III., Chap. II.; Buckle, History of Civilization, Vol. I., 32 *seq.*; Spencer, Principles of Sociology, Vol. I., §15; Réclus, Earth and its Inhabitants, Europe, Vol. V., Asia, Vol. I., where he treats of tribes in Scandinavia and Siberia. See further, Felix, Der Einfluss der Natur auf die Entwickelung des Eigenthums.

[1] Herbert Spencer, Principles of Sociology, Vol. I., §15. He further illustrates the correctness of his position by citing "the still more miserable Fuegians" in the southern hemisphere. He says: "These beings, described as scarcely human in appearance, have such difficulty in preserving the vital balance in face of the rapid escape of heat, that the surplus for individual development is narrowly restricted; and, by consequence, the surplus for producing and rearing new individuals. Hence the numbers remain too small for exhibiting anything beyond the incipient social existence."

roaming through the woods without tents, and seeking temporary shelter in caves or the hollow trunks of trees. A slight sleigh carries all of their effects, and they will journey with it thousands of miles, always retracing their steps with unerring certainty. Signs and natural objects constitute their language. The woman in labor flees to the forest and is confined unaided, at the risk of perishing in the snow or rain.[1]

Situation, embracing waters or mountain fastnesses, or swamps or plains, has had a marked effect upon the human being. Arid wastes have prevented civilization and governments from settling there; indeed, as they encroached, as is even now the case in Central Asia and Northern Africa, civilization which previously existed disappeared. In the United States, not to mention the great Desert of Sahara or the Desert of Mongolia, there are vast wastes, unpeopled and uncultivable, which require the investment of millions and a method of amelioration not yet begun, on the part of the Federal Government, to make them habitable. The relation of mountains to social movement is shown in Montenegro. "The Montenegrins are the kinsmen of the Servians of the Danube, but their life of almost incessant warfare, the elevation and sterility of their country, as well as the vicinity of the Albanians, have developed special features among them. The quiet life of the plains is unknown to the Montenegrin; he is violent, and ready at all times to take up arms; in his belt he carries a whole arsenal of pistols and knives, and even when working in the fields he has a carbine by his side. Until recently the price of blood was still exacted, and a scratch even had to be paid for." Blood vengeance was hereditary among them until quite recently. "Compared with the Servians of the Danube, the Montenegrin is a barbarian."[2] Mountainous life seems to have begotten a hardier,

---

[1] Réclus, Earth and its Inhabitants, Asia, Vol. I., 338, 340, 358, 359. See for other illustrations, Roemer, Origin of the English People and Languages, 10, 11.

[2] Réclus, Earth and its Inhabitants, Europe, Vol. I., 181. As to the Albanians see *ibid*, pp. 115 *seq.*, especially 121.

more valiant disposition than the life of the plains. The Cantabrians, whom Strabo admired so much, and who are supposed to be the ancestors of the Basques, were superior to their neighbors in independence of spirit and valor, and the descendants of the Basques, or such of them as yet live in the valleys of the Pyrenees, may still lay claim to greater push than their southerly neighbors. The Swiss of the Middle Age far excelled most of his neighbors in independence of spirit, enterprise and energy, though now, on account of his narrow and somewhat insulated industrial and political existence, he lags behind. The mountainous tribes of India are distinguished from tribes of the plain and the swamp, by greater activity and energy, though in so far as they are insulated and remain unaffected by English or even Chinese influences they are now less developed in civilization than other, formerly inferior, tribes. Mountainous life, where accompanied by sterile soil, is apt to keep people backward. It tends to keep warlike tribes from following industrial occupations and from adopting industrial customs and usages.[1] It tends in numerous present localities to keep the people who are confined to it in a somewhat primitive and backward condition. Moonshiners, that is, illegal whiskey distillers, are usually people of this class, who are simple and unintelligent, yet brave enough to oppose, however fruitlessly, the United States Government, in breaking up their practice. In the mountainous regions of some of the United States, especially where the soil is sterile, development is slow and law is not frequently invoked. On the other hand, high and fertile plateaux are much sought after and frequently support an excellent population. In the higher lands of Palestine and Persia the best population is probably now to be found. The cultivated mountain lands of Central Asia yield better results and maintain a better civilization than most of the parched neighborhoods on the plains.

In temperate climates, however, the plain, so-called, is apt,

[1] See Principles of Sociology, Vol. I., §17.

upon the whole, to yield the best results in development and civilization. Earlier diverse factors no doubt contributed toward this, some of which emanated from mountain regions, and some came from less elevated torrid regions where vegetation was varied and abundant and gave time and room for reflection, however limited that might be.[1] The inhabitants of desert tracts, as well as those of mountain tracts, are difficult to consolidate; facility of escape, joined with habits of life adapted to sterile regions, greatly hinder social subordination. Conversely, social integration is facilitated within a territory which, while it is able to support a large population, affords facilities for coercing the units of that population; especially if at the same time it is bounded by regions offering little sustenance, or peopled by enemies, or both.[2] The long-continued independence of the Highland clans of Scotland, and of other mountain tribes, may be cited to sustain the one position, while Egypt and Chaldea might be cited as fulfilling the conditions to social integration. The prairies of Illinois facilitated a much more rapid growth than the mountains of West Virginia, North Carolina or Tennessee. And the like may be predicated of that vast territory now covered by the States of Kansas, Nebraska, and portions of Missouri, Iowa, Texas, and other States. What comparison can be drawn between the mountain regions of the Rockies, or parallel ranges, and the valleys and plains of California?

In addition to the diverse influences exercised by mountain and valley or plain, one should note other differences due to the configuration of territory. Wet, marshy territory deters and delays development, as is attested by the swamps of Virginia, Florida, Louisiana and Arkansas, while well-drained and undulating country invites population and thrift. The swamps of the South are the occasion of much backwardness in their growth in the United States. They have kept

[1] On the effect of an extensive *flora* and *fauna* see Principles of Sociology, Vol. I., §§18, 19.

[2] Spencer, Principles of Sociology, Vol. I., §17.

back civilization in southern Europe,[1] and where rivers and seas have inundated and made wet and impassable subsiding territory, civilization has in some instances been compelled to withdraw. Rome to-day feels the detrimental effects due to marshy soil, and Memphis, Tennessee, may, probably, in no small measure, trace the devastating effects of yellow fever to the swamps of Arkansas, to the west of her. Sometimes swamps prove havens of refuge for an oppressed or conquered people, and too often they become the asylum of criminals.

Oceans, inland seas, bays, estuaries, lakes and rivers have been the resort of mankind, and have served as channels of communication, of intercourse, and developing industry and commerce as much, if not more than any other physical element already referred to. The Nile, Euphrates, Tigris, Jordan, Ganges, Indus, Irawaddi, Yang-tse-kiang, Oxus, in Africa and Asia, mark out, upon an extended scale, the seats of earliest known civilization and political existence. The Volga, Danube, Dnieper, Po, Tiber, Rhone, Rhine, Elbe, Weser, Seine, Thames, etc., early attracted trading or defensive stations or seats. The favorable situation of Phoenicia, Greece, Italy, and other lands contiguous to great bodies of water, facilitated the rise of city commonwealths, and the commerce and agriculture which these presupposed and required. And on this account, in no small degree, we have the phenomenal development which has given us the philosophy, the arts of government, the sculpture and architecture, the history, poetry and drama, the jurisprudence and elaborate sacrificial cult, and the maritime customs which we trace down to these sections. Mr. Grote says: "The ancient philosophers and legislators were simply impressed with the contrast between an inland and a maritime city; in the former, simplicity and uniformity of life, tenacity of ancient habits and dislike of what is new or foreign, great force of exclusive sympathy, and narrow range both of objects and ideas;

---

[1] For instance, the "Landes," in France.

in the latter, variety and novelty of sensations, expansive imagination, toleration and occasional preference for extraneous customs, greater activity of the individual and corresponding mutability of the state."[1] In Northern and Western Europe, the aggregation of tribes occurred first in the vicinity of bodies of water. And the same rule holds regarding the people who colonized the Western Hemisphere. The early Spanish and English settlers of North America selected the sea-coast or some river for the purpose of settlement. And every consecutive step westward evinced the same choice. Probably among the earliest words now extant are the names of oceans, seas, or important rivers and other waters, or other natural features.[2] "Mountains and rivers still murmur the voices of nations long denationalized or extirpated." Towns may be destroyed, the sites of human habitations may be removed, but the ancient river-names are handed down from race to race; even the names of the eternal hills are less permanent than those of rivers.[3] Over the greater part of Europe —in Germany, France, Spain—we find villages which bear Teutonic or Romanic names, standing on the banks of streams which still retain their ancient Celtic appellations.[4]

The character of the soil has likewise played a part in man's movement. The aridity of sandy wastes, the flooding of lands, the formation of alluvial deposits, have contributed to prevent even the pursuit of a pastoral occupation, or have furthered the development of agriculture, municipal life and industries. There are no signs of pastoral or agricultural or municipal life in the deserts of Turkestan, Arabia, Africa, or

---

[1] History of Greece, Vol. II., p. 296. See on the influence of physical configuration, etc., *ibid.*, Part II., Chap. I., from which the above extract has been taken.

[2] *Cf.* Taylor, Words and Places, pp. 27, 130.

[3] *Ibid.*, p. 130.

[4] *Ibid.* *Avon* (Celtic) means water; *Wick* (Norse) means bay; Don, Dvina, Danube, Donau, Ganges, all mean *river*. Volga means *holy river*. Words and Places, p. 330; Réclus, Europe, Vol. V., 346, 365. Mississippi means Father of Waters.

Mongolia. And the like may be said of the great western desert region of the United States. Yet warlike spirit and the first forms of political life, so far as implied in a militant career, are promoted by such wastes, at least in Arabia, and, if "cowboys" and Indians may be cited, perhaps in the United States. The luxuriance of vegetation, as well as its utter absence, may depend upon soil, and may seriously impede the growth of civilization; as is attested in tropical climes.

With these universal factors, as far as the earth is concerned, man began his career. And their influence has been instrumental in shaping, in limiting man's activity ever since. They are implied in the evolutionary environment by which he is conditionated. Waiving the detailed discussion of the evolutionary physical influences from without, under discussion, which can best be studied in the works of natural historians, such as Darwin, Huxley, Quatrefages, Schmidt, Müller, Haeckel, Romanes, and in the volumes of Herbert Spencer on biology, I have confined the present inquiry to general evidences of those influences. Observing how exceptional, in contrast with surrounding nations, has been the development of the Swiss, and the rise and maintenance of their present cantonal form of government, and the prevalence of pursuits which their mountain life has superinduced, we see there the effect of what is due to their peculiar physical surroundings, the result of centuries of independent and active life such as their surroundings coöperated to produce. Similar conditions have conspired to produce the republic of San Marino in Italy. Situated in the Apennines, its inhabitants have been able to maintain a separate continuous political existence through many centuries. "San Marino, with some neighboring hamlets, constitutes a 'most illustrious'[1] republic, and is now the only independent municipality of Italy." England itself has had a peculiar growth, doubtless due to its insular position. On this account, coupled

[1] Réclus, Earth and its Inhabitants, Europe, Vol. I., p. 284.

with the limited area of agricultural lands it possesses, the means of agriculture have been insufficient for the demands of its growing population, and the doctrine of free trade has found an abiding place. And this doctrine of free trade, in its present broad features, is perhaps maintainable there because of the relation which England bears to numerous colonial appendages; a relation which requires the use of a large merchant marine as carriers, for these colonial possessions are separated from her by vast expanses of ocean. The vast extent of territory in the United States, embraced within variant climatic zones, facilitated the growth of an antagonism of interest between the North and the South; the condition of the North conspired to make slavery unprofitable and undesirable, while the condition of the South had an opposite effect. From these conditions resulted the spread of manufactures in the North, the spread of plantation life in the South. Another consequence was the extension of the doctrine of protection, introduced by the fathers of the Constitution of the United States, in the North, for the continued protection of manufacturing industries, while the South, devoted to agricultural interests, saw its advantage to lie in a free trade. The ultimate outcome of this antagonism was war and emancipation. Now, the physical conditions of the South remain such, with a large mass of emancipated negro population, as to render agriculture very burdensome and frequently unprofitable. The physical conditions of the South have produced a more inflammable temperament than is peculiar to the colder clime of the North, and this, in light of the negro problem, does not brook the same control, nor present the same self-control, which is possible to a people in colder climes. The problem is how to deal properly with these embarrassing conditions. No doubt time will have to yield its modicum to its solution. Before it can be properly dealt with theory will have to be less ambitious and aspiring, and physical conditions will have to be taken into account. Further evolutionary effects of physical phenomena have been shown already in the quite contracted social stage which the tribes in the north of Europe, Asia and America have attained.

The elements referred to have not only left an impress upon human society and laws as above indicated, but they may be credited with a more conspicuous influence. The jurisdiction of admiralty courts in England depended at one time, and doubtless still depends, upon the ebb and flow of the tide. In the United States it depends upon the navigability of waters. Thus physical characteristics solely determine the extent of this jurisdiction, and this even if we say, with the Supreme Court of the United States, that it "extends wherever vessels float and navigation successfully aids commerce,"[1] or with an inferior federal court that it extends over canals.[2] The courts are often called upon to ascertain and define this jurisdiction by reference to physical data, as in the canal case. Thus, while contracts having relation to navigation may be within the jurisdiction of federal courts, in admiralty, it is made the duty of these courts to determine what are such contracts. A sailor has such a contract for his services upon board ship, though the service may involve loading and unloading in port, but a day laborer for a vessel lying in port has no maritime claim.[3] What is such a craft as is within such jurisdiction is also sometimes an interesting question,—a barge, canal-boat, a raft have been held to be such. Mr. John M. Gould, of the Boston bar, has written a treatise on "The Law of Waters," including riparian rights and public and private rights in inland and tidal waters, embracing 816 pages. He has chapters on "property in tide waters at common law," "property in tide waters in this country," "rivers and lakes," "the public right of navigation," "riparian rights," etc. Under each one of these chapters, interesting, and not always easy, questions are treated. The ships belonging to and controlled by the sub-

---

[1] The Hine *v.* Trevor, 4 Wall., p. 555; The Montello, 11 Wall., p. 411.

[2] Malony *v.* City of Milwaukee, 1 Fed. Reporter, p. 611.

[3] *Cf.* Desty, Federal Procedure (6th ed.), p. 69 *seq.*

jects of a nation are said to belong to that nation, and the jurisdiction of that nation extends over the navigation of the ship. In other particulars the oceans are said not to be subject to the exclusive dominion of any nation, except that portion which lies within a certain distance from the coast. Since cannon have come into use, their presumed range tends to fix the distance.

The existence of water manifests itself in other forms. The differences, based upon the extent and character of salt water as distinguished from that of fresh water, are important.[1] "Beyond the point to which the sea ebbs and flows, the soil is *prima facie* in the riparian owners, and the right of fishing private," as held in Ireland.[2] And a similar doctrine seems to prevail in England.[3] But in the United States a great deal of diversity of opinion exists regarding this question, depending upon the size of the rivers and other, mostly physical, conditions.[4] In delivering the opinion of the Supreme Court of the State of Tennessee, in the case of Elder against Burrus,[5] Judge Turley, in behalf of the court, said: "All laws are, or ought to be, an adaptation of principles of action to the state or condition of the country and to its moral and social position. There are many rules of action recognized in England as suitable which it would be folly in the extreme, in countries differently located, to recognize as law; and, in our opinion (the) distinction between rivers 'navigable' and 'not navigable,' causing it to depend upon the ebbing and flowing of the tide, is one of them. The insular position of Great Britain, the short courses of her rivers and the well known fact that there are none of them navigable above tide-water but for very small craft, well warrants the distinction there drawn by the common law."

[1] *Cf.* Gould, Waters, §51.

[2] Ir. Rep., 2 C. L., p. 143.

[3] Gould, Waters, §52.

[4] *Ibid.* §56 *seq.*

[5] 6 Humphrey's Reports, p. 366. See also Ray, Negligence of Imposed Duties, pp. 286, 373, 386, 444.

He then speaks of countries where streams are long and large and navigable to a great extent above tide-water, in which the civil law governing there has adopted a very different rule.[1] In some other particulars the common law of England relating to waters is inapplicable to this country. For instance, the right to divert the water of flowing streams, which at common law is denied to one person at the expense of others along the stream, is held to exist in the Pacific States with reference to miners, the first *appropriator* obtaining property therein for mining purposes.[2] The claim to the water is, however, said to be merely usufructuary, it is said not to be in the *corpus* of the water, and continues only with possession.[3] The only value which water has to the miner would seem to be while it is in his possession or under his control; after it flows away beyond his reach it is no longer appropriated by him. It can only be usufructuary. Water may be appropriated for the use of different pursuits, and may be employed at alternate periods by different appropriators.[4] Subterranean streams are not subject to the same doctrines regarding diversion that surface streams are at common law; neither are surface waters, falling waters, or snows subject to the same doctrines.[5] In England, and probably in the United States, gathering waters in reservoirs sometimes involves extraordinary care and liability; if the reservoir bursts and the water escapes, creating damages, the party owning and controlling it will sometimes be held liable even though there is no negligence, upon the theory that one who keeps on the premises anything likely to do mischief if it escapes (such as a wild beast) must keep it from injuring

---

[1] See Institutes, Lib. II., Tit. I., 1, 2. *Flumina autem omnia et portus publica sunt. Ideoque jus piscandi omnibus commune est in portu fluminibusque.* Tit. I., §2.

[2] Atchison *v.* Peterson, 20 Wall., p. 507 *seq.* See also Coffin *v.* Left Hand Ditch Co., 6 Colo. 443.

[3] Eddy *v.* Simpson, 3 California, p. 249; Kidd *v.* Laird, 15 *ibid.*, p. 163.

[4] Smith *v.* O'Hara, 43 *ibid.*, p. 371.

[5] Cooley, Torts (1st ed.), pp. 574, 575, 580.

others by escaping from its confinement, at his peril.[1] The breaking of a dam which confined the waters of an artificial lake, used for pleasure purposes, resulted in great destruction of life and property at and around Johnstown, Pennsylvania. Here liability depends upon the form of keeping and storing water—a subject that may yet be prolific of considerable litigation. In New Orleans, where wells and cisterns, and perhaps good river water, for drinking purposes, seem to be impracticabilities, does the same liability exist with reference to the tanks in general use there? Freshets do not always entail liability on owners of dams, where they are of an extraordinary nature. Filthy water may be a nuisance,[2] and to render drinking water unwholesome may be a crime.[3]

Easements in air and light can be obtained by use.[4] In many countries "there is a natural right to the use of all the light and air which flow naturally to land; but light and air differ from water in this, that whereas the natural right to the flow of the water of a natural stream is paramount, and no man is justified in obstructing that water or preventing it flowing in its ordinary course to the land of other persons,[5] the natural right to the flow of light and air is subordinate to the right incident to property, which every man has, to build on his own land."[6] Artificial light produced by electricity and gas, and cold air produced by artificial means, may give rise to legislation and decisions peculiar to new phenomena.

Offensive noises, embracing the barking of dogs, noises of billiard rooms, blowing of steam whistles, ringing of bells and jarring of machinery, etc., may be nuisances;[7] and the inge-

---

[1] Ryland *v.* Fletcher, 3 House of Lords Cases, pp. 330, 339; Cahill *v.* Eastman, 18 Minn. 324.

[2] Cooley, Torts, p. 567.

[3] Bishop, Criminal Law, Vol. I. (5th ed.), §491.

[4] Goddard, Easements (Bennet's ed.), p. 28 *seq.*

[5] We have seen how this may be modified by physical environment and the development of occupations peculiar to such environment.

[6] Goddard, Easements, p. 31.

[7] Cooley, Torts, pp. 599, 600.

nuity of man will hereafter beget new questions resulting from the prevalence of noises and odors not yet settled. Offensive odors, numerous in kind, such as are produced by soap and candle factories, livery stables, gas manufactories, breweries, slaughter houses, and the like, are frequently held to be nuisances.[1] When epidemics prevail, climatic conditions form the basis of severe and stern regulations against the existence of odors and other things productive of disease.

From what has been said and the illustrations given, it will be quite apparent that the physical elements referred to have had a marked influence upon social growth and the creation of laws, not only in the past, but also in the present; and it is also quite certain that they will have as great an influence in the future in the same direction. Further instances will suggest themselves. He who deals with all the sources of law must reckon with them, and the problems of the future in politics and laws will not be resolvable without a consideration of the bearing of these factors.

SECTION II.—THE PHYSICAL AND SOCIAL FACTORS IMPLIED IN INDIVIDUAL EXISTENCE AND IN HUMAN AGGREGATES.[2]

It falls in with the course of this work to consider now the physical elements involved in individual existence, and in the existence of greater or smaller bodies of individuals, so far as these bear upon laws. A few remarks will also be presented on the physical elements implied in animal existence in their relation to laws. It was said in the jurisprudence of Rome in reference to legal personality that, as his physical being, so does man's legal being begin at birth; from that time he exists as person. Birth is the complete severance from its mother of a living being of human form. That which is not yet born, but is still within the mother's womb, is

[1] Cooley, Torts, pp. 601, 602.

[2] See Felix, Der Einfluss der Natur, Sitten u. Gebräuche auf die Entwickelung des Eigenthums.

not yet a person; the possibility of its becoming such is, however, recognized, and therefore law has anticipated an unborn future personality. A moment of life is sufficient to produce important legal changes. With death not only does the physical existence expire, but likewise the legal existence. The deceased one is no longer capable of rights (*rechtsfähig*).[1] Other systems of civilized law agree with the Roman in saying that a physical existence is a prerequisite to legal capacity for rights. But they do not agree with it, nor with each other, in determining when the physical life begins that shall yield the requisite legal status. Some made a difference between the sexes, with reference to embryonic existence.[2] The being when born need not be rational.[3] In some systems the being must not be a monstrosity.[4] Thus we see how the law takes cognizance of a physical being, depending upon physical effects; or, in other words, how physical characteristics have left their telling impress. Nor does it confine itself to these details. By constitutional guarantees preservative of life, liberty and security; by provisions against murder, mayhem, assault and battery, rape, self-annihilation, exposition of the body, it takes cognizance of the same physical elements in diverse ways.

The operations of the nerves it is forced to recognize in treating of insanity. The capacity of a *non compos mentis* is still the subject of painful ignorance on the part of judges and lawyers, who approach the matter theoretically, and not as though the mind were dependent upon the neural system. Want of capacity of children, of married women, and the need of legislation for prodigals and spendthrifts, all involve mental characteristics that are based on neural factors. Destruction of sight is classed under the crime of mayhem, and it is cognizable in other different forms, as for instance when

---

[1] Zrodolowki, Das römische Privatrecht, Vol. I., pp. 171, 172.

[2] Compare Mayer, Rechte der Israeliten, Athener u. Römer, Vol. II., §121; Blackstone, Commentaries, Book I., p. 123 *seq.*

[3] Holland, Elements of Jurisprudence, p. 66.

[4] *Ibid.*

the credibility of an eye-witness, or the negligence of a company whose agent is affected with color-blindness, is in question. Want of hearing is likewise an element with which the administration of the law deals, as regards, for example, negligence or the credibility of witnesses. The author has personal knowledge of a case where a deaf clergyman attempted to swear away the character of another person, by testifying to the reputation of the latter for probity and truthfulness. He seemed not to be aware that he was impeached by his own deafness. Taste has engendered the use of liquor and tobacco; and the use of these has been the basis of much past and will be far more of future legislation and decisions. It has contributed to produce a marked and somewhat inconsistent change of views in at least one Supreme Court of the United States. Thus, the Supreme Court of the State of Arkansas, before the subjects of prohibition and temperance were agitated in that state, in determining what was a privilege, and hence subject to be specially taxed under the constitution of the state, held that only those things could be regarded as privileges which, at common law, required a franchise from the government, such as the right to take toll, keep a market, fair or ferry, and it refused to hold that to keep a billiard saloon was a privilege.[1] At that time intoxicating liquor was in use and was sold—indeed it has been used all over the civilized world for centuries; but after the agitation of prohibition and temperance had brought about a sentiment unfavorable to the sale of intoxicating liquors, the same court held the same provision to permit the imposition of an almost prohibitory special tax on the sale of such liquors.[2] It was abuse in the use of liquors, and the effect of such use upon the consumer and upon interested wives and children, that produced the sentiment for and enactment of prohibitory legislation. These are factors implying mostly physical or material elements.

---

[1] Stevens *v.* State, 2 Arkansas Reports, p. 291; Gibson *v.* Pulaski County, *ibid.*, p. 309.

[2] 26 Arkansas Reports, p. 523; 27 *ibid.*, p. 625; 38 *ibid.*, 641.

It may not be out of place to add, that the theories of prohibition are forcing legislation beyond the need of these evils; legislators lose sight of the ineradicability of the desire to use, and the occasional absolute need of alcoholic stimulants, and by doing so they become instrumental in making laws in disregard of physical elements. The consequences are as yet problematical. But an insidious disregard of the law may result, which will tend in the long run to become detrimental to that respect for law upon which good government depends.

In many other ways laws take note of the individual physical personality. As already suggested, death or dissolution begets new rights and duties in the law. It may increase the widow's and children's means under administration and dower laws, or under acts like that of Lord Campbell, giving causes of action against railroads where death has been produced by their fault. In the shape of life tables, life annuities and life insurance, the law takes cognizance of individual existence, as it does in those constitutional guarantees already mentioned relating to life and liberty and property—life, liberty and property which imply fresh, unpolluted air and water, under certain restrictions, and a place to move in; which imply, moreover, restriction of prior rights growing out of the spread of cities upon occupations which thus become detrimental to the peace and comfort of others.

What must, however, not be lost sight of is that man alone, unassociated, could never have created a custom or legal rule; had he lived but a single member of his kind upon the face of the earth, he would never have formulated or breathed into conscious life a custom or a law. Some sort of aggregation between human beings is requisite before a custom or law can arise.

There is no disagreement among those who are authorities, respecting the fact that man has always been a gregarious animal,[1] in this respect showing analogies, though superior

[1] Compare Spencer, Principles of Sociology, Vol. I., Chap. I., and succeeding chapters; Lindsay, Mind in the Lower Animals, Vol. I., Chap. XXI. See last two chapters of this work.

in kind, to the characteristics of other animals. Mr. Leslie Stephen forcibly reminds us that when we speak of man it is of man with his normal accompaniments. "To say that man would be better or worse if he had no stomach is to put together words which have no real meaning whatever. . . . You might describe a statue as a man without organs, but this is simply to play with words unless we confine our reasoning to properties dependent exclusively upon external forms. By 'man' we mean a being belonging to a given class and varying within the limits determined by the essential properties of the class; and amongst these essential properties we must, of course, reckon dependence upon a race."[1] The logical outcome seems to be that "every man is both an individual and a social product, and every instinct both social and self-regarding."[2]

As man started upon his earthly career in company with others, forming with them some aggregate possessed of some social instinct, it may be well to idealize the kind of instinct the earliest form of aggregation presents to us. Mankind is passing from the age of unconscious to that of conscious progress,[3] and the beginning of organization, like that among animals and insects, was not the result of reflection, but the outcome of an impulse. The earliest, most primitive creature is not entirely devoid of some kind or form of association. As far as we can see into the most primitive condition, it appears that the human infant has been helpless longer, requiring maternal care for a longer period than other animals. So it appears, from the outcome, that the feeling of maternal instinct lasted longer. "The prolonged helplessness of the offspring," says Mr. Fiske, "must keep the parents together for longer periods in successive epochs; and when the association is so long kept up that the older children are growing mature while the younger ones need protection, the family relations begin to become permanent.

---

[1] Science of Ethics, 95.

[2] *Ibid.*, 96.

[3] Tylor, Anthropology, 439.

The parents have lived so long in company that to seek new companionships involves some disturbance of ingrained habits."[1] What follows in the evolution of other social forms is thus outlined by the same author:[2] while the parents are thus becoming more attached to the family group, "the older sons are more likely to continue their original association with each other than to establish association with strangers, since they have common objects to achieve and common enmities, bequeathed and acquired, with neighboring families. As the parent dies, the headship of the family thus established devolves upon the oldest, or bravest, or most sagacious male remaining. Thus the little group gradually becomes a clan, the members of which are united by ties considerably stronger than those which ally them to members of adjacent clans, with whom they may indeed combine to resist the aggressions of yet further outlying clans or of formidable beasts, but to whom their feelings are usually those of hostile rivalry. It remains to add that the family groups thus constituted differ widely in many respects from modern families, and do not afford the materials for an idyllic picture of primeval life. Though always ready to combine against the attack of a neighboring clan, the members of the group are by no means indisposed to fight among themselves. The sociality is but nascent; infants are drowned, wives are beaten to death, and there are deadly quarrels between brothers. In the primitive clan all the women are the wives of all the men." "This state of things is just that which natural selection must assist and maintain so long as the incipient community is small and encompassed by dangers."[3] Some matters remain unconsidered by Mr.

---

[1] John Fiske, Outlines of Cosmic Philosophy, Vol. II., 344; Herbert Spencer, Principles of Sociology, Vol. I., Part III., Chap. II. See Chap. III., Sec. II., *post*, for a discussion of domestic relations.

[2] Fiske, 344, 345.

[3] See more fully Chap. III., Sec. II., and Chap. IV., *post*. W. Robertson Smith (Kinship in Arabia) has revealed a great deal of valuable information upon the early matriarchal and subsequent patriarchal condition of the early Arabians and Hebrews.

Fiske in the above extract that modify his views. The physical environment of man may in one locality be favorable to the maintenance of life, elsewhere it may be unfavorable; the one may at certain times and under certain circumstances contribute toward aggregation of families, or of members of families into tribes or clans, and the other may tend to produce an opposite result. If beasts of prey or other enemies do not threaten and the means of subsistence are large, a primitive group may hold together and grow, when the opposite result would have to take place if the means of subsistence were hard to find. In the former event children might be permitted to live, when in the latter infanticide might prevail. In the regions of Arctic ice infanticide and a life of small family groups would prevail, while in torrid regions tribal life would be matured. While the conditions of labor are unfavorable, as in the icy regions, few groups, and these far between, might live together in peace, whereas elsewhere multiplying numbers would produce conflicts. Mountainous life might produce, as already seen in the preceding section, a spirit of adventure and war which in more favored regions would be greeted by the feebleness of an easier, more peaceful life. We may say, however, that sociality will begin where, through variation, there is less tendency than usual for the individual to disperse widely; and that, allowing for further variation, mankind will tend, by survival of the fittest through adaptation, to preserve the largest, best aggregated social forms or bodies. The impulse that makes all animal life struggle to maintain existence, in mankind assumes new phases with the development of its gregarious tendency. Not less than gregarious animals does man, sooner or later, obtain pleasure from the presence of his mates and by their actions—a pleasure which is but a phase of that satisfaction in existence which the lower animal feels; and the maternal and dependent feelings which the female animal and its young will feel are surely not wanting among at least some primitive human beings. And these feelings are the early aspect of what later, in the course of later impact, growth, change and experience, become sympathy and love and family affections, to subserve which the customs and laws came into existence that now, in their latest form, constitute the basis of our text-books on "Domestic Relations."[1] While clan life is a form of aggregation which does not follow quickly upon the heels of the most primitive social forms, Mr. Fiske's outline, with some qualifications, is a fair summation of early human social development; and it shows that aggregation is a spontaneous product, the result mostly, if not entirely, of physical factors.

It is interesting to observe how far savage tribes have advanced to a state of legality. In the note[2] we give a list of

---

[1] See Chap. III., Sec. II., *post*, for fuller views on this subject.

[2] Mr. Lindsay's researches covered inquiries into the moral condition of savages or primitive races in East, West, South, and Central Africa, Ceylon, Malay Peninsula, Andaman Islands, North and South America, Australasia, New Zealand and the Fiji Islands. He sums up his evidence in the following list of negative and positive moral qualities or conditions:

Negative conditions:

1. No sense of sexual decency, modesty, chastity, virtue, purity, propriety or shame.
2. No marriage tie or rite.
3. No family arrangements.
4. No love—maternal, paternal, conjugal, parental, filial or fraternal.
5. No idea of paternity or of other relationships.
6. No kindness to or consideration for each other, whatever the natural or other relationship.
7. No respect for woman or sex.
8. No compassion, pity, sympathy for suffering.
9. No mercy.
10. No regret, remorse, self-reproach, or repentance.
11. No gratitude or other form of response to kindness received.
12. No sense of guilt or criminality.
13. No idea of duty or responsibility.
14. No conception of right and wrong, of moral good or evil.
15. No sense of justice or equity.
16. No respect for the rights of property or possession. (See Chap. III., Sec. I., *post*.)
17. No self-denial or self-control.
18. No knowledge of truth.

moral qualities discovered among them, as noted by W. Lauder Lindsay. The list given does not exhibit a noteworthy moral status. It is a status which the same author, in comparing it with that of the lower animals, considers in no way superior to that of animals.[1] He says: "It has to be remarked that the moral virtues are illustrated mainly by or in those animals that have directly or indirectly received their moral training from man—such animals as the dog, elephant and horse." He could have safely added others.[2] From which we confirm the previous argument, that the early aggregations and the resulting customs are of spontaneous production, just as are the animal's, and are not due to any self-conscious reflection and resulting effort. It may be that already far back in human history a low moral status may,

---

19. No honesty.
20. No ideas of honor.
21. No generosity, magnanimity, or charity.
22. No respect for or obedience to authority of any kind, unless embodied in the form of superior power.

Positive conditions:

1. Indiscriminate or promiscuous association, mingling or intercourse of the sexes, and of all ages.
2. Lust, lewdness and debauchery.
3. Desertion, including exposure and mutilation of or insults to the young and aged, sick, weak, or disabled and dead.
4. Cruelty to, including the torture of captives or enemies, and pleasure in witnessing the sufferings of the victims.
5. Bloodthirstiness, propensity to murder, including cannibalism.
6. Dishonesty, envy, covetousness, greed, proneness to theft, robbery, plunder of all kinds and degrees.
7. Prevalence of perjury, mendacity, lying.
8. Selfishness.
9. Ingratitude, including the repayment of good with evil.
10. Treachery, deceit, cunning.
11. Dominance of the instincts, appetites and passions. (Mind in the Lower Animals, Vol. I., pp. 164–166.)

[1] *Ibid.*, Chap. II., p. 175 *seq.*

[2] As ants (Romanes, Animal Intelligence, p. 58 *seq.*); bees, *Ibid.*, p. 155 *seq.*; monkeys, *Ibid.*, p. 471 *seq.* See Lubbock, Ants, Bees and Wasps, pp. 23, 285 *seq.* Spencer, Principles of Ethics, Justice, Chaps. I. to III. inclusive.

where the environment was favorable, have become somewhat ameliorated, and customs have obtained a better character.[1] And the time did come when not only household or tribal life gave place to a larger clan life, but likewise when patriarchal life was succeeded by municipal organization, and when municipal organization became merged into a still larger aggregate.[2]

The aggregation was in each instance builded upon physical units, whose activity, though become more conscious and intelligent, was largely a spontaneous impulse that moved on and spent its force in producing social effects. The process of cohesion by which a family—or rather a group centered around some woman—became a larger group or the basis of other independent groups, might occur among savages, but it was more apt to occur among people who had attained some mode of a settled life, as the tribes of Germany and Gaul. A warlike tribe might cohere, based on some kind of association around or descent from a woman, and driven by a disposition for adventure, make war and predatory excursions on others—a disposition most likely created by scarcity of sustenance and animal desire after females. In countries where the soil and nature yielded a prolific supply of berries or roots or plants, life would be less militant, and a rude mode of agriculture, by digging for roots, etc., would be introduced. The warlike overcoming the more peaceable and better-supplied groups and making slaves of their women and others, ultimately yielded large aggregates and a system of slave labor. Where flocks could be herded, these would be attended to by slaves or the women; where roots had to be dug or a supply of berries secured by some care and attention, a primitive form of labor by slaves and women was introduced. One need or one possibility brought the other. The larger group involved militancy, slavery, chase, and the

[1] See Tylor, Anthropology, Chap. XVI.; Lubbock, Prehistoric Times, pp. 580–586.

[2] See later chapters of this work.

tending of herds or that kind of agriculture which consists of digging for roots by means of sticks. If any thought is involved in this process, it is that form of thought which comes from practice and usage, and is retained because the brain retains it in the form of memory. Usage and practice, combined with the most efficient resisting forms of aggregation, are the means of survival. These are natural elements whose evolution and survival are implied in the battle of life. And with larger forms of aggregation, assuming the shape of clans, or towns, or cities, or nations, a greater elaboration of channels of communication, of preservative energy, of divisions of work and an increasing cohesive power resulted.[1] "It is a principle in physics that, since the force with which a body resists strains increases as the squares of its dimensions, its power of maintaining its integrity becomes relatively less as its mass becomes greater. Something analogous may be said of societies. Small aggregates only can hold together while cohesion is feeble; and successively larger aggregates become possible only as the greater strains implied are met by that greater cohesion which results from an adapted human nature and a resulting development of social organization." On the other hand, "as social integration advances, the increasing aggregates exercise increasing restraints over their units." "The forces by which aggregates keep their units together are at first feeble and, becoming strenuous at a certain stage of social evolution, afterwards relax, or rather, change their forms."[2]

The opening and maintenance of roads and bridges and the establishment of fortified places constitute features of increasing aggregation and distribution of population, to which society owes a vast deal of communication, transportation, locomotion, and the establishment of cities. The need of these was felt early in the history of our modern nations,

---

[1] Spencer, Principles of Sociology, Vol. II., Part V., Political Institutions.

[2] Principles of Sociology, Vol. II., §§451, 452.

as is evidenced by the importance which was attached to the *trinoda necessitas*, or threefold duty required of the most favored, and enforced with considerable strictness, of rendering military service, repairing bridges and maintaining fortifications;[1] also to maintain the roads and keep watch and ward.[2]

Cities, moreover, do not find their origin only at strong places of defence.[3] Other natural conditions, as we have seen and shall further see,[4] co-operated to produce them, such as the proximity of a body of water, or a road. Many cities date their beginning from the fact that they were fording places,—such as Ox*ford*, Here*ford*, Hert*ford*, Bed*ford*, Strat*ford*-on-Avon, Staf*ford*, Walling*ford*, Guil*ford*, Chelms*ford*, Iel*ford*, Rom*ford*, Ayles*ford*, Dart*ford*, Frank*furt*, Lem*förde*, etc.[5] "At the spot where the Roman road crosses the Aire, the name of PONTEFRACT (*ad pontem fractum*) reminds us that the broken Roman bridge must have remained unrepaired during a period long enough for the naturalization of the new name."[6] A number of towns still show their proximity to early roads and bridges. The Danish word *gata* means a street or road, and in Scandinavian districts of Great Britain the word *gate* designates the same thing; therefore, when we see towns within such districts having streets or roads ending with *gate*, we may affirm their proximity to roads; of which Briggate or Bridge street and Kirkgate or Church street in

---

[1] *Cf.* Stubbs, Const. Hist. of Eng., Vol. I., p. 76, note 4, also pp. 95, 105, 184, 190; Maurer, Markenverfassung, §91; same, Hofverfassung, Vol. I., §143; Waitz, Deutsche Verfassungsgeschichte, Vol. IV., p. 25 *seq.*; Stubbs, Select Charters, p. 153.

[2] Zoepfl, Deutsche Rechtsgeschichte, Vol. II., §40, IV.; Schrader, Handelsg. u. Warenkunde, Chap. I.

[3] *Cf.* Taylor, Words and Places, pp. 81, 148, 149, 172, 333; Roemer, Origins of the English People and English Language, pp. 124, 187, 466; Woolsey, Political Science, §153; Arnold, Verf.-Geschichte der deutschen Freistädte, Vol. I., p. 3; Freeman, Eng. Towns and Districts, *passim*.

[4] Chap. IV., *post*.

[5] Taylor, Words and Places, pp. 169, 331. See Chap. IV., *post*.

[6] *Ibid.*

Leeds are evidences.[1] Brixton, Bruges, Innsprück, Weybridge, Briançon are derived from the vicinity of bridges.[2] The influence of roads, bridges and cities upon laws still remains manifold.

The maintenance of roads, the travel upon roads, the casualties upon roads, including railroads, their use as post and military roads, as channels of communication between place and place, and the beneficial or blighting effect their management may entail, form the basis of a vast amount of legislation and many decisions. Relative to railroads alone, governments are occupied every year with measures to regulate them, under forms of incorporation, or police regulation, or the exercise of eminent domain.[3] The management of these extraordinary media of commerce has called into existence at the instance of receivers of courts, principally in the United States, certificates of indebtedness, issued under the orders of the court, with the assent of the litigating beneficiaries, for the purpose of maintaining and operating railroads. The exercise of the power is partly based upon the obligations of a common carrier and a mail carrier which the court assumes when it takes possession and, through its receiver, manages a railroad; it is also grounded, among other things, in that rule of public economy which requires the highways to be kept in repair. "The public is entitled to protection in the continued use of the railway as a king's highway." Though the beneficiaries are usually required to assent to such orders, practically the proceeds of the certificates are employed for many things not for their benefit, and their consent is "only colorable and constructive . . . The schoolboy creeps like a

---

[1] Taylor, Words and Places, p. 168. See same authority for other evidences, pp. 331, 332.

[2] *Ibid.* 332.

[3] Upon this subject consult Schrader, Handelsg. u. Warenkunde, Chap. I.; Herbert Spencer, Moral, Political and Aesthetic Essays, p. 251, Railway Morals and Railway Policy; see also Wharton, American Law, §§422, 446, 482, 489, 490; Pierce on Railroads; Green's Brice, *Ultra Vires;* Mills, Eminent Domain; Woolsey, Political Science, Vol. I., pp. 40, 221; Vol. II., pp. 399–401.

snail unwillingly to school. In some sense he goes voluntarily, and so consents to go because he is compelled and cannot make a successful resistance. In a majority of cases where receiver's certificates are made a prior lien upon railroad property, some portion at least of the holders of the senior liens give no more voluntary consent to the issue than this. They assent because it is idle to refuse."[1] These are an entirely new species of commercial paper.[2] I cannot resist the temptation to refer to another birth or product of railroads. It is an old doctrine among English and American lawyers that when a trespasser, whatever his good faith may be, attaches a thing to the soil of another, the thing so attached becomes the property of the owner of the soil. That rule has been slowly modified;[3] and now in the case of railroads it has been wholly departed from, notwithstanding that railroad companies exercise the right of eminent domain to acquire lands against the will of the owner, and are required to pursue the course of condemnation prescribed to them by law. The question has invariably arisen in reference to the action of railroad companies in putting roadbeds and rails—a track—upon another's lands either without having previously condemned the lands in the mode provided by law, or have proceeded in condemning them against the wrong person. The courts in the United States, with a few exceptions, now hold that the owner cannot compel a railroad company to pay him for a track it located upon his land under the circumstances mentioned, even though he in no way encouraged it.[4] The

---

[1] Chas. Fiske Beach, Jr., Receiver's Certificates, 3 Law Quarterly Review, pp. 430, 431, 439; also now to be found in the same author's work on Receivers, chapter on Receiver's Certificates. See also to same effect, Meyer *v.* Johnson, 53 Ala., pp. 237, 348.

[2] See same article of Mr. Beach.

[3] See Jones on Liens, Vol. II., §§1131–1139; 90 N. C. 111; 30 Md. 352; 2 Pet. 137; 20 Kans. 434; 77 N. C. 188; 2 Dev. 376; Schouler, Personal Property, §§114–118.

[4] 70 Ala. 227, 232; 87 Pa. St. 28; 34 Kans. 158; 42 Wis. 538; 20 Fla. 616; 63 Miss. 380; 14 Oregon, 519; Pierce on Railroads, p. 219; 15 S. W. Rep. 188; see *contra*, 36 Ind. 463; 47 Cal. 515; 31 N. J. Eq. 31; 97 Mass. 279; 124 Mass. 118; 35 Ohio St. 531.

courts say, quoting from the Oregon case referred to in the note: "In modern times, for the encouragement of trade, manufactories and transportation, and owing, no doubt, in part to the increased value and importance of personal property, many things are now considered as personalty which are attached to the soil. The necessities and conveniences of an advancing civilization have demanded a relaxation of the strict rule, so that now attachment to the soil is only one of the several conditions to help in determining whether a given thing belongs to the realty .... In view of the rights delegated by the state to [the railroad corporation in question]; the purposes for which they are conferred; the public use for which the land is condemned; the just compensation required to be paid for its appropriation; and the great interest the public has in the successful operation of the road—it seems to us that these elements plainly distinguish the acts of a corporation, although technically a trespasser, in building its road upon lands without proper authority therefor, from the acts of a common trespasser, in affixing chattels [*i. e.* roadbed and rails] to the freehold, and to render inapplicable the strict rule of law which would treat such improvements as fixtures and part of the realty."[1] Here then is another consequence, unforeseen, of railroad construction. It will be noted how this opinion indicates the interdependence between railroads and other physical creations of social aggregates; also the reference to physical elements contained in this opinion will be noted, such as "personalty," "soil," "trade," "transportation," "public use," "compensation," "appropriation," etc.

Among the commonwealths of North America commissions are being created to regulate the management and fares of railroads, and Congress has also attempted the same upon what must be regarded as an extraordinary scale of magnitude. Whether this will prove beneficial cannot be foretold

---

[1]See the case in 14 Oregon 519; also reported in 13 Pacific Reporter, p. 300. And also Jones *v.* R. R. Co., 70 Ala. 227, 232; Justice *v.* R. R. Co., 87 Pa. St. 28; Newgass *v.* R. R. Co., 54 Ark. 140, 146.

with any certainty. These measures involve a hasty and perhaps too extensive an artificial regimen over railroads—a regimen that is producing consolidation of roads upon gigantic scales of magnitude, and which may culminate in centering more power over larger territory, by means of these expeditious methods of locomotion and intercourse, in the hands of a few speculating and daring men than even exists at present, and cities of great magnitude, if not states, may thus be made and unmade. The tariff these impose may operate like a protective tariff upon some communities, like a blighting one upon others. It is a grave question whether the congressional measure has been builded upon a careful study of the present and prospective factors involved, of which physical elements constitute a large part.

Among roads, rivers and other channels of intercourse by water are to be embraced. The influence of rivers and water has been partially treated under another head. Here we may consider the use social aggregates make of them. Thus, they become highways of intercourse whereby different sections are brought together politically, as occurred with the French settlements in Louisiana, Illinois and Canada, by means of the Lakes, the rivers of Illinois, Indiana and Ohio, and the Mississippi; they afford the easiest means of communication among a people who have not yet felt the need of cutting roads through the wilderness; they have formed barriers of protection to people; they have afforded food to the inhabitants of the earth. And in our modern day the poverty-stricken can find upon bodies of water that are public a right to fish and thus to maintain life without infringing on other's rights. The use of rivers and other bodies of water for intercourse is recognized in legal systems, in the codes of law regulating navigation on internal waters, upon the ocean and inland seas. The intercourse between social aggregates is what led to such systems, developing with the size and needs of such aggregates. They originally were based on what resulted spontaneously from the acts and methods and medium of navigation. But reforms and additions have been made which are contained in the notions which experience has shown to be beneficial; which therefore owe their origin to more or less thought. The mills of earlier and later days, and the legislation thus engendered, from the early *Hof* or *Dorf* to the present New England Town, depend upon river and streams. Canals and roads were created by social aggregates for needs that were felt, and were the basis of much controversy at certain stages in the history of government. The Suez Canal and the canals of Asia, Egypt, Europe and the United States filled positive needs, and were and are the subject of legislation and rights which courts and nations enforce.

The early mills, agriculture and herding of flocks implied social aggregation. The earliest form of agriculture in the shape of any sharp-pointed stick for digging roots resulted only after some form of aggregation made it needful, and the onerous character of labor required to develop it made any advance in it depend upon the existence of a class which was in more or less subjection to the others of a given group. The herding of flocks is hardly practiced as early as the practice of digging for roots, but it is possible for it to have existed among many aggregates as to whom agriculture was limited or perhaps non-existent. Both herding and husbandry are emanations from the pursuit after sustenance. So they are both the outcome of favorable physical surroundings, and they have proven prerequisites in the formation of such aggregates as are required in the formation of states. They are the bases of regulation and regimen far back in the history of mankind.[1] And this regulation and regimen keep pace with the changes and progress or retrogression of the mass. The earliest forms of pastoral and agricultural communities seem to show a community holding

---

[1] Tylor, Anthropology, p. 214 *seq.*, p. 418 *seq.*; Spencer, Principles of Sociology, Vol. II., §538 *seq.* See also Seebohm, English Village Community, p. 437. See Chap. III., Sec. I., *post.*

land in common without individual ownership, amongst whom, as judged by later practices, the regulation thereof was the result of practice and experience.[1]

The development of social aggregation implies, therefore, beside roads, pastoral life and agriculture. We know that without these property in land would not have been possible, neither could the early communal political organization have come into existence. Without these the possibility of any kind of coöperation needful to city life would have been prevented, and municipal life would never have found a being. It would then have been impracticable for a civilized aggregate, such as a State, to find a basis for existence. Our present laws contain, as historical results, a vast number of regulations which bear on land ownership, that had a beginning in and for many centuries depended upon a pastoral life and agriculture; and modern codes contain numbers of regulations showing a dependence of the social aggregates upon this use of land. I shall treat of this subject more fully hereafter.[2]

The use of weapons, the practice of war, is another incident of social aggregation.[3] It was certainly a very early phenomenon. Forcible resistance or attack are the phenomena of animal life, when bent on securing subsistence or satisfying passionate impulses. And these aspects of acquisition or defense come up through all stages of human existence. They develop into self-help and the combined defensive energies of the family group. Roving families compelled to seek for food, subjected to severe vicissitudes, as already hinted at, would

---

[1] See Hanssen, Agrarhistorische Abhandlungen, Vol. II., p. 84 *seq.*; Maurer, Markenverfassung, Appendix; same, Dorfverfassung, Appendix; Seebohm, Eng. Village Community; Laveleye, Primitive Property; Spencer, Principles of Sociology, Vol. II., Part V., Chap. XV.; Maine, Village Communities. See Chap. III., Sec. I., *post*.

[2] *Cf.* Chap. III., Sec. I., *post*.

[3] "In rude societies all adult males are warriors; and, consequently, the army is the mobilized community, and the community is the army at rest."—Spencer, Principles of Sociology, Vol. II., §515.

be more inclined to attack, and by natural increment of experience develop a militant state or condition. Neighboring tribes subjected to similar conditions, when coming into collision, would engage in strifes. The weakly, the more peaceable, would need protection. They would ultimately be merged in other more warlike groups, becoming their slaves, or, where possessed of superior traits, their equals or superiors. The discipline thus engendered, enlarging with the group and with the needs and successes and defeats it suffered, would become amplified in details and severed in form, presenting increasingly with its vicissitudes a stricter subordination, or it would succumb to disintegration resulting from want of subsistence or from defeat in wars. The character of warfare typifies the character of the mass engaged in it. Among the lowest races there is no organization. All the men go out, in a desultory sort of way, and the wars are not very bloody; the women sometimes assist. The picture which Champlain drew of a battle between his Indian allies and the Mohawks shows how very primitive was their mode of warfare.[1] It presents two swarms of men with bows and arrows, who approached close to each other and delivered their arrows. Champlain and two French arquebusiers in a few minutes defeated the Mohawks with a few well directed shots. Among more developed tribes warfare is much more serious, difficult and imposing. Many of the tribes of Asia and Africa have shown far superior skill in the military art to these lowest races, with each advance presenting a larger or more compact aggregation, better arranged and disciplined and governed. And the history of mankind has been in a large measure the history of the military art.[2] That it was which conspired to

---

[1] Narrative and Critical History of the United States, Vol. IV., p. 120. *Cf.* last two chapters of the present work.

[2] Consult Spencer, Principles of Sociology, Vol. I., §259, Vol. II., Part V., Chap. XII.; Tylor, Anthropology, p. 221 *seq.*; Hallam, Middle Ages, Vol. I., p. 255 *seq.*; Roemer, Origins of the English People, etc., p. 144 *seq.*; Bancroft, History of the United States, Vol. II., Chap. XXXVII.; Green, Making of England, p. 164 *seq.*; same, Conquest of England, pp. 66, 67,

consolidate tribal and municipal organizations, thus creating larger territorial social aggregates. It created a head and a kind of political existence among loose formations. We know that without it no Roman Empire, nor Merovingian or Carolingian dynasty would have been possible, and that Europe today would be without any such social aggregations as it has. The importance of the military art can be seen by reference to what it has lost in social evolution. Setting out with that period in which the army is coextensive with the adult and male population, and a body-politic has not yet formed, we observe how it eventually becomes specialized. "There is the restriction in relative mass which, first seen in the growth of a slave population engaged in work instead of war, becomes more decided as a settled agricultural life occupies freemen and increases the obstacles to military service. There is, again, the restriction caused by that growing costliness of the individual soldier accompanying the development of arms, accoutrements and ancillary appliances of warfare; and there is yet the additional restriction caused by the intenser strain which military action puts on the resources of a nation, in proportion as it is carried on at a greater distance. With separation of the fighting body from the body-politic at large, there very generally goes acquirement of a separate head. Active militancy ever tends to maintain union of civil rule with military rule, and often causes reunion of them where they have become separate; but with the primary differentiation of civil from military structures is commonly associated a tendency to the rise of distinct controlling centers for them."[1] The factors that imply a militant condition of the tribe will likewise account for that disposition which regards robbery of strangers as legitimate; human life, on its own account, of comparatively little value; cruelty and slavery as natural; and agriculture and the herding of flocks

414, 415, and see the whole of these two works, and generally Spencer's Descriptive Sociology. For development of Roman military discipline, see Marquardt, Röm. Staatsverwaltung, Vol. II., Part III.

[1] Principles of Sociology, Vol. II., §521.

and the practice of peaceful professions as menial. And these conditions, as we know from European history, will not die out until the body-politic is formed upon those broader bases implied in recent and most modern state formations. The savage disposition in mankind, its animal impulses and passions, promoted by association among human beings, have succumbed slowly to the moral suasion and influence of a developing humaneness; the one was more a physical, the latter a more mental impulse. And the feelings of anger, fury, malevolence, by which individuals are influenced, are surviving remnants of those same animal impulses.[1] That the law has dealt with this impulse needs no telling. Malice makes crime more atrocious, civil offenses more grave. But the law has dealt only with acts; the motive is punishable only when manifested in acts, and the acts indicate the motive.[2]

The products of military life have been, speaking of physical conditions, aggregations of individuals in increasing cohesive form; construction and maintenance of roads; creation and maintenance of slavery or serfdom; the maintenance of status as opposed to contract; demand for fortresses; demand for arms, ammunition, ordnance, etc. And as these came into existence there were born regulations, rules, customs, laws (call them what you will) relating to the needs of a community engaged in war, increasing as the community enlarged. From rules inhibitory of desertion or cowardice, among early tribes, and modes of treating captives, down to the elaborate rules embraced in modern military codes and treaties and hospital service, one can trace up the evolution of rules of military conduct growing up with the practice of war, while social aggregates broke up and reformed or merged in other aggregates or ceased to exist. And one

---

[1] Compare Spencer, Data of Ethics; Tylor, Anthropology, p. 405 *seq.*; Bain, Emotions and the Will, p. 179 *seq.*; Leslie Stephen, Science of Ethics, p. 236; Martineau, Ethical Theory, p. 172 *seq.*; Mind, Vol. VIII., pp. 61, 415, 562.

[2] Bishop, Criminal Law, §§204 *seq.*; Stephen, History of Criminal Law, Vol. II., p. 110 *seq.*; see Woolsey, Political Science, Part II., Chap. VIII. For earlier aspects of criminal law, see Post, Bausteine, etc., Vol. I.

can trace to wars the continuance of barbarousness down to our own day in many forms, and the sanguinary character of codes up to a very recent day in some countries and the continuance of such codes in other countries. The practice of war, like the practice of other things, begets a taste for it and a corresponding disposition; and thus military art may tend, when aided by the existence of large, well-formed and compact social aggregates, to become a factor promotive of anti-social anti-humane rules. But no one can legislate for armies and for their proper management who attempts to do so by reference to theory only. Many physical conditions must be studied and borne in mind before a successful campaign can be assumed. Von Moltke's knowledge of French territory, French railroad capacity and other resources formed a base for legislation that facilitated a most extraordinary campaign. The knowledge of Russian power has had an effect upon European legislation; the contiguity of Russian dominion upon English legislation.

Barter and trade are other incidents of social aggregation. It would be difficult to imagine any extended co-operative life without these factors. They have followed close upon early forms of aggregation and have kept pace with development. The practice appears in the "swapping" among children, and in a similar act among early beings. Many savage tribes show that they understood the practice. The Indians of North America in the days of the first settlers used "wampum" as a medium of exchange; the Australian tribes carry stone, valuable for making hatchets, hundreds of miles and accept in return therefor products they prize. The *Iliad* speaks of barter.[1] The Esthonian word *raha,* money, in the related language of the Laplanders means fur. In Russia

[1] VII. 472 ff. Oxen formed the basis of barter. *Ibid.* II. 449, VI. 236, XXI. 49, XXIII. 703 ff.; Odyss. I. 431; Jevons, Money and the Medium of Exchange; Schrader, Handelsgeschichte u. Warenkunde, Chap. IV. The evidence points to ornaments as the first forms of money. Schrader, *loc. cit.* The earliest forms of barter were probably gifts given in exchange for gifts. *Ibid.* 9, 10.

kung, money, means marten. The Danes used cattle and, after they had progressed in agriculture, grain in barter. Cattle were used among the early Germans, Irish, Scotch and Anglo-Saxons. The Kirghises use horses and sheep, wolf-skins and lamb-skins. Among the Persian nomads sheep or, when held in subjection in the cities, corn, straw and wool are used in exchange. Cattle are used in barter by the Tartars and the Tscherkessens.[1] In Rome *pecunia*, which originally meant property, riches, wealth, wealth in cattle, later came to signify money; it was derived from *pecus*, which meant cattle or, collectively, a herd. *Pecus* is said to be related to the Gothic *faihu*, Anglo-Saxon *feó*, German *vieh*, English *fee*, all derivations of the same root *paçu*, and all mean cattle. The early swapping we know has evolved into the vast and multitudinous transactions of commerce that now occupy the attention of a vast number of the inhabitants of the world. The methods whereby this has been accomplished embrace means of transportation, regulated between town and town by tolls or duties—tolls and duties that were the forerunners of the tariff policies of nations. So these methods embrace places of trade, such as markets and fairs, from early days to our own day; and now also market-places and expositions, all of which are the occasions of no little legislation and a great many decisions.[2] Banks, coinage, commercial paper and securities, bailments, telegraphy, intercourse between nations, states, cities and other localities, manufactories, shipping, invention, even science, more or less directly represent methods whereby commerce has become so large an element of human activity. And all of these constantly imply the use and need of physical objects, also aggregations and aggregate unity and action depending as much, if not more, upon spontaneous growth as upon self-conscious origination.

---

[1] Compare Roescher's Political Economy, Book II., Chap. III.; Tylor, Anthropology, p. 281 *seq.*; Hallam, Middle Ages, Vol. II., p. 527.

[2] A splendid inquiry into the early history of trade is to be found in Schrader, Handelsgeschichte und Warenkunde.

Roads, bridges, fortifications tend to add new aggregates to those already existing. They contribute to make agriculture, the military art, and barter and trade more extensive, effective and influential. And these severally act and react upon each other when utilized by the growing aggregates. They do nothing by themselves, yet they shape the molding and evolving forces of social aggregates, and they incidentally tend to make and unmake customs and laws.

The influence of social aggregation upon jurisprudence now meets with general recognition.[1] It has been affirmed that the legal unit was the family;[2] and from that point the history or development or growth of law has been traced up. The customs expand with aggregation into larger social forms, and (as social aggregations become more complex and numerous,) assume more and more those forms which approach nearest to our present laws. When city and national life come into existence they are based on social aggregations previously existing, and upon that mass of customs and forms which represent the sum of acting and

---

[1] Ihering, Zweck im Recht, Vol. II., 142; Wharton, American Law, Chaps. I. and II.; Stephen, Science of Ethics, Chap. IV.; Spencer, Principles of Sociology, Vol. II., Political Institutions, esp. Chap. XIV.; same, Data of Ethics, Chap. VIII.; Fiske, Cosmic Philosophy, Vol. II., 240 *seq.*; Amos, Science of Law, Chap. IV.; an article by Prof. S. W. Dyde, in Mind, Vol. XIII., 549 *seq.*; Lecky, History of European Morals, Vol. I., 130 *seq.*, and other portions of the same work; Courtney, Constructive Ethics, 26 *seq.*; Frederick Pollock, Essays in Jurisprudence and Ethics, Chaps. VIII. and XI.; Montesquieu, Spirit of Laws, Book I., Chap. III.; Markby, Elements of Law, Chap. I.; Holland, Elements of Jurisprudence, Chap. IV.; Clark, Practical Jurisprudence, 149 *seq.*; Savigny, Heutigen R. R., Chap. II.; Holtzendorf, Encyclopædia der Rechtswissenschaft (Systematischer Theil), *passim*, esp. see first article on the Philosophical History of Jurisprudence; Fowler, Progressive Morality, *passim*.

[2] Maine, Ancient Law, 128 *seq.*; Miller, Philosophy of Law, 47 *seq.*; Hearn, Aryan Household, *passim;* Essays in Anglo-Saxon Law, 122; but see Chap. III., Sec. II., and Chap. IV., *post.* The earliest form was not the family as much as it was a group of so-called kinsmen, clustered around a female or females. For an illustration see W. Robertson Smith, Kinship in Arabia.

doing of these aggregates. Some customs or laws are peculiar to aggregates—thus those customs or laws which control in the deliberations and movements of such aggregates with reference to each other. The leagues of early Grecian commonwealths, of the free-cities of the Rhine, the Hanseatic League, the treaties between nations, and a growing mass of rules governing the relations between members of united or confederated states, all imply legal relations and indefinite legal problems. In our modern day the relations between the nation and the state, between the nation and the townships, counties and cities, and between the state and its subdivisions, have given rise and will continue to give rise to important legal positions and problems.[1] The commerce clause of the United States Constitution, which originally contemplated the power to impose a tariff for protective purposes,[2] seems in this to now militate against State integrity and to require a different interpretation on this account.[3] In any event, up to quite recently the superior prevalence of State loyalty completely dropped from the public consciousness the original moving causes of that clause. The sense of State and county integrity has been creating a sentiment adverse to the exercise of any control over cities and counties by Federal tribunals. Corporate life has found a great expansion in the shape of municipal and especially private corporations; and the continual increase of these, and the vast wealth and influence they are securing, is begetting a sentiment adverse to them. Therefore legislation concerning railroad and insurance corporations is becoming stricter and more extended. Corporate life, of the kind just mentioned, has introduced that lack of sympathy between employer and employed which is increasing the discontent of the employé,

---

[1] A reference to Cooley, Constitutional Limitations, will confirm this statement.

[2] Tariff Hist. of the U. S., by David H. Mason, Part I.; Crit. and Nar. Hist. U. S., Vol. VII., Chap. IV. See also the last chapter of this work.

[3] Reports Am. Bar Ass'n, Vol. XI., 247 *seq.*, a paper by J. Randolph Tucker.

and is manifesting its results in strikes, in socialism and anarchy. So, too, furnishing as it does tremendous leverage to men of exceptional financial skill, this corporate life is putting political entities at the mercy of a few, and is becoming the means of vast accumulations in the hands of the few at the expense of the many. It is also loosening the cords of family life in favor of luxury, over-indulgence and skepticism. The law deals with all of these circumstances, or ought to. How can it do so properly, save by a recourse to the fundamental causes of evil; save by a study of those elements which have rendered possible these growths? The aggregation of individuals is looked at, in certain particulars, with more or less concern by governments, and the laws reflect this sentiment. In many European countries it is a crime, more or less severely punishable, for men to assemble together at certain times and places, no matter what the occasion. Socialistic and communistic movements are condemned and punished with severity. And in our own law certain combinations, whether called trusts, pools, or by other names, are treated as criminal conspiracies.[1]

Not only in the form of States, cities, towns and the like is law moulded and fashioned by aggregates; not only by the family or tribal groups is it affected; it is likewise affected by those aggregates which are formed for purposes of trade in different centers or places; by those aggregates which contemplate the regulation of benevolent and penal establishments, and by those aggregates which embrace the "humanity" of a given period. All sorts of such forms are continually arising and dying out, leaving their effect upon the laws that are extant.[2]

---

[1] See Wright, Criminal Conspiracies, with Corssen's addition thereto. Two or more persons are essential to constitute a conspiracy, *ibid.* 127. But a man and wife are not capable of so conspiring, *ibid.* Conspiracy has been said to be "a breathing together." 28 Fed. Rep. 808.

[2] See Bacon, Benefit Societies and Life Insurance, Chap. II. Beside corporate associations may be mentioned unincorporated associations, partnerships and clubs. See *Ibid.*, Chaps. I. and II.

The individual himself changes under the influence of social aggregation. In some respects his personal freedom becomes more restrained, either as slave or serf or dependent; in some particulars, that is in the opportunities and capacity for accumulation and the superior means of preservation thus afforded, he may secure a less precarious means of existence and obtain a larger personal enjoyment than he previously had. And the law reflects, in multiform particulars, these effects. His mental condition, which is least dependent upon physical factors, nevertheless exhibits the effect of such development, as social aggregation superinduces, in a developed brain, in inherited feelings, in social aptitudes. And the dependence these have upon physical elements is easily seen when lesions or physical taints produce abnormal conduct in this or that particular. The brain is now regarded as the seat of the mind, and its physical characters are too obvious for discussion,[1] and the law which recognizes the causes of insanity, or mental disease, in a diseased brain, looks with suspicion at the will or contract of the undeveloped mind or brain of the infant, of the weakened mind or brain of the inebriate or idiot or those afflicted with senility, and it makes allowances for the more emotional and susceptible natures of women, especially wives, and contains provisions for the protection of all of these; these provisions are rules which have come up with the growth and development of society, thus illustrating the recognition of social and physical elements as controlling factors.

The position of the individual in the early village community, typified in the Russian *mir* of to-day, is radically different from that occupied by him in the United States. His rights and duties were less comprehensive and detailed.

---

[1] Compare Bain, The Emotions and the Will; same, The Senses and the Intellect; Spencer, Principles of Psychology; Lewes, Problems of Life and Mind; Maudsley, Body and Will; same, Physiology and Pathology of the Mind; Sully, Sensation and Intuition; same, Illusions; Wundt, Grundzüge der physiologischen Psychologie; Ribot, Diseases of Memory; same, Diseases of Will; Luys, The Brain and its Functions.

His place in the body of which he was a unit was of more consequence than now, but his freedom of action was more restricted. The existence of frequent wars and a militant organization begot and maintained in ancient Rome a feeling of patriotism and reverence for power that rendered possible the deification of emperors and the enforcement of that apotheosis by laws. The industrial development of later ages has produced a regard for promises and oaths that is evidenced in the laws against perjury and in favor of the enforcement of contracts to an extent unknown in ancient times. And these influences have colored the lives of individuals as they have given character to the age and the state. The drift of modern communities seems to be towards democracy and a kind of socialism.[1] In the heart of Europe, under the Berlin Treaty, a great extension was given by monarchical nations to democratic tendencies, and was forced upon all of the parties thereto by circumstances based upon mutual distrust. So in England and the United States, laws aiming to provide for and protect the masses, in utter opposition to the doctrine of *laisser faire*, have been all along on the increase.[2] Poor laws, laws relating to land-ownership, laws providing for state ownership of railroads, telegraphs, etc., mechanics lien laws, laborers lien laws, are evidences of the moderate form of socialism. But other graver aspects of a similar tendency may be found in the disposition to make laws interpretable and applicable as in the judgment of any jury may seem most appropriate.[3] That democracy produces good results and political self-control has been exemplified on more than one occasion in the United States, especially after heated presidential elections. And that an extravagant application of democratic theories may tend to annihilation is well illustrated by anarchism. Both result

[1] Compare Hosmer, The People and Politics, and see Political Science Quarterly, Vol. III., 549 *seq.*; Graham, Old and New Socialism.

[2] Herbert Spencer, The Man versus the State.

[3] See the instructions given by the trial judge in the anarchist trials of Spiess and his confederates, Northeast Reporter, Vol. XII., 865.

from combinations, and both react in forming the legal status and feelings of individuals. In the United States those who have become identified with its democratic institutions display largely a feeling of deference and obedience for law and courts; while those who have become transplanted there, and do not care to become identified with its institutions and body-politic, aim to annihilate the governments and laws there prevailing by means of assassination, fire and dynamite, in spite of the fact that they invoke with vehemence, even frenzy, the protection of the government and laws when called to account for their atrocious doctrines. The effect of aggregation upon the individual was illustrated by the history of slavery in the United States after the Federal Constitution was adopted. Introduced into the country by traders, it flourished both in the North and South, until climate and soil in the North demonstrated the need of that thrift and toil which are inimical to serfdom; these begot economy, great energy, careful regimen and thought, and an unfavorable field for slave and other unprofitable labor. In the South manufacturing was not followed; there the cultivation of tobacco, corn and cotton, and the great heat which rendered exertion painful, produced a favorable region for the employment of slave labor. The needs and demands of the latter and the lack of such needs on the part of the former produced that antagonism which culminated in abolitionism and secession and war. The resulting emancipation has produced new social problems with which political parties, legislators and courts have been, and will continue to be, called upon to deal. The emancipation movement was the prolific cause of many urgent laws, and its results will be still further seen in the multiplication of other not less urgent laws.

Before concluding this chapter I venture to mention the productive agency which animals have played in the formation of laws. One needs but to be reminded of humanitarian laws for the protection of animals, in order to understand that

---

[1] See Chap. IV., *post*.

their presence has given rise to serious controversy in the field of law. Vivisection is thus lamed and rendered impotent of results, when it ought not to be improperly checked. Laws against estrays, vicious animals, and for the licensing of animals result from their presence and use in societies. That they are capable of ownership and value needs not to be told.

NOTE.—Mr. A. L. Lyall, whose familiarity with Indian institutions and history will not be questioned, says: "No better example [than India] could be found of the force with which needs and risks of a primitive age can bind men together by *spontaneous combination*, for the purposes of social preservation and continuity."[1]

Professor Woolsey affirms: "There is no highly civilized society which, if its history is traced back, does not contain some vestiges of a type of polity, which may fairly be supposed to be connected with and to have *grown out* from the first institutions of mankind. There is no savage or uncivilized race which cannot in its institutions be referred back, on the supposition of degeneration or of natural departure, to social forms that *grew* out of the family state or out of something like it."[2]

Dr. Hosmer, who has written a remarkable book on politics, says that "communities of human creatures—'bodies politic'—are organisms that have an existence marked by definite stages of growth and decay; and the changes that take place in that existence do so regularly within certain limits, and under the influence of *external physical conditions, or of impulses originating in the vital resources of these bodies.* They have their physiological history, and the facts of this history recur with certainty in the same circumstances. Politics—as a classification of these facts—the digestion of

[1]A. L. Lyall on Sir Henry S. Maine, Law Quarterly Review, Vol. IV., 132.

[2]Theodore D. Woolsey, Political Science, Vol. I., §137 *seq.*

the facts involved in the relations of men in political communities, and in the relation of such communities to one another—is as clearly a physical science as natural history—of which, indeed, it is a further part, for it is a habit of the animal man to construct states."[1] He has written a profound treatise which tends to show how one form of government has flowed from the other, in the consecutive growth of mankind; becoming revealed in spite of the bloom and wreck of many nations.

The purely physical aspects of aggregates in the production of law are well illustrated by Professor Sheldon Amos, in his works on the science of law and the science of politics.[2] In one place he says: "The object for which the rules which constitute a nation's law are made is the determining of the mutual relations of the human beings who form the community."

"The whole community may be regarded as composed of an active crowd of multitudinous atoms, incessantly crossing one another's path and interfering with one another's freedom of movement. The influence of family life and of the simpler forms of agricultural and industrial co-operation tend, of themselves, at the very birth of the state, to create within the realm of this confused atomic action an increasing number of fixed groups or centers of independent movement. About the same time another series of events is taking place, giving rise to the phenomena of law. These events are of a different description in different communities. Either the groups spontaneously enlarge themselves and the village absorbs the family, or some one or more of the originally co-equal groups enlarge in numbers or increase in importance out of proportion to the rest. Or the whole community becomes subjugated to the sway or influence of some already organized state. What is of importance, however, to notice

---

[1] G. W. Hosmer, The People and Politics, 22, 23. See also Miller, Philosophy of Law, Lecture IX.

[2] A Systematic View of the Science of Jurisprudence; Science of Law, and Science of Politics.

is that, in every case, the final result is the adjustment of the limits of free movement of the various groups constituting the community, in respect of their capacity for disturbing each other."[1]

"Physical relations involve and generate jural relations, in the case of self-conscious beings. Person and property have created the state just as truly as the state has created them. Or rather, as in an organic body, each part is a means and at the same time an end." In the same chapter progressive integration in the formation of law is insisted upon.[2]

No person has shown more conclusively the play of aggregation in the production of law than Mr. Herbert Spencer. One cannot single out portions of his work to illustrate this. The Principles of Sociology disclose it in a most marked manner. The formation of groups, their compounding and recompounding, are emphasized as accompanying social evolution, and law is shown to be one of the products. It would appear from what he has written that the evolution of human beings necessarily involved social evolution and social products, and that law was a spontaneous outcome.[3]

"Wenn wir in der Betrachtung des Rechtsverhältnisses von allen besonderen Inhalt desselben abstrahiren, so bleibt uns als algemeines Wesen desselben übrig das auf bestimmte Weise geregelte zusammenleben mehrerer Menschen. Es liegt nun sehr nahe, bei diesem abstracten Begriff einer Mehrheit überhaupt stehen zu bleiben, und das Recht als eine Erfindung derselben zu denken, ohne welche die äussere Freiheit keines einzelnen bestehen könnte. Allein ein solches zufälliges Zusammentreffen einer unbestimmten Menge ist eine willkührliche, aller Wahrheit ermangelnde Vorstellung: und fände sie sich wirklich so zusammen, so würde ihr unfehlbar die Fähigkeit der Rechtserzeugung mangeln, da mit dem Bedürfniss nicht zugleich die Kraft der

---

[1] Science of Law, 78, 79.

[2] Wm. Galbraith Miller, Philosophy of Law, 230.

[3] Principles of Sociology, Part V., Chap. XIV. *Cf.* also Data of Ethics, *passim*, and his recent work on Justice.

Befriedigung gegeben ist. In der That aber finden wir überall, wo Menschen zusammen leben, und so weit die Geschichte davon Kunde giebt, dass sie in einer geistigen Gemeinschaft stehen, die sich durch den Gebrauch derselben Sprache sowohl Kund giebt, als befestigt und ausbildet. In diesem Naturganzen ist der Sitz der Rechtserzeugung, denn in dem Gemeinsamen, die einzelnen durchdringenden Volksgeist findet sich die Kraft, das oben anerkannte Bedürfniss zu befriedigen."[1]

[1] Savigny, Heutigen röm. Rechts., Band I., §8. See Savigny's and Spencer's views compared in Wharton, Commentaries on American Law, §106. See also *post*, Chaps. III., IV.; also Holtzendorf, Encyklopädie der Rechtswissenschaft, Systematischer Theil, 602.

CHAPTER III.

THE EVIDENCES OF PHYSICAL AND SOCIAL FACTORS IN LAW.

SECTION I.—IN THE LAW OF PROPERTY.

Though procedure may have been largely instrumental in giving early expression to law among archaic communities,[1] it does not seem to have been its first producing cause. The most primitive form of procedure known, self-help, which is practiced by animals far down in the scale of organization,[2] and which is an utterance of that physical impulse which manifests itself in the defence of food, mates, offspring and habitation—this simplest, earliest form of procedure implies possessions, valued possessions. Whether land or other objects were the first occasions of recognized ownership is a question of interest. Though it does not seem to be of pressing importance in the present discussion, I discuss it briefly. There are those who think that personalty rather than land formed the first basis of ownership.[3] Next to defence of life, the capture and retention of food are the earliest forms of acquisition; the acquisition of mates, of slaves, and of habitation is later. No doubt movable objects first became the basis of property. And with them came relations, even if unexpressed and unconsciously felt, of *meum* and *tuum*. From thence came the disposition which is

---

[1] As to which see *infra*, Sec. IV. Also see Pollock, Torts, 21. Felix mentions some savages who have no idea of acquisition of property. Felix, Der Einfluss der Natur auf die Entw. des Eigenthums, p. 3.

[2] See Spencer, Data of Ethics, Chap. II.

[3] Compare Spencer, Principles of Sociology, Vol. II., Part. V., Chap. XV., §§536, 537; Essays in Anglo-Saxon Law, "The Anglo-Saxon Procedure," Part V., 227, and other parts of the same essay; Schrader, Handelsgeschichte u. Warenkunde, 57 *seq.*

implied in early notions of seisin.[1] The acquisition of food is a primary instinct or impulse which is so all-pervading that it seems the earliest form of acquisition and the presumption, in the absence of countervailing evidence, of ownership. It is not unlikely that the possession of mates and slaves, involving war and capture, may have antedated land ownership among some early tribes. Schoolcraft, speaking of the Comanches, says: "They recognize no distinct rights of *meum* and *tuum*, except to personal property, holding the territory they occupy, and the game that depastures upon it, as common to all the tribe; the latter is appropriated only by capture."[2] Of the Brazilian Indians it is said that "scarcely anything is considered strictly as the property of an individual except his arms, accoutrements, pipe and hammock."[3] Treating of beings in a similar state of savagery, another author says that "personal or individual property was chiefly what each wore or carried."[4] The same author affirms that "among the lower races the distinction which our lawyers make between real and personal property appears in a very intelligible way. Of the land all have the use, but no man can be its absolute owner. The simplest land law, which is also a game law, is formed among tribes who live chiefly by hunting and fishing. Thus, in Brazil, each tribe had its boundaries marked by rocks, trees, streams, or even artificial landmarks, and trespass in pursuit of game was held so serious that the offender might be slain on the spot."[5] "At this stage of society in any part of the world, every man has the right to hunt within the bounds of his own tribe, and the game only becomes private property when struck."[6]

---

[1] That seisin of personalty as well as of reality existed, see F. W. Maitland, The Seisin of Chattels, Law Quarterly Review, Vol. I., 324 *seq.* See authorities in last preceding note.

[2] Principles of Sociology, Vol. II., §537.

[3] *Ibid.*

[4] Tylor, Anthropology, 420.

[5] *Ibid.* 419; Spencer, Principles of Sociology, Vol. II., §538.

[6] Tylor, *loc. cit.*

The same customs do not prevail everywhere among similar tribes. Yet we know from numerous accounts that the Indians, in colonial days, in North America, valued territorial possessions, not because they were the basis of such rights as now exist, but because their life and habits made such acquisitions dear to them in the same way that the animal values his food or his lair or his cave.

Hunting, trapping, fishing and grubbing for roots were known to the savage; his life impelled him to these. And "even while he feeds himself, as the lower animals do, by gathering wild fruit and catching game and fish, he is led by his higher intelligence to more artificial means of getting these. Rising to the next stage, he begins to grow supplies of food for himself. Agriculture is not to be looked on as an impossible invention, for the rudest savage, skilled as he is in the habits of the food-plants he gathers, must know well enough that if seeds or roots are put in a proper place in the ground they will grow."[1] Agriculture, as other attainments, was a gradual acquisition. Habits are slow to change, especially when there is as little intellectual incentive to change as prevails among early people. The hunting state is not voluntarily abandoned to take up either a pastoral or an agricultural occupation. When we first observe either of these occupations they are the compulsory duties of the women, the dependent ones or the serfs.[2] The search for food may prevail among the men, but it will be that which is peculiar to the hunting life, the digging of roots or the primitive cultivation of plants being forced upon those who could be compelled to do this work. When the phenomenon arises, the need for its existence has previously forced its adoption upon the group, and this would not take place until the group had enlarged to embrace women and serfs; that is, it would arise as members were added to the group who had to live, but could not live except in the digging and cultivation of

---

[1] Tylor, Anthropology, 214.

[2] See, in this connection, Ross, Early History of Landholding among the Germans, 126, note 6.

roots and plants, because weakness, or opposition on the part of the controlling members, would render it impracticable for them to subsist by the chase as the stronger members subsisted. Though frequently asserted, it is not always true that the agricultural stage followed the pastoral stage. There are localities where pastoral life prevails because the territory is most favorable to it and not as favorable for agriculture; so there are localities where a pastoral occupation is not practicable, at least in early stages of development. The agricultural stage may follow upon the nomadic life of hunting and fishing; the pastoral may follow it also; and either of these may follow the other according to environment. In Arabia, southern Russia, and on the western plains of the United States a pastoral life would be likely to prevail. In the alluvial lands of rivers, where forests interfered with herding, agriculture would follow the hunting state, especially if plants would grow with little effort. The earliest forms of agriculture would be with sticks, just as digging for roots might be carried on. The planting would be less likely to be in ridges than in holes, and the things planted would be such as were familiar to the neighborhood and as would be seen to grow. The pointed stick, hitched to a pole and yoked to oxen, was the plow of the ancient Egyptian, and his hoe was a pointed stick. The Australian and other tribes use the stick; the early Swedes used a primitive kind of hoe consisting of a forked stick or what resembled it.[1] Among the early North American Indians the principal implement of agriculture seems to have been the hoe, for which they often used the shoulder-blade of the bison fixed into a handle of wood. Wild rice, which was gathered by the women, formed, next to the chase, the principal article of food in Michigan, Wisconsin, Iowa, Minnesota, as well as the

[1] Tylor, Anthropology, 216 ; Spencer, Principles of Sociology, Vol. II., Part V., Chap. XV.; Rawlinson, History of Ancient Egypt, Chap. VI.; Gomme, The Village Community, 279 *seq.*; such was also the practice in early days of ancient Greece. Schrader, Sprachv. und Urg., 417. See *ibid.* Part IV., Chap. V.

upper valleys of the Mississippi.[1] There is some advance in the character of implements and modes of cultivation between the earliest forms and those employed by the North American Indian, and a still further advance between these and the implements and modes of agriculture in use among the ancient Egyptians; also between the earlier and later inhabitants of ancient Greece.[2]

It is not my purpose to write the history of agriculture. But this is noticeable, that larger social aggregates bring in their train a development of agriculture, as they do of a developed pastoral condition. And these occupations are in a measure prerequisites to this aggregation in any enduring form. When we observe it in Europe, agriculture assumes somewhat primitive forms, yet we note the prevalence of a certain series of customs regulating the relations between the tribes and the territory that betoken a growth beyond what is indicated by purely savage tribes. Among the aborigines of Britain whom Caesar speaks of, the inland ones did not sow corn, but fed upon flesh and milk.[3] The inhabitants of Kent, however, followed agriculture, and so did many of the tribes of Gaul.[4] The Suevi, he says, were constantly engaged in war and hindered from the pursuits of agriculture; nevertheless some agriculture existed, which was carried on by those who stayed at home. Among them there was no private or separate land, nor did they remain more than one year in one place for the purpose of residence. They did not live much on corn or grain, but subsisted mostly on milk and flesh, and engaged largely in hunting.[5] Of the Germans he said that they did not pay much attention to agriculture, and that a large portion of their food consisted of milk, cheese and flesh; no one had a fixed quantity of land or his

---

[1] Lubbock, Prehistoric Times, 539, 540. See also *ibid.* 287.

[2] Schrader, Sprachv. und Urg., Part IV., Chap. V., 416, 417.

[3] *Interiores plerique frumenta non serunt, sed lacte et carne vivunt pellibusque sunt vestiti*, D. B. G. Lib. V., 14.

[4] *Ibid.*, also Lib. IV., 1.

[5] D. B. G. Lib. IV., 1. See Elton, Origins of English History, 119.

own individual limits.[1] Caesar gives his idea why this was so, but it is not sustained by later investigation.[2] Tacitus wrote 150 years later than Caesar, and in his day the Germans had no cities, but lived scattered and apart, "just as a spring, a meadow, or a wood attracted them."[3] They lived in rude habitations and villages, each household group having a habitation and a space around it. Their agricultural toil consisted in scratching rather than plowing the soil, and their crops of wheat and rye were small. They cultivated the land in common, and their fields were continually shifted. Tacitus' expression, "*Arva per annos mutant et superest ager,*" has formed the basis of some controversy.[4] Landau contends[5] that it shows the prevalence already at this time of what is known as the three-field system of agriculture; a system prevalent at a certain stage of social growth, and of which further mention will be made presently. Upon this theory Landau, relying upon the long continuance of agricultural customs, bases the statement that there was no material change in the system of agricultural landholding from this early day up to the prevalent system of landholding in the middle age. Dr. Hanssen, however, puts a different, and I think more accurate, interpretation upon this text of Tacitus. It signifies to him that such agriculture as was then a necessity was carried on under the open-field system in its simplest form—the plowing up of new ground each season, which then went back to grass.[6] It reminds him of that wild, primitive condition

---

[1] D. B. G. Lib. VI., 22.

[2] Compare Seebohm, The English Village Community, Chaps. VI. and VII., and *passim*; Landau, Territorien, Part I., Die Flurverfassung; Hanssen, Agrarhistorische Abhandlungen, Vol. I., Art. 2, Wechsel der Wohnsitze und Feldmarken in germanischer Urzeit.

[3] Germania, XVI.; Seebohm, The Eng. Village Community, 338 *seq.*

[4] See Hanssen, Agrarhistorische Abhandlungen, Vol. I., 126 *seq.* The quotation is from Chap. XXVI. of the Germania. The language is sometimes translated as follows: "The arable lands are annually changed, and a part left fallow."

[5] Territorien, 61.

[6] Agrarhistorische Abhandlungen, Vol. I., 128, 129. To same effect see Seebohm, The English Village Community, 412.

observed among barbarians, according to which new fields are continually selected, and the cultivation of the soil makes allowance for an indefinite number of years during which the land lying fallow may recuperate. There is then so much land and so sparse a population that no limitations are met with in the quantity any tribe may enjoy.[1] The simpler system of open-field husbandry carried on by the free tribesmen and Taeogs of Wales seems to have been in its main features identical with that described by Tacitus. It was an annual plowing up of fresh grass-land, leaving it to go back again into grass after the year's plowing.[2]

The form of landholding extant in Europe until quite late in the middle age, and widely prevalent, is that communal mode known as the three-field system, or analogous systems not radically distinct from it. This implies a surrender of tribal shifting-possession and the submission to fixed settlements. The three-field, or later form of open-field, cultivation implies a given territorial area containing a given collection of habitations, surrounded by a small lot of land, in the rear of or surrounded by which is a wide expanse divided off into more or less numerous strips, which are allotted to the different members of the community entitled to share in the product of the common fields. These strips were separated from each other in the earlier days not by hedges but by green balks of unplowed turf; there were "long" strips and "short" strips, but generally the normal strip was identical with the mode of land measurement. In England the statute acre was thus identical with the normal strip, that is, a furlong of 40 rods or poles, 4 rods in width. The strips are in fact roughly cut "acres" of the proper shape for plowing. The furlong is the "furrow long"—that is, the length of the drive of the plow before it is turned. The acre marked the extent of a day's plowing,[3] and is very ancient, dating back to German usage a thousand years ago.[4]

---

[1] Seebohm, The English Village Community, 369.
[2] *Ibid.* [3] *Ibid.* 2, 124. [4] *Ibid.* 3.

The whole arable area was divided off into such strips, each township embracing thousands of them. Throughout their whole length the furrows in the plowing run parallel from end to end; the "balks" which divided them being, as the word implies, two or three furrows left unplowed between them.[1] A common field-way gives access to the strips, running along the side of the furlong and the ends of the strips, or a strip running along the length of the furlong inside its boundaries and across the ends of the strips is utilized. This is called in English communities "head land." All the owners of the strips in a furlong have the right to turn their plow upon the head land, and the owner of the head land must wait until all the others are plowed before he can plow his own. When a hillside formed part of the open field the strips almost always were made to run, not up and down hill, but horizontally along it, and in plowing the custom for ages was always to turn the sod of the furrow down hill, the plow consequently always returning one way idle. Every year's plowing took a sod from the higher edge of the strips and put it on the lower edge, the result being that after a while the strips became long, level terraces one above the other, and the balks between them grew into steep rough banks of long grass covered with brambles and bushes.[2] There were other features of this form of open-field cultivation, but they cannot be mentioned here. The strips were allotted according to some number or mark for each sharer, and each received in regular order a strip, then the first again took a strip and the allotment went on as before until the arable land was exhausted. A division was made every year. The producing factor was the day's plowing, which constituted the

---

[1] Seebohm, The English Village Community, 4. *Balc* is said to be a Welsh word; and when the plow is accidentally turned aside and leaves a sod of grass unturned between the furrows, the plow is said to "balc." For a further explanation see Gomme, The Village Community, 75 *seq.*

[2] Seebohm, English Village Community, 5, 6; Gomme, The Village Community, 84 *seq.* See Gomme for evidence of its great antiquity, *loc. cit.*, 75 *seq.* Also the authorities cited in note 2, p. 76, *infra.*

basis of early divisions; making division depend on actual usage. Connected with these "village communities" so-called were rights of common pasturage in fields that lay fallow, of mast and fuel, and for habitations, in the woods. They were rights that only came to be valued when these communities by increase and migration came to impinge upon one another.[1] This open-field mode of cultivation, carried on in common, is a later form of that communal holding of territory which, already existing among purely nomadic tribes, in a condition of barbarism, did not cease to exist until the rise of cities and the accumulation of property in individuals put a stop to it.[2] It left its impress on the manorial holdings of Europe and other countries;[3] upon courts and procedure. From these communal groups by direct descent come the jury and the Parliament. The Roman doctrines of succession or inheritance were derived from this form of property-holding.[4]

An *outline* of the process of development of early landholding would indicate the following.

Beginning in the continuance of the group or mass composing an early kinship group upon a given territory, as the group enlarges and slaves and women do labor and the

---

[1] Compare Seebohm, The English Village Community, Chap. XI.; Waitz, Deutsche Verfassungsgeschichte, Vol. I., Chap. IV.; Hanssen, Agrarhistorische Abhandlungen, *passim*; Ross, Early History of Landholding among the Germans, 24, 25; Woolsey, Political Science, Vol. I., 52 *seq.*; Stubbs, Constitutional History of England, Vol. I., Chap. II., 10 *seq.*; Maine, Village Communities in the East and West, Lecture III., 78 *seq.*; Hearn, The Aryan Household, Chap. IX.; Von Maurer, Markenverfassung, Chap. I., Einleitung; Landau, Die Territorien, 116; Meitzen, Die Ausbreitung der Deutschen in Deutschland.

[2] Laveleye, Primitive Property, 3, 4. That the Greeks and Italians passed through similar forms see Schrader, Handelsg. und Warenk., p. 149 *seq.*; Seebohm, English Village Communities, Chap. IX.; Scrutton, Commons and Common Fields.

[3] Seebohm, The Eng. Village Community, 8 *seq.*; Waitz, D. V. G., *passim.*

[4] Leist, Graeco-Ital. Rechtsgeschichte, Book I.; Holmes, Common Law, 343; Maine, Ancient Law, Chap. VI.; Fustel de Coulanges, Ancient City, Book II., Chaps. VI., VII.

surroundings are favorable, social forms grow into a cultivating or herding body, which, as the group throws off other groups, or as the groups otherwise increase in number, become circumscribed in area. At first the cultivation is temporary and intermittent. The natural vegetation may be burned on the surface, and grain may be sown in the ashes, or plants may be placed in holes or cavities made rudely with the sharp stick or the rude hoe or plow. Where the soil is plentiful it rests for a long series of years. In this way the Tartars cultivate buckwheat, and many tribes still cultivate land. Later on, a small portion of the land is successively put in cultivation, according to the triennial rotation, developing into the three-field system, the greater part remaining common pasturage for the herds of the village. Afterwards the cattle are better tended, the manure is collected, and the fields are enclosed. Roads and ditches are marked out, and the land is permanently improved by labor. Then the fallow is curtailed, powerful manures are purchased in the towns or devised by industry; capital is sunk in the soil and increases its productiveness.[1] This meager outline does not show how gradual the change was, and how the necessities of each recurring situation *forced* the tribe or group into the use of new expedients rendered familiar by the surroundings. Each succeeding step in the progress is an increment of experience, produced spontaneously for the most part.[2]

Let us note a few more of the stages and characteristics of the development referred to, and the regulations by which these forms of landholding were controlled.

Like the beasts of the field, the forest Veddahs wander about in small family groups, destitute of any political organization

---

[1]Laveleye, Primitive Property, pp. 4, 5; Hanssen, Agrarhistorische Abhandlungen, Vol. I., *passim*; Landau, Die Territorien, Book I., Part I.; Digby, History of the Law of Real Property, Chap. I., Sec. I., §1.

[2]See Taylor, The Origin of the Aryans, *passim*, and *cf. ibid.*, pp. 186, 193. The effect of Dr. Isaac Taylor's works will unquestionably be to clear up many obscure questions relating to early life. See also Schrader, Sprachv. und Urg.

or of any definite religious notions. Nomad hunters, they live almost exclusively on flesh, which till recently was eaten raw. They build no huts, dwelling under the branches of trees or in caves.[1] All the possessions they took note of were what an animal would value. The Tasmanians looked upon those who came upon their hunting grounds as enemies.[2] Legal authority was unknown to them in their primitive state; so was real property.[3] Among the Fijians slaves exist, and the lands are cultivated by them. The women are utilized for similar purposes, frequently being treated in the same manner as beasts of burden. They do field work, carry heavy loads, etc.[4] In Arabia slavery exists. Some of the Arab tribes are still low in the scale of civilization, and recognize no general head, but are subdivided into countless bands following a nomadic life. The Bedouin Arabs are not savages, they have a developed pastoral life. They assert title in the soil, and visit with bloody revenge a trespass. They recognize the possession involved in the places of habitation of their different groups. The women sometimes herd the flocks, milk the goats, and go to war.[5] Among the Todas, nearly every *mund*, that is, group or subdivision or clan of the tribe, has its duplicate and triplicate areas, to which they migrate at certain seasons, both for the sake of fresh pasturage and with a view of escaping the inclemency of situations exposed to the west monsoon rains and wind. Each clan has grazing and forest land of its own, which is divided between the different lesser groups,

---

[1] Réclus, Asia, Vol. III., p. 370. See J. Davy, Travels in Ceylon, p. 118; Bailey, in Transactions Eth. Soc., N. S., II., p. 281. See also for tribes in a similar condition, Tacitus, Germania, Chap. 46; Réclus, Primitive Folk, Chap. I.

[2] Bonwick, Daily Life and Origin of the Tasmanians, p. 83.

[3] Tasmanian Jour., I., p. 253; Bonwick, *supra*, 83.

[4] U. S. Ex. Ex., III., p. 97; Erskine, Jour. of a Cruise among Islands of the West Pacific, 214.

[5] Compare J. Petherick, Egypt, the Soudan and Central Africa, 57, 136, 178; Palgrave, Journey through Central and Eastern Arabia, 1, 27, 35, 274; Burkhardt, Bedouins, I., 356; Rambles in the Deserts of Syria, 9; Smith, Kinship in Arabia, *passim*.

each group being located on its own land. These so-called villages are the respective abodes of a family or intimately related portion of a clan whose cattle are herded together. The land belongs to the village community for the time being and cannot be alienated. The milk and what grain is gathered are divided among the members of the village each day. The unconsumed balance and the cattle are considered the property of the males of the community.[1] The women are the menials among them. Among the Iroquois the individual could not obtain the absolute title to land, but he could reduce unoccupied lands to cultivation to any extent he pleased, and so long as he continued to use them his right to their enjoyment was protected and secured. No one among the Koosas of South Africa possesses landed property; the individual sows his grain or seed wherever he can find a convenient spot.[2] Among the Israelites, a pastoral and an agricultural people, communal forms of holding undoubtedly prevailed, for they had no private ownership in land; in fact, possession, communal possession, was at the base of their customs.[3]

Putting together and comparing evidences of early Irish and Welsh holdings, it appears that the chief of the tribe corresponds less with the lord of a manor than a king. His office is not hereditary, but elective. The tribesmen are men of the tribal blood, and equal blood with the chief. They, therefore, are not serfs. They are not allodial holders, for they hold *tribal* land. The *taeogs* are not generally the serfs of the free tribesmen, but, if serfs at all, of the chief. They are more

---

[1] Marshall, A Phrenologist among the Todas, 59, 206. See also Spencer, Principles of Sociology, Vol. II., §538.

[2] Spencer, *supra*, §538.

[3] S. Mayer, Rechte der Israeliten, Römer u. Athener, Vol. I., §102. See as to what extent this was also true of the Athenians, *ibid.*, §104. See also his views regarding the Romans, §103. See also *ibid.*, Vol. II., §152 *seq.* *Cf.* Hirsch B. Fassel, Das Mosaisch-Rabbinische Civilrecht, Vol. I., §304 *seq.*; Schrader, Sprachv. und Urg., Part IV., Chaps. V. and XII.; Leist, Graeco-Ital. Rechtsgeschichte, Book I.; same, Röm. Societas; Hermann, Griechische Antiquitäten, Vols. I. and II.

like Roman *coloni* than mediæval serfs. But they are easily changed into serfs. The slaves in household or field service, more or less numerous, are, like the cattle, traded, and are reckoned as cattle. These three tribal orders of men, with their large households and cattle in the more or less nomadic stage of the tribal system, move about from place to place, and wherever they go, what may be called tribal houses must be erected for them. These houses are built of trees newly cut. "A large straight pole is selected for the rooftree. Six well-grown trees, with suitable branches apparently reaching over to meet one another, and of about the same size as the rooftree, are stuck upright in the ground at even distances in two parallel rows—three in each row. Their extremities bending over make a gothic arch, and crossing one another at the top each pair makes a fork, upon which the rooftree is fixed. These trees supporting the rooftree form the nave of the tribal house. Then, at some distance back from these rows of columns or forks, low walls of stakes and wattle shut in the aisles of the house, and over all is the roof of branches and rough thatch, while at the ends are the wattle doors of entrance."[1] Here the free tribesmen composing a household, if such it may be called, (perhaps it was a later form of the kinship group,) comprising several generations, lived together. In later Welsh law, the name for the separate divisions (*Gwelys*) made by the central columns of the house,

[1] Seebohm, The English Village Community, 239. Mr. Elton, quoting Herodian and Dion Cassius, speaking of a people who inhabited the Grampians before the day Mr. Seebohm speaks of, says: "They had no towns, or fields, or houses, but roamed on the wild and waterless mountains, or in deserts or marshy plains. Their scanty existence was gained in hunting, though they got some small supplies of food from their herds and flocks; and they eked it out with herbs, with fruit and nuts, and even with the bark of the trees in the forest. They lived naked and barefooted, in a savage community, without any organization of state or family; and even the wives and children were regarded as the property of the horde." Origins of Eng. Hist., 169, 170. See following pages in same chapter. The Aryan hordes, he claims, were more advanced when they came into Europe. *Ibid.* 161.

described the shares which descendants had in the property left to them. In the times when the tribesmen shifted from place to place, the local names were taken from natural characteristics, the streams, the woods, the hills which marked the site. The *weregild* or compensation for blood was the means of satisfying those who permitted themselves to be appeased.[1] By the Irish custom of gavelkind, the inferior tenantries were partible among all the males of the sept, both bastards and legitimate; and, after partition made, if any one of the sept had died, his portion was not divided among his sons, but the chief of the sept made a new partition of all the lands belonging to that sept, and gave every one his part according to his antiquity.[2] The sept was a smaller body than the clan or tribe. The latter was a large and miscellaneous body, whose relationship of blood with the chief and the mass of free tribesmen was a mere fiction. The sept was a much smaller body, whose proximity to a common ancestor was close enough to admit of their kinship.[3] Among the German tribes in a later day than that already mentioned, especially where *höfe* or villages existed, the land was divided into habitations and areas around them, the arable lands, the pasture lands and the wood lands. Within the *hof* the kinsmen or villagers dwelt. Each habitation was surrounded by its own area or yard. Each household had the absolutely exclusive use and enjoyment of the dwelling and

---

[1] See regarding Welsh and Irish landholding, Seebohm, The English Village Community, Chaps. VI. and VII., from which the above statements are taken. See also Maine, Early History of Institutions, Lectures IV., V., VI., VII., in which the development of Irish land law is shown. See on this subject also articles by Judge O'Connor Morris in the Law Quarterly Review, Vol. III., p. 133; Vol. IV., p. 1.

[2] Sir John Davis, as quoted by Maine. See Early History of Institutions, 186.

[3] Maine, Early Hist. of Inst., 186, 187. The analogy between this picture and that of the Todas seems to be striking. See *supra*. There seems to be an advance, however, in the Irish system, for inheritance of some kind seems to be recognized. "According to his antiquity" seems to point to inheritance or descent.

this area, under the regulations of the tribe. These separate households, which were regarded as appurtenant to the habitations, were entitled to shares in the arable land, pasture land and wood land. The house determined the share of the field, the field the share of the pasture; the pasture and house determined the share of the forest.[1] Serfs seem always to have existed.[2] The allotments were made and held subject to an elaborate code of regulations.[3] Some of these will be mentioned presently. Hanssen, whose recent inquiries into the subject make his judgment worthy of being accepted, says that the *hof* and *dorf*, with their parts and open-field characteristics, are out of one and the same mold. The family or household tie which formed the basis of the *dorf* and embraced the *feldmark* was already created at the time of the settlement in Germany; this family tie was founded on early notions of kinship. This personal tie was cemented and strengthened by the tie produced by living and cultivating or herding together.[4] It became expressed in the word "Nachbarschaft," that is, neighbors collectively; not in the sense that is intended when neighbors in cities are spoken of. "We neighbors" signifies the collective members of the *dorf* in their aggregate unity.

Among these common regulations grew up and were observed, were enforced through many centuries, undergoing

---

[1] Von Maurer, Marken-Verfassung, §20; Waitz, Deutsche Verfassung-Geschichte, Vol. I., Chap. IV., p. 121, Vol. III., Chap. V., Vol. V., Chap. IV.; Landau, Die Territorien, Part I.; Hanssen, Agrarhistorische Abhandlungen, Vol. I.; Hearn, Aryan Household, Chap. IX., p. 219; Grimm, Rechtsalterthümer, Book III., p. 491 *seq.*; Meitzen, Ausbreitung der Deutschen, etc.

[2] Meitzen, Ausbreitung der Deutschen, 15; Zoepfl, D. R. G., Vol. II., §7, par. II.; Germania, Chap. XXV.

[3] See Von Maurer, Marken-Verfassung, Appendix, Nos. 4, 5, 6; Dorf-Verfassung, Appendix; Hanssen, Die Dorfwillküren, etc., in his Agrarhistorische Abhandlungen, Vol. II., 84; Grimm, Rechtsalterthümer, Book III.

[4] Die Dorfwillküren, etc., in Agrarhistorische Abhandlungen, Vol. II., 84.

little change until they finally, when writing became more general, were transcribed in more durable form. The neighborhood must appear at a certain place upon the sound of the bell or alarm; regulations regarding the tending of bulls, kine, swine, the removal of stones from the fields which are to be cultivated, the covering up of the roads or ways which may have been dug up, the prevention of estrays, the building of chimneys or flues, the management of the plow in the field, grazing of horses and cattle, use of fire, disposition of the manure, preservation of boundary stones, burials, and numerous other details of their village life can be found.[1] They are not entirely alike in any two communities, some being fuller of details than others. But all sorts of things are regulated, and sometimes in the most primitive mode. Nor have such rules yet ceased to exist.[2] They certainly existed in England when the Pilgrims came to America, for we see these bringing them along.[3] We shall see in a later chapter how the regulations of these early social aggregates influenced procedure through the court-leet and the court-baron. And such regulations partly constituted the basis of customs upon a large scale in larger social forms.[4]

The quest after sustenance and other animal pleasures begot antagonism, animal and savage antagonism, and war, and these begot slavery and oppression of the weak. The captives and the weak members followed the occupation which necessity forced upon them and superior power forced

---

[1] Hanssen, Agrarhist. Abh., Vol. II., 107 *seq.*

[2] Contemporary Review, July, 1881, W. Steadman Aldis, Notes from a German Village.

[3] Johns Hopkins University Studies, Vol. I., Number II., The Germanic Origin of New England Towns, by Herbert B. Adams; Number IV., Saxon Tithingmen in America, by the same author; Village Communities of Cape Ann and Salem, same author, being Numbers IX. and X. of same volume. See also similar phenomena in Maryland, same volume, Numbers VI. and VII., Parish Institutions of Maryland, by Edward Ingle, and Old Maryland Manors, by John Johnson.

[4] *Cf.* Maurer, Mark-, Hof-, Dorf- u. Stadt-Verfassung; Waitz, D. V. G.; Hanssen, Agrarhist. Abhandlungen.

them to continue.[1] This has already been affirmed. But note the deduction: the warrior contemns the labor of the women and the slaves; his occupation is war and chase; theirs to dig for roots or tend the herds or to pursue agriculture and herding. The slaves do not always remain such, nor does a group remain intact. The kinship group, if it can be called such, receives into it the slaves, and in time what was the occupation of the weak and the dependent would become the duty of many others. The prowess attending war always kept up a class of independent or free men, whose occupation was to govern and to pursue war, hunting, fishing, etc. These formed the governing element in the Grecian *kome* and *polis*. The dependent element gave rise to an industrial class. The one expanded in one direction, the other in an opposite direction; one made for war and tyranny, the other for peace and industry. The development of the one led to a nobility and armies, the development of the other to commerce, manufactures and industrial cities. Both were gradual in their expansion, each acted and reacted on the other, and both largely involved unconscious processes.[2] Property on an enlarged scale, individual property, was an outcome. Let us note still further the development of property. The feudal system, which constitutes so conspicuous an element in English law, is by no means peculiar to it. That system came, it is said by some English jurists, from the Normans who conquered England; but this is only partially true.[3] Feudalism, that is, that system of landholding which implies a relation between lord and vassal, in virtue of which the former gives protection while the latter renders homage and service, not only prevailed on the continent of Europe, but it likewise prevailed wherever the military art had so far developed as to create a nobility as distinguished from those who

---

[1] Speaking in his Rechtsalterthümer of *liegende habe*, Grimm says: "Jene nach altstrengem Recht kann nur Freien zustehen," 491.

[2] Worship of gods may have tended to establish classes also. See Ancient City, Book IV.; Leist, Graeco-Ital. R. G., Book I.

[3] Digby, History of the Law of Real Property, Chap. I., Sec. II.

were of inferior classes. There are some evidences of its existence in Rome, for Mr. Seebohm traces some of its incidents to Rome.[1] It existed in Japan,[2] in China,[3] Greece,[4] among the tribes of the Caucasus.[5] And elsewhere evidences of its existence will be found. The word probably is a Latin recoinage of a word sprung from an old Teutonic root (Lombardian *fin*, Old High German *fehu* [*vieh*], Gothic *faihu*) signifying cattle or property; cattle being an early form of property, antedating the definite existence of feudal forms.[6] Feudalism is to be seen in the old Roman *obsequium*.[7]

The indications are, as may be seen in those localities where feudalism is now in a state of formation, as among the tribes of Asia, that where capture of women and the creation of serfs became a practice, the needs of the group or groups in question had developed beyond a mere family form, and that warfare had, in addition to the chase and search for sustenance, become an outgrowth, a spontaneous feature of developing social existence. And as war is not possible unless it gives opportunity for the development of headship or chieftainship, the natural result of war was superior prowess, superior possessions of women or serfs or cattle or land, among the divisions which were made by the members of the tribe. I take it that the very earliest form of owner-

---

[1] The English Village Community, 263 *seq.* See also S. Mayer, Rechte der Israeliten, Römer u. Athener, Vol. II., §134, p. 62 *seq.*; Marquardt, Römische Stadtsverwaltung, Vol. I., p. 3 *seq.* See Latin *obsequium.*

[2] Griffis, The Mikado's Empire, index, Feudalism.

[3] Laveleye, Primitive Property, 265.

[4] *Ibid.* See also Fustel de Coulanges, Ancient City, Book II., Chap. VII., Book IV., Chap. V.

[5] Réclus, Earth and its Inhabitants, Asia, Vol. I., 56; *Ibid.* 58; *Ibid.* 93; *Ibid.* 95; *Ibid.* 114.

[6] Digby, History of the Law of Real Property, p. 32, note.

[7] See Leist, Zur Geschichte der römischen Societas. *Cf.* Latin Vocabulary, *Obsequium.* For similar ancient Greek evidences see Platner, Beiträge, etc., Chap. V.; Leist, Graeco-Ital. R. G., Book I.; the existence of the doctrine of primogeniture among them would seem to sustain the same position. Meier and Schömann, Att. Process., Vol. II., pp. 573, 574.

ship was common ownership among a group of greater or lesser size, and that the extension of groups not only led to different occupations, but also led to the valuation of new and more numerous objects. In any event, when we see social forms beyond the mere early kinship group, we see serfdom, especially where a pastoral or agricultural life has come to be followed; and these imply the pursuit of warfare and the existence of a class devoted to military pursuits as distinguished from those following the pursuit of accumulating sustenance. In the large amount of testimony at hand relative to the development of modern governments and institutions one can hardly fail to discover innumerable evidences of these statements.[1]

The beginnings of feudalism, as the word indicates, are not to be confined to possession or enjoyment of land, they may be traced even in a pastoral condition.[2] The chief who was recognized as the possessor of superior herds or shares, though little, if at all, more than the head of a family group, except that his prowess may have contributed to give him command over groups instead of over individuals, would be as much the factor of feudalism as the later *cyning* or king. The likelihood is that the beginnings of manorial life—the prevailing characteristic of developed feudalism—must be traced to that form of holding which implied inferior herdsmen or cultivators of the soil and independent lords or freemen. Such a condition Mr. Seebohm thinks existed in England in pre-Norman days, and if we may trust the evidence of the comparative jurists and historians of Germany and France, existed there as far back as authentic history goes. Evidence

---

[1] The views of Fustel de Coulanges (Ancient City, Book II., Chaps. VI. and VII.) seem to attribute a different course of development in ancient times to the Hindoos, Greeks and Romans; but they can be reconciled by the observation that he attributes a too elaborate constitution to the ancient household or kinship group. It was rather more barbarous in form than he seems to think. *Cf.* Smith, Kinship in Arabia; Réclus, Primitive Folk.

[2] Maine, Early Law and Custom, 341 *seq.*, esp. 346. See *supra* note 7.

points to the same phenomena in ancient Greece.[1] Yet the cultivators and herdsmen had in a measure improved their condition, becoming an essential part of the village or place of repose, and obtaining a larger recognition by others in the administration of the affairs of the group. And this condition might have continued to improve had not wars imposed, as the groups embraced larger territorial bounds, an increased burden of duty on the militant portion. The manorial status is an outcome of war and conquest on the one hand, and of a class devoted, at first by compulsion and necessity, and later by inheritance and habit, to the tending of flocks and domestic duties. The common fields and hearths are the product of the latter class; the forms of administration of kings and kingly bodies, with national parliaments and courts, are a product of the militant class; though to the maintenance of both, in the war of human and other elements—that is, to the survival of those found best adapted—each was a contributing and indispensable factor. From the play of both and the tendency of social aggregates to coalesce and produce ramified coöperative industrial and militant factors, it would result that the agricultural class and their holdings would become developed in certain directions and qualified in others. The force of arms would, as its power became greater, reduce to an iron subjection the purely agricultural class. But on the other hand, from among its votaries would come those elements of industrial growth implied in barter and trade. The militant condition contributed to the production of landlordism in the hands of a few. The earlier industrial conditions maintained landholding in a communal and quite stationary form. The military baron and the industrial burger produced the city life to which enlightened humanity owes so much; for the early mediæval city is the product of an ecclesiastical foundation, with its military bishop and assistants, and the tradesmen and handicraftsmen who gathered there, or of some fortified place with its dependents engaged in defense, and

---

[1] *Cf.* references, note 7 *supra.*

those who fed them from the field and herds, or some developed communal form of agricultural life, such as the village community or *hof.* In some localities the city is a development of camp life, the very thoroughfares showing signs of its origin; elsewhere, the walks, and the different quarters of the city, show it to have been a fortified place of defense; again, the clustering of houses around some cathedral shows visibly the dependence which the place had upon the church; and not infrequently the long single important street betrays the presence of that village life still to be seen among the communities of Europe. And if we look to the early charters or liberties of cities, we shall see that all of them owed their early prominence and their later influence to some power or potentate possessing a military significance.

Developing city life, with its municipal mayor and council and polity, and the effect this had upon the splitting up of communal forms of holding into individual holdings and ownership, and the accumulation of large holdings into the hands of individuals through kingly grant, tended to impair the prevalent, perhaps the only early form of ownership, that is, the communal or joint ownership of the kin, family or larger group. The later enclosure of fields produced by the obvious disadvantages resulting from a communal form (whereby individual incentive was counteracted, and agricultural stagnation threatened a permanent existence), or produced by lordly tyranny and force, tended in time to enlarge the field of individual ownership in land.[1] And the development of statehood, whereby tribal and other forms melted away into larger masses, and family groups tended to embrace only those connected by consanguinity, likewise tended toward individual ownership, because it produced a larger field for individual enterprise and thought.

[1] See Arnold, Geschichte des Eigenthums, etc.; also Law Q. Rev., Vol. V., No. 1, an article by Mr. Pike on livery of seisin of incorporeal hereditaments, and Scrutton, Land in Fetters; same, Commons and Common Fields.

The later forms of ownership owe much to the city organization. The doctrine of rent, as an incorporeal hereditament, lying in grant, is probably most largely an outcome of city life; prior to that time it was a service payable in kind, and was as capable of seisin as land was, for both represented but the product of the land; the product was alone capable of individual ownership or control.[1] The very notion of individual ownership was foreign to the early forms of thought respecting lands.[2] It needed some form of social aggregation such as city life, with its increasing departure from the previous tribal or village life, with its aggregation of gilds and industries and houses and streets, and the political forms that grew up with these, such as a mayor or council, city judges, a mint and a polity, to completely destroy the notion of property which is peculiar to a tribal or earlier condition—a notion of property which, except regarding immediate sustenance, wear and implements, relates to movables as well as to immovables, as is apparent from the early doctrine of succession.[3] When barter and trade have grown beyond simple exchange such as barbarians practice, movables are assured a wider influence upon human development than before, and when the construction of warehouses and residences follows in the wake of trade, landholding must cease to remain communal.

Yet while this evolution and change goes on, the influence of military discipline and effects will be observed in the control still retained, even to our day, over great aggregates of property in cities and towns by the nobility; also by that mode of succession which devolves upon a single successor

---

[1] Mr. Ross, in his Early History of Landholding among the Germans, takes a different position, but he is not sustained by the great mass of inquirers.

[2] See and compare Scrutton, Land in Fetters, and Commons and Common Fields; Hanssen, Agrarhistorische Abhandl., Vol. I., 484 *seq.*, Die mittelälterliche Feldgemeinschaft in England nach Nasse, etc.

[3] See Maine's Ancient Law, Chap. VI.; Holmes' Common Law, Lec. X.; Hearn, Aryan Household, 190; Spencer, Principles of Sociology, Vol. II., §536 *seq.*; Fustel de Coulanges, Ancient City, Book II., Chap. VII.

the landed possessions of the ancestor, implied in primogeniture[1]—two consequences which the new settlement of lands in America tended to check and in a large measure eradicate. Such discipline and effects are observable in the doctrine that to the crown, or king or sovereignty, belonged originally all lands—a premise not true except where conquest had eradicated all prior possessions or rights, yet a necessity of thought, because to no one else could be attributed, especially in a large and growing social aggregate, the ownership of unoccupied or forfeited lands. It is noteworthy, too, that as aggregations became larger and more heterogeneous in composition and more ramified in pursuits, militant discipline became broader in outline and more rigorous and unelastic; likewise the serfdom became more severe and galling, until industrial agencies tended to introduce a more correct notion of man's general capacities, and the church and philosophy secured a better appreciation of man's general worth. Industry in a measure tended later on to reverse the good effects thus secured, by introducing a refined form of slavery such as is exhibited in the history of the United States and the West Indies; of which some evidences can also be found in Roman history.[2]

Some countries, because of the peculiar physical surroundings to be found there, disclose a somewhat different course of development than that above indicated. Such is the case among the cantons of Switzerland and of the republic of San Marino. It is likewise the case in the United States. In the production of this exceptional development, the mountains of Switzerland (the Alps) have had large influence; and as to the United States, a broad ocean and a development free from restraints of baronial and kingly rule have had great weight. Mention has already been made of the influence of the physical factors referred to upon laws, and they

---

[1] See, on the abolition of primogeniture in ancient Greece, Ancient City, Book IV., Chap. V.

[2] See Zrodolowski, Römisches Privat-Recht, §§25–28.

need not be further treated in this connection; but it will not be amiss to observe some phases of development in Switzerland in the matter of landholding, due to the physical surroundings.

Miaskowski, whose researches into Swiss landholding are accepted as authority,[1] traces up its history from the establishment of those early village forms of communal holding which are to be found all over Europe in early days. In the Middle Age extensive lordly holdings with serfs existed, and to this became added the holdings of churches and monasteries, which came to cover the land like a web. A few holdings confined to a single family are to be found, but these seem by ultimate occupation by a larger group to have developed or evolved into village holdings—a development the opposite to what is to be seen elsewhere in Europe during the same period, because the power of the barons elsewhere in Europe increased at the expense of the peasantry, while it became broken in Switzerland. The development of communal holdings otherwise developed here as elsewhere in Europe, until the agrarian form of association became superseded by the requirements of a freer industrial activity, though some peculiarities in this development may be noted. In virtue of the splitting up of the holdings of the members of a given community through inheritance and otherwise, it came to pass that a great variety of large, small and still smaller possessors disputed with one another for the enjoyment of communal privileges, of constructing homes on their portion of the village devoted to the erection of homesteads, and of enjoying the right of pasture and wood upon the commons and in the woods of the community. The right of being heard in the determination of the policy which should control the community was likewise asserted by these, and their obligations regarding duties and taxation to main-

[1] See Hanssen, Agrarhistorische Abhandlungen, Vol. I., 513 *seq.* See for evidences of development of landholding in New England, in addition to authorities already cited, Weeden, Economic and Social Hist. of New England, Vol. I., Chaps. III. and VIII.

tain the community were the source of considerable dispute. The right of homestead gave rise to great controversy, which has continued on to the present day, giving rise in turn to many different regulations aimed to prevent a disturbance of previous holdings, and especially the confusion resulting from too much division of a share or right of enjoyment allotted to the separate members of the community. The impracticability of maintaining the village integrity led to an appropriation of the common pastures and woods among individuals, and to individual forms of competition in industry that militated strongly against the village customs and conservative forms and notions. Enclosures of given parts became in this way more numerous. To what extent these enclosures produced regulation cannot be told, but they were at first permitted under certain conditions and for certain periods only, and the products which might be cultivated were not infrequently prescribed, for the protection of others who adhered (were bound by custom and disposed by long-continued practice to adhere) to the communal forms and products of agriculture. Notwithstanding, the cultivation of cereals gave gradual place to the raising of cattle, and the export of cheese became the principal industry. And now a danger threatens—the dependence of Switzerland upon the outside world for the most of her requirements has been rendered much too great, in the interest of cheese manufacture, which of late years has not proved profitable. The capacity of self-maintenance, peculiar to Switzerland in earlier days, has largely ceased to exist—too much so, indeed. The growth of cattle-raising has largely, driven by the impossibility of extending it where it came into contact with the agricultural village communities referred to, led to the occupation and enrichment by toil and effort of the higher and more sterile lands of the Alps. These and the custom of sending the cattle to graze in the higher regions in the hot months have led to many regulations peculiar to the occupation of higher mountainous districts. Regulations prohibiting the pledge or transfer of any part of these regions to outsiders; regulations providing that only the cattle fed in winter from the hay of the valleys might graze in certain mountainous pasturages; that the surface required to feed one cow should constitute a unit of landholding for purposes of taxation; that the use of the pasturages should be under prescribed limitations as to time and quantity, in view of the danger of irreparable waste; regulations relative to the maintenance of forests and mountain roads, etc., exist. These regulations are modified when they come into contact with the needs of the cities of Switzerland, and many cantons have local regulations occasioned by special necessities of their situation. The strife of a communal life with adverse physical elements and the spread of industrial activity have superinduced long-continued and bitter controversies, and the end is not yet. But the comparative area of the nation is so limited that the conservative elements peculiar to an agrarian people maintain a *status quo* which cannot be found elsewhere among the enlightened nations of Europe, and government is largely a matter of local and personal concern.

In the low country, in the north of Europe, the liability of the people to overflows gave rise to peculiar agricultural customs and to forms of landholding that have not an exact counterpart elsewhere.[1] So on the banks of the Nile early communal customs were affected by its periodical overflows.[2] On the shores of Newfoundland may be found at this day a people whose life and regulations are merged in and colored by the single pursuit of fishery, among whom the native currency is some form or product of the fish. The changes in the land system of England have been partly indicated by Mr. Thorold Rogers[3] and Mr. Scrutton.[4] In the first half of

---

[1] Hanssen, Agrarhistorische Abhandlungen, Vol. II., 330. See also Elton, Origins of English History, 51.

[2] Leist, Graeco-Ital. R. G., 106, 107; Kuhn, Röm. Stadt-Verf., Vol. II., 472 *seq.* The like might be said of the effect of the Euphrates and Tigris.

[3] Work and Wages.

[4] Land in Fetters, Chap. VII.; also, and more fully, Commons and Common Fields, Chap. IV. *seq.*

the 14th century the method of cultivation in England was, on the domain land of the manor, by laborers employed by the lord or his bailiff, who were paid out of the money commutations which had taken the place of the personal services due from the copyhold tenants. There were two classes of landholders, landlords and laborers. "The copyhold tenants had their homestead and stock from their lord, and were bound in return to perform personal service in tilling his domain land, a service which by this time had usually been commuted into fixed money payments, with which he had hired laborers to cultivate his domain." Alienation of land usually took place by the hands of the lord. The plague of 1348, '49 and '61, in which nearly half the population are estimated to have perished, changed matters. It produced a scarcity of help and a rise in wages. The landlords undertook to meet this by statutes prescribing the limit of wages, and by enforcing performance of personal service again. The discontent thus produced gave rise to the peasants' revolt of 1381. The outcome was that lands were let out on leases, and not infrequently it led to sales of small holdings. This brought to notice the restraints on alienation which existed, produced by the ingenuity of casuistical lawyers. The Wars of the Roses killed out the barons and gave room for some land acquisition upon the part of the commercial class. This tendency led to a commercial regimen in the cultivation and alienation of lands. It was seen that lands for pasturage were most profitable, and acquisition and enclosure of large tracts for this purpose occurred to such an extent as to call the attention of the country to the danger which threatened the small farmers and yeomanry, who were thus becoming deprived of their livings.[1] An act was passed to meet this, in addition to other acts in favor of alienation, which provided "that no house to which 20 acres of land was attached should be destroyed." In another act it was provided "that a suitable dwelling-house

[1] See this danger shown by Scrutton, Commons and Common Fields, Chap. IV. *seq.*

should be maintained for every 40 acres of land." And there were other acts against excessive sheep-farming and enclosures. "The cultivation of England by lord and peasant gave way to a system of culture by lord, farmer and laborer; commercial reasons led to large farms, and the desire of new landowners to found a family prompted the accumulation in one hand, and the invention of devices to keep on the land the grasp of that hand, though dead."

Those writers who have studied the subject well have not hesitated to affirm that the growth of cities has contributed to produce our nationalities.[2] This is not, however, the place in which to pursue that inquiry further; it will present itself for examination further on. What, however, is of importance to note is that the customs of trade, those customs which have developed the use and importance of movable and immovable objects, and have expanded both by the artifice of a representative of value, have their most prominent impetus in cities.[3] There, as already seen, we look for a development of the custom of receiving or exacting interest, not in the shape of a duty or charge resting upon the possessor of the soil, but in the shape of a *quid pro quo*, a consideration for use.[4] And there rent, as it is now used and as it is understood by English-speaking people, found its first home.[5] The early services were those of subjects or dependents, not such as were the result of bargain or trade.[6]

---

1 The above summary is taken from Scrutton, Land in Fetters, Chap. VII.

2 Arnold, Verfassungsgeschichte der deutschen Freistädte, Vorrede; Arnold, Geschichte des Eigenthums in den deutschen Städten, *passim*; Waitz, D. V. G., Vol. VII., 418, 419; Freeman, English Towns and Districts, Preface; Stubbs, Constitutional History of England, Vol. I., 403 *seq.*; Schwebel, Deutsches Bürgerthum, *passim.*

3 See Schwebel, Deutsches Bürgerthum, *passim*; Arnold, Eigenthum in D. S.

4 See Arnold, Eigenthum, etc., 45, and Chaps. III. and V.

5 See Arnold, *loc. cit.*

6 See Seebohm, English Village Community, Index, Services of Villani; Spencer, Principles of Sociology, Vol. II., Part V., Chap. XVI.; Ross, Early History of Landholding among the Germans, 126, 146; Roescher,

Remembering that the use of money is comparatively late, and that while barter of articles is the only known mode of exchange there is no probability of the idea of rent as now understood, much less of interest, we see at once how true the position taken must be. It needs a growth of custom and habit such as city life and traffic produced to segregate from things the idea of absolute or qualified ownership. I cannot agree with those who claim that possession is an extension of the notion of ownership.[1] The probabilities are that possession was the fact upon which the earliest groups based their views of ownership. We see this not only in the views already indicated, but also in their views of tradition and early remedies,[2] and their inability to abstract, hence to separate in idea, the notion of possession from that of ownership. But it is doubtless true that the extension of experience and modes of user and enjoyment of property have not only led to *individual ownership*, but the extension of ownership by its segregation from actual possession. This is how seisin became different from possession; how use and ownership became separable; how incorporeal hereditaments came to lie in grant.[3] The process of development of language from things the senses perceive to abstract notions is thus revealed in the domain of law. It will be seen, as one should easily

---

Political Economy, Book III., Chaps. II. and III.; see Arnold, *supra*, 207; Roescher, Political Economy, Vol. I., Book II., Chap. III. See also Garlanda, Philosophy of Words, 136, 137; Taylor, Words and Places, 297 *seq.*

[1] Holmes, Common Law, Lecture VI., and authorities therein cited; Spencer, Principles of Sociology, Vol. II., Part V., Chap. XV.; Maine, Ancient Law, Chap. VIII.; Laveleye, Primitive Property, Chap. XVII.; Essays in Anglo-Saxon Law, 55; 3 L. Q. Rev., 32 *seq.*; Ihering, Der Grund des Besitzes-Schutzes; same, Besitzwille. But see Ross, Early History of Landholding among the Germans, Notes 143, 144, who is opposed in his views by the great weight of authority. See also Hanssen, Agrarhistorische Abhandlungen, Vol. II., 84 *seq.*; Landau, Die Territorien, *passim*; Seebohm, The English Village Community, *passim.*

[2] See section on Procedure, *post.*

[3] See as to this, Law Quarterly Review, Vol. V., On Livery of Seisin of Incorporeal Hereditaments. See Ihering, Besitzwille.

anticipate, in every domain of law. There is no branch that has not grown from early conditions unless it be of recent creation, and the way the different topics are made up in our arrangement of legal heads betrays the legal patchwork which we call precedent. As each subject is explored we have it revealed to us that the law of the courts and the bar is largely the expression of what the bench and bar have said, as occasion called for expression, regarding mooted points bearing upon the relations of beings to one another and to objects around and about them.[1] It does not pretend to be a logical invention based on syllogisms, nor a philosophical, nor even scientific subject treated in a thoroughly systematic way, worked out in all details.

Property nowadays embraces not only land and movable objects, but it also embraces choses in action and the use or enjoyment of privileges or rights in or over land and objects. The idea or notion itself has expanded as society has developed new features in this regard. Commercial paper has expanded to embrace notes, checks, bills of exchange, negotiable bonds of manifold kinds, debentures, rentes, bank notes, the national currency, and book accounts. All of these have in view the delivery, sooner or later, of objects of tangible value; sensuous objects that have some more real value than mere slips of paper possess. These are *representatives* of value, or convenient means of exchange. Their origin is not clear, but that they are the outcome of the extension of barter is undoubted. At their base lies a *causa* or consideration, or material existence, not a mere figment of the mind. The servitudes that rest upon land in diverse forms are the creatures of user or imply user. The doctrine of hypothecation involves the notion of pledging, and still retains, even in the shape of mortgages, the notion that possession goes with it unless the

[1] See Hanssen, Agrar. Hist. Abhd., Vol. I., 112, where he says, respecting land development in the district of Trier, that it justifies the position regarding private landownership all over Germany and Scandinavia, that it resulted from the rarer and rarer use and eventual abandonment of the practice of early forms of division and distribution.

contrary be stipulated. In Germany, mortgages of land are representatives of part of the property, and when recorded are transferable as such. Franchises, such as rights of ferriage, markets, private corporate functions and privileges, have in view material, objective gains, not mental development, except where corporations are organized for literary, moral, æsthetic, religious or benevolent purposes.

The growth spoken of could not fail to leave its impress upon law. The feudal customs relating to the alienation of property, the tenures by which they have been held, some remnants of which still color the law of real property, the different phases of developing ownership implied in uses, trusts, servitudes and bailment, and other incidents markedly show this. The doctrine of warranty is a derivation from it, the outcome of those early practices of putting forward the person who had made tradition, usually some person of larger powers than those who vouched to warranty. The modes of transfer were at first visible modes of tradition, corresponding with that appreciation for matters which the senses solely took note of in earlier days. The bringing a person to the place and putting him upon it, the handing over of some part or emblem of the premises, the delivery of property, the making and delivery of deeds, all imply tradition or a handing over of some representative object. A gift is not complete without delivery or its equivalent.[1] A sale implies delivery.[2] Property descends and is divided, though in an intangible form. The doctrine of descent is a slow develop-

---

[1] Wharton on Contracts, Vol. I., §496; Chitty on Contracts (11th Am. ed.), Vol. I., 60; Flanders *v.* Blandy, 12 Northeastern Reporter, 321; Peters *v.* Construction Co., 34 Northwestern Reporter, 190.

[2] Mr. Benjamin says that there must be a concurrence of the following elements to constitute a sale: 1st. *Parties* competent to contract; 2d. Mutual assent; 3d. A *thing*, the absolute or general *property* in which is *transferred* to the buyer; 4th. A *price* in money made or promised. Mental and physical elements are here intimately blended. In early days tradition was not distinguished and abstracted from the mental attitude of the parties; that happened only when courts and lawyers, in obedience to later experience, created the abstraction.

ment of tribal into later forms of landholding, bearing many traces of the day when the property was still looked upon as a corpus belonging to the family group.[1]

The development of leasing or renting has called into existence new relations with physical objects, such as fire and other forms of waste or destruction, and doctrines relative thereto; also doctrines relative to the objectionable or permissible uses to which property may be put. The doctrines of nuisance largely grow out of abuses to property following in the wake of developing societies or aggregations. Pledges, which were perhaps among the earliest forms of tradition of movable objects, and which were, as we shall see, a natural outcome of the disposition to seek relief and security against wrong, implied the actual transfer of the object and the continued retention thereof. And in our day possession is essential to a pledge. The mechanic's lien upon personal property likewise implies possession. It was on account of actual possession or dominion forming the basis of recognition that the early people of western Europe recognized only the right of the bailee to proceed against the wrongdoer for a loss sustained while in the bailee's custody.[2] The growth of cities and towns has

---

[1] Holmes, Common Law, Lec. X.; Maine, Early Hist. of Inst., Lec. VII., 188 *seq.*; Hearn, Aryan Household, Chap. VI. An evidence of this fact is to be found in what has been called the custom of borough-English, whereby the youngest son obtained the homestead; which was widespread in earlier days, and is the product of the custom of those who were attached to the soil and cultivated it, whereby the last or youngest of the sons received the hearth and the home and its attendant privileges. See Hearn, Aryan Household, 82, 83; Maine, Early Hist. of Institutions, 223, 224; Scrutton, Land in Fetters, 10, 62; Glanville, VII., 3; Elton, Origins of Eng. Hist., Chap. VIII. Mr. Elton shows the wide prevalence of the custom and attributes it to early religious practices. Its advent where noticed is more or less overshadowed by the right of primogeniture. See Elton, also Ross, Early History of Landholding among the Germans, 104, and note 226. My explanation of this would be that the class who were cultivators retained the custom of so-called *junior right*, while the warrior class favored primogeniture. See further upon this subject, *infra*, Section II.

[2] Holmes, Common Law, 166; Scrutton, Roman Law and the Law of England, 188; Essays in Anglo-Saxon Law, 202, 203, 204.

produced such results as dedication of streets and ways by estoppel, enjoyment of proper light, pure air and reasonable quiet, likewise the varying uses to which single, large buildings are put by different tenants, whereby relative duties are entailed on tenants toward each other and with landlords. In consequence of modern city growth, doctrines relating to party walls have found a necessary existence, even contrary to the wishes of the landowner. The character of buildings and the dangers ensuing from improper construction and deleterious maintenance in municipalities have given rise to a mass of regulations and new features in the criminal code.

Enough has been said upon this subject to show how physical and social agencies play a part in the law relating to property. Much more could be said, as the reader can easily surmise.[1] The physical objects of ownership form the very basis of that branch of the law and the indispensable factor to the development of all other branches. The growth of social aggregates has depended upon these,—upon their existence, and the means of sustenance and the traffic they afforded. Each stage of growth has varied and multiplied the forms of use of these objects and added to their number. Social aggregation has acted back upon them, giving rise to new possibilities in their use. And whatever of invention there may have been involved, the basis and the prime element of it all was the physical object acted upon by men, adapted in use to the physical environment by which man was surrounded, which formed a necessary factor in his calculation. We cannot say of these objects and the law which their varying uses produced, that these were to mankind as the canvas is to the artist. The canvas is a comparatively insignificant element in the construction of the work. Not so, however, these objects; they more frequently than otherwise oblige man to adapt himself to them and the surroundings that environ both.

The need of bearing in mind the importance of physical

---

[1] See this Chapter, Section 3.

and social factors in the growth of the law of property is exemplified in the disposition to view property as an evil *invention,* and in the agitation, more or less revolutionary or anarchical, to overthrow it. The overthrow of property is an impracticable end. It is a notion that forms part of civilized existence; so bound up in its growth and development as to be inexpungible therefrom. The notion itself, not only in Rome, but in modern nations, is not synonymous with untrammeled control; for the exercise of the privilege of eminent domain, taxation, police control in its different forms, and the relative duties which owners owe to each other and the public, assume the existence of a large deduction therefrom. Property, like possession, is a relative term, and it expands with the increments of experience bearing upon the use and abuse of earthly possessions. The theories of those who would annihilate property are not based on any proper conception of the growth of jural notions; and the ideas of those who think that the declaration of jural notions by courts or writers can stay for good the drift of developing or changing communities is, likewise, gratuitous and unfounded.

And when the protection of property more and more becomes the desideratum of constitutional law, as reflected in the pages of Magna Charta, Bills of Rights, and our constitutional provisions, in one form or another, in numerous connections and ways, we observe the movement meagerly indicated which in more detail is illustrated by the pages of this chapter. We shall see the influence of property in the formation of constitutional law in the earliest *demos,* when we come to discuss constitutional law.[1]

SECTION II.—THE LAW CONCERNING DOMESTIC RELATIONS.

In the recent work of Geddes and Thomson, on the Evolution of Sex, the position is advanced and supported by

---

[1] See the last two chapters of this work.

references to the works of those scientific inquirers who have devoted themselves to this special branch, that intercourse between male and female is a matter of gradual evolution, occasioned as the growth of anatomical and physiological characteristics induced change of life. Intercourse in one form or another is shown by them to be a fundamental characteristic of all human beings, lying deep in the framework of organic life. And one of the incidents thus disclosed is the essential difference in constitution which eventually distinguished the male from the female, a difference whose physical results affected the emotional as well as the intellectual life of both. We may be sure that from the very first intercourse was a physical phenomenon which human beings practised.

The tendency occasioned by this characteristic to induce aggregation in lesser groups is found among many animals, and has always been found among mankind. The gregarious habit which distinguishes the bovine, the equine and the wolf likewise makes itself manifest in the very earliest stage among mankind.[1]

There are then two physical characteristics invariably distinguishing mankind in its earliest stages—*intercourse* and *aggregation*. Incidental to these are those universal impulses which seek satisfaction in allaying *hunger* and *carnal desires*. Thus we have brought before us elements which are found in animal life below the stage of the human being, and which, without a single normal exception, impelled mankind from its earliest stages.

No satisfactory account of the *origin* of the human being has yet been given, but all the evidence points to his evolution from a non-human condition. However this may be, when mankind is seen in its earliest stages, forms of aggregation exist, also customs of various kinds, customs at first purely barbarous.

The *familia*, the family, is an organization, if such it can be called, which finds an existence only when more families

---

[1] Geddes and Thomson, Evolution of Sex.

than one in a collective group are noticeable.[1] The worship of the *manes* of a family group is a copy of the worship of a tribal chief. The two may have come up in a like way, or the one may have reacted upon the other. But, however this may be, we may rest assured that in the worship of *manes*, *penates*, the ghosts of dead chiefs or heads of families, the family group obtained that *adherence* to a hearth which aids to create a household in our modern sense.

Mr. Elton says that the early inhabitants of the Grampians, who antedated the Celt, "lived naked and barefooted, in a savage communism, without any organization of state or family."[2] And this is likewise predicable of other savages.[3] The word "family," another writer says, is not known to early tribes; their first form of social grouping was the "household," meaning thereby "an organized permanent body, distinct from its individual members, owning property and having other rights and duties of its own. . . . Over it the house-father presided with absolute power, not as owner in his own right, but as the officer and representative of the corporation. . . . The tie between the members was neither blood nor contract, but community of domestic worship. . . . It included servants and dependents. It included children by adoption. . . . Its one great aim was the perpetuation of the *sacra*."[4]

---

[1] Schrader, Sprachvergleichung u. Urgeschichte, 568; Friedrich Engels, Ursprung der Familie, Chap. II. and page 65. The probabilities seem to be that the worship of gods originated only after the necessity of chieftainship produced fear of a ruler, and worship of his shade after death. But see *contra* Fustel de Coulanges, Ancient City; Hearn, Aryan Household. *Cf.* Leist, Graeco-Ital. Rechtsg., Books I. and II., especially page 96; Platner, Beiträge, etc.; Schrader, Sprachv. u. Urg., Chapter on Familie u. Staat.

[2] Origins of Eng. Hist., 170.

[3] McLennan, Studies in Ancient History, 430 *seq.*; Transactions Ethn. Soc., N. S., V., 45; Encyclopædia Britannica, "Family."

[4] Hearn, Aryan Household, Chap. III., §1. To the same effect is Fustel de Coulanges, Ancient City, Book II., who attributes to it the early constitution of the law of succession, primogeniture, and the growth of city life. He seems to lose sight of the fact that the earliest possible forms of

It is not at all likely that such an organization existed among the earliest people as that indicated in the quotation from Mr. Hearn's work.[1] The group among these is one of shifting individuals, and the notion of communal property only comes into existence after the group has assumed somewhat permanent characteristics. I am tempted to believe that the first social groups are kinds of associations of individuals, partly founded on blood relation, and partly on primitive forms of aggregation and the need of mutual support.[2] In no correct sense can family life be affirmed to be the earliest form of social aggregation. The members of the earliest group were probably those who clustered or flocked around or became associated with some woman or women of the group. The first social forms are matriarchal in character. The tribe is the term usually employed to denote the first form of organization not based exclusively on relationship. (Really relationship is a notion foreign to the mental conceptions of savages.)[3] We have no complete knowledge of the development of the tribal group; the term tribal being itself of vague signification. It was not originally large, but it necessarily became larger, as we have indicated in Chapter II. Those agencies that drive beings on to the procuring of sustenance and the satisfaction of animal passions, conspire among animals to change the personnel of groups. It was so of primitive human groups. They disappeared by merger in other groups or by destruction. The outcome was a large group

---

grouping are incapable of the worship he predicates, and that the form of family he has in view is coeval with a developing city life. See Taylor, The Origin of the Aryans, p. 186.

[1] Smith, Kinship in Arabia, reveals the early matriarchal condition and the form of earliest *kinship* organization. *Cf.* Réclus, Primitive Folk, Chapter on the Nairs.

[2] Both tended to produce the association.

[3] See as to confirmation of this view, Spencer, Principles of Sociology, Vol. I., § 318; Gomme, Village Community, 39 *seq.*; Smith, Kinship in Arabia; Starcke, Primitive Family, last chapter. And see *post* Chap. IV. What is said in Chapter II., Section II., *ante*, must be taken as qualified by what is here said.

or series of groups. Or, if intercourse was peaceful and the pursuit of sustenance did not press against the means of livelihood of others, a favorable increase among the same group might occur.[1]

The place of woman, of progeny, at this stage of life was not always well defined, nor did defined rights as such exist for them. If the group had not attained the pursuit of war, but was peaceful, it is possible that the women might retain a better place compared to the other adults than in groups addicted to war.[2] The latter occupation would tend to render them subordinate and oppressed. All who were not warriors would be resolved into an inferior class; the pursuit of war would of necessity put the non-militant individuals into the inferior class. The women captured in war were on the same basis as the serfs. There was in the earliest stage no adoption. The female infants might be killed if in the way, the male would be permitted to live, tended somewhat as young animals are tended by the female progenitor. The time comes when the young escape from the control of those who are their elders and are left to get food for themselves, are left to their own devices, and the time likewise comes when the elders become antiquated and an encumbrance, for whom neglect and starvation or destruction by the other members of the group is the ordinary lot.[3] The practice is followed because

---

[1] The effect of ancestral worship in forming family groups and customs contemporaneously with the expansion of early city life, is finely shown by Fustel de Coulanges, Ancient City, Book II. The *phratria* is a form of this association, preserving its domestic features. See Platner, Beiträge, etc., Chap. V., and Leist, Zur Gesch. der römischen Societas. Smith, Kinship in Arabia, discloses much excellent material for the reconstitution of the earliest forms of social grouping, and he fully sustains the text.

[2] *Cf.* Réclus, Primitive Folk, chapters on the Esquimaux and Kolarians.

[3] Grimm, Rechtsalterthümer, 487; Tylor, Anthropology, 410; Lubbock, Prehistoric Times, 447, 470, 501; Réclus, Primitive Folk, 38; Felix, Einfluss der Sitten u. Gebräuche, etc., 383. It is not likely that worship of ancestors, purely domestic, would go on with such treatment of the old. It is remarkable that the gods who are worshipped as tribal or household gods are usually "males."

it is natural, not because the savage being has *devised* a cruel system. And the practice is acquiesced in as natural by those affected. We do not see in all this any elaborate scheme of relative rights and duties which mark the domestic relations of our modern day.[1]

The *status* thus defined continued on with variations, changing, as groups consolidated, into larger territorial aggregates having political significance, and the place of *status* which marks the condition of early society was replaced by increasing individuality and the elements underlying *contract*. The relative place of marriage, husband, wife and child changed with these social revolutions.[2] Promiscuous intercourse or what was its equivalent, and absence of knowledge of home —the domestic place of woman—became changed and superseded by other characteristics. War led to man's supremacy, to the increase of coherency and importance and size of groups, to slavery, to the spread of a pastoral and an agricultural life. Unless women were exceptional, or unless the group had enlarged to self-maintaining size, with woman as the head, women would become more and more the dependent members of the social forms and would be little more than the captives in war. Children would become more strictly bound to discipline of their elders. Man would become the head and owner of the children and be known as such. After a while, as in Rome, the power of the household group would be segregated from the larger consolidated body-social, and the *patria potestas* would thus become an assured fact. With this development the capture of women might change for the bargain and sale of women; the utter serfdom and menial position they occupied be exchanged for a more tolerable condition, such as comes with the recognition of the more civil-

[1] See Waitz, D. R. G., Vol. I., 53.

[2] The fear of the dead and the belief in ghosts, culminating in the worship of household, tribal and national deities, likewise served eventually as a cement in the consolidation of human groups and tended to keep them together and to color their development. See Fustel de Coulanges, Ancient City, Books I. and II.; Engels, Der Ursprung der Familie.

ized notions of maternity. In Rome woman had attained a very high place in many instances, as also in Palestine and in the Athens of Pericles.[2] Nevertheless she was not a *person* within the meaning of legality for most purposes, nor were the children permitted to be recognized as legal persons.

Women are still bound to men, in marriage, by ties that are not contractual but are of a physical coloring. Status still describes the character of the married state. They are, except where they are put entirely upon the plane of *femme sole,* still incapable of contracting with their husbands,[3] and the language which confers upon them the power of disposition of their property as if *sole* has been inadequate to root out such relics of status as *right of curtesy,*[4] the incapacity on the part of the wife to bind herself with reference to her property by title bond[5] or other executory contract,[6] or to appoint an attorney to convey for her.

In other words: When women were sought as animals seek to satisfy their cravings for females, the woman was an object of value, and this gave her ample assurance of existence. She appears to have, like animals, enjoyed an equal place with males, except where the practice of war rendered her dependent and subordinate. Then, as already said, her position became more menial and she became degraded to the condition of the serf. There was no large change of mental action involved in this, simply because she had originally borne the aspect of a thing of value. Her

---

[1] See Mayer, Rechte der Israeliten, Römer u. Athener, Vol. II., §222 *seq.*; McLennan, Primitive Marriage; Spencer, Prin. of Soc., Vol. I., Part III. See also *ante*, Chap. II., Sec. II.; and Marquardt, Privatleben der Römer, Part 1.

[2] Felix, Entwg. des Eigenthums, Vol. II., Part II., 346 *seq.*

[3] Zrodolowski, Das römische Privatrecht, Vol. II., 278; Puchta, Institutionen, Vol. II., §219; Amos, Roman Civil Law, 276 *seq.*; Mayer, Rechte der Israeliten, etc., Vol. II., §231; Kelley, Contracts of Married Women.

[4] Neely *v.* Lancaster, 47 Ark. 175.

[5] Stidham *v.* Mathews, 29 Arkansas 650.

[6] *Ibid.;* also Chrisman *v.* Partee, 38 Arkansas 31; Benton Co. *v.* Rutherford, 33 Arkansas 640.

[7] Holland *v.* Moon, 39 Arkansas 120.

condition was probably rendered a little harder, though there is no evidence that she appreciated this fact at that time. Her right to sustenance at all times in savage life depended largely upon her own efforts, and the birth of children did not long incapacitate her.

When women came to be purchased instead of being captured, the condition of society must have been improved, even though the purchase was in the nature of a barter. "The history of marriage in early German law is the history of its gradual enfranchisement from the forms of a sale."[1] There was no consensual but a real contract, in which the price or things to be delivered were given on the one side and the woman on the other; indeed the delivery of the purchase price carried along the right to take the woman. The betrothal and marriage went together. The laws of Ine and Alfred show the introduction of a new principle. The bargain is binding if the purchaser paid or handed over a small sum or thing in trade as earnest money; this is the German *handgeld, arrha,* the Lombard *launichild.*[2] This led to the point where no price was paid but only a promise was made. Eventually the price was given to the woman and was called her morning-gift. It was distinct from the Roman *dos,* which was originally given by the father of the bride. But both of these tended to become merged in one and the same thing when it came to turning over to the widow her dower-right.[3]

---

[1] Essays in Anglo-Saxon Law, 165. That this was not peculiar to early German customs, see Post, Bausteine für eine allgemeine Rechtswissenschaft, Vol. I., §29 *seq.*; same, Ursprung des Rechts, Chapters III., IV. and V.; same, Die Geschlechtsgenossenschaft der Urzeit und die Entstehung der Ehe. Felix, Entwickelungsgeschichte des Eigenthums, Vol. II., Part II., Chap. B.; W. Robertson Smith, Kinship in Arabia.

[2] See further, *ante* pp. 56, 57.

[3] Essays in Anglo-Saxon Law, 170; Grimm, Deutsche Rechtsalterthümer, 441. "Die Ehe wird für vollzogen angesehen, wann die Decke Mann und Frau *beschlägt* * * * das *Bett beschritten* ist." On the succeeding morning the wife receives from her husband a respectable gift called morning-gift (*Morgengabe*). "Schon in der Pactio Guntheramni et Childeberti (Greg, Tur. 9, 20) werden Dos und Morganegiba unterschieden."

Among the Anglo-Saxon tribes in Britain the wife continued under the control of her spouse, owing him obedience. In her own sphere as housekeeper she had attained some independence. The husband was a co-possesser of her property, including the morning-gift. The husband, or the husband and wife, or the wife alone, conveyed her property. Gifts were regularly made to husband and wife together, which were held in common; her property was not answerable for his debts nor his for her debts. A homicide committed by her had to be atoned by her kin. The wife's kindred protected her property from alienation by the husband. At his death the wife was entitled to all of her property, including the morning-gift, or if there was no such gift then half of his property. Divorce by mutual consent seems to have been permitted.[1] Some of these privileges exceed those which the wife had later, when a military life and conquest had imposed new conditions favorable to males and unfavorable to females upon the country. In France these rights remained pretty intact except with reference to divorce, but in England the wife lost some of her individuality, though upon the whole her place in the family became much better defined.

The growth of the community, the consolidation of tribes into a national mass with a national polity, furthered the rise and development of separate family groups. These groups were already well developed when Rome, through the clergy, imposed its doctrines upon the English Isle. The modern notion of family took hold and grew, and at least in England the wife ceased more and more to be a mere servant whose identity was wellnigh lost sight of. She became the emotional, the moral element of the family group that made

---

Grimm, *loc. cit.* That *dos* and *morgengabe* became identified as one, see *ibid.* 442. See also Zoepfl, Deutsche Rechtsgeschichte, Vol. III., §81c; S. Mayer, Rechte der Israeliten, Römer u. Athener, Vol. II., §225 *seq.*, esp. §227; Digby, Hist. of the Law of Real Property, 112–116. For similar phenomena among Semitic people, see Smith, Kinship in Arabia.

[1] See Essays in Anglo-Saxon Law, 176 *seq.*

mostly for righteousness; and the husband remained the warrior, her baron or lord, the legal possessor of their joint property. She became incapable of controlling her separate property in person or through her kinsmen; became incapable of contracting for herself except, possibly, for necessaries; her husband became liable for her torts, for her sustenance; they could not make gifts to or contract with each other, and so on.

The children, as the family group developed, obtained recognition by the community, their property was protected through representatives, though their earnings during minority still remained their fathers', and their inability to contract continued. In our modern day the married woman is again securing some old Anglo-Saxon rights and some new ones, and is being saddled with liabilities, and minors are being held accountable where they perhaps would not have been chargeable in earlier days. Yet the condition of married women and children remains largely that of status rather than of contract so far as concerns the marriage relation; while the servants or menials have become amenable to a doctrine of agency or contract.

The modern family is an aggregate, which American law assumes to exist in providing homestead rights and rules of succession for the provision of the widow and children. The solidarity of husband and wife still remains a recognized fact, as does the relation of husband, wife, child and servant in reference to the doctrine of defense of each at the hands of the others.

It is noteworthy that the law does not deal with the internal regimen of the modern family, except so far as it is presented in outward acts affecting a larger social interest. It deals principally, if not entirely, so far as domestic relations and rights are concerned, with external acts or with physical objects. It does not probe the mind and seek to fathom and regulate motives and emotions. What it does in this regard is by way of anticipation, and it punishes or repairs the injuries it takes cognizance of only when revealed by some form or mode of external action.

To what extent the law should ignore the doctrine of status and put women upon a plane with other persons is still a much debated question. Its improper solution may tend to weaken the ties of society and again introduce that social disintegration which marked the decline and fall of the Roman Empire. The *intellectual* effort which is being put forward to give woman the franchise and office, and married women full right to undertake business and contract and convey away their property as men may do, is the culmination of that tendency of social development which marks the decadence of status and the adoption of contractual relations. Its outcome seems to be to make the marriage tie *solely* contractual in its nature, and hence to despoil family life of that cement which is implied when marriage is treated as a sacred and binding status depending on hereditary conditions no less than on contractual relations. Courts and lawyers cannot solve the difficulty, they will go with the stream. Yet if they can open the minds of the people to the physical factors that play their part in the formation of the family and in promoting its lasting growth and effects, they may avert the evil implied in a too extensive enfranchisement of women.

Connected with the subject of the family and of property is that of succession and inheritance. Prior to that form of status which implies the existence of a group bound together by ties of natural descent and aggregation there is no likelihood of a succession in the event of death. In succession the acquisition of things and their retention is implied. It is affirmed, and it may be true, that the notion of succession is the outcome of an early practice of preserving the worship of ancestral spirits.[1] The most natural form of inheritance is that which contemplated an equal division among the

---

[1] Maine, Early Law and Custom, Chap. IV.; Hearn, Aryan Household, Chap. III., §6; Fustel de Coulanges, Ancient City, Book II., Chap. VII.; Leist, Graeco-Ital. R. G., Book I.

descendants.[1] And this is the form of distribution which early prevailed regarding movables.[2] But the community-life and holdings of early days were not consistent with such a mode of succession. The ownership was not in the individual, and consequently at any one's death there was no idea of inheritance.[3] If, as was the case generally among patriarchal groups, some one person represented the communal group, had the same powers as the *patria potestas*, the person who succeeded him was likely to be at first the best male representative who could defend and maintain the possessions of the group. This was not at first necessarily the male child.[4] The line of succession would fall upon that person who was the individual of the group adapted, under all the circumstances, to take up the functions of representative. If intercourse was promiscuous, and no family life, in a modern sense, had developed, such a representative might be other than child, and, if military practices had not intervened to prevent, might be in a female. The prevalent practice seems to have been in a later day to select a male representative who was the nearest in the line of succession to maintain the worship of the household gods.[5] A military life engendered those factors which made for social cohesiveness and *political* unity; it likewise introduced military autocracy, kingly rule, and that mode of obtaining land which is implied in kingly grant. As is stated in another chapter, it likewise led to the establishment of a family integrity as understood nowadays. Then it was, except

[1] Ross, Early Landholding among the Germans, 24 *seq.*, 53; Maine, Early Hist. of Inst., 195. But as to who are such descendants see Engels, Ursprung der Familie; Leist, *loc. cit.*

[2] Hearn, Aryan Household, Chap. VII., §6.

[3] Hanssen, Agrarhist. Abh., Vol. I., 77, "Wechsel der Wohnsitze u. Feldmarken in germanischer Urzeit."

[4] Spencer, Principles of Sociology, Vol. I., Part III., Chap. IX.; Hearn, Aryan Household, Chap. VII., §3.

[5] Maine, Early Law and Custom, Chap. IV.; Hearn, Aryan Household, Chap. III., §6; see, however, Morgan, Ancient Society, Part III., for a different view. See also Engels, Ursprung der Familie, etc.

where agricultural customs had introduced a different mode of succession, that the eldest male became the heir of the family holding.

In Anglo-Saxon times, among the tribes inhabiting western Europe, the mode of succession was like that which prevailed in Britain. There the landed possessions were those of the family; but the family's private property gradually became the private property of the individual. *Yrfe-land*, heir-land, was originally inalienable, and the question of intestate succession did not arise with regard to it, for if the family died out the land reverted to the community. The next step in its development into private property was attained when the head of the family obtained rights over the land by consent of the members of the family. Then we find private ownership and power of alienation outside of the family by consent of the king and *witan*. Ecclesiastical influence introduced wills, which were first used to endow ecclesiastical institutions. In intestacy the estate was sometimes divided among all the children, from which we have the Kentish custom of gavelkind. The land which was attended with the privilege of alienation is to be found principally among that class of holders who held of the crown by military service, the privilege of alienation being extended, where possessed, by the king. If the king did not extend this privilege it reverted to him upon the death of his donee. In England the Norman Conquest led to the forcible ejection of the more prominent Saxon holders from their holdings, but the mass of cultivators were not disturbed. On the continent of Europe the modes of holding land corresponded in the main with those of Great Britain, and the Conquest introduced into England no material change, except that it fastened upon the Anglo-Saxon people a more elaborate

[1]Scrutton, Land in Fetters, Chaps. I., II. and III.; Hearn, Aryan Household, Chap. III., §6; Zoepfl, Deutsche Rechtsgeschichte, Vol. III., 112 *seq.*; Maine, Early Law and Custom, Chap. IV.; Waitz, D. V. G., Vol. I., 54 *seq.*; Grimm, Deutsche Rechtsalterthümer, 466 *seq.*; Sheldon Amos, Roman Civil Law, Part II., Chap. V.

and stricter form of manorial ownership. The duty of rendering military service among the English became stricter and the doctrine of primogeniture found more and more practical application. The small holders who were not in the condition of dependents of the soil now gradually became such, rendering definite service and holding a socage tenure from king or lord, while the mass of tenants whose status remained unchanged continued in the communal enjoyment of their possessions, rendering services as before. The custom of alienation was not known among them until the increase of population, the growth of the cities and the spread of industrial and commercial activity led to the desire for individual progress and culminated in a departure from communal customs. Enclosures likewise tended to the same end: all of which has been discussed in another chapter. But the result was that the tendency toward alienation increased, and lands, except where manorial customs or rights intervened, became alienable. But the doctrine of primogeniture had fastened on the land, through the spread of baronial influence, prevailing, except where the agricultural cultivators had finally established and obtained recognition for an older or different mode of succession. Trade, too, tended to overthrow a military mode of succession. We note that borough English and gavelkind remained modes of succession alongside of primogeniture; both relics of early tribal life.[1] We note also that multiform other customs prevailed in different manors and localities, indicating that in a large measure, before national unity began to form, and national courts and other agencies began to create a national policy, each community had its own peculiar customs of succession and descent.[2]

---

[1] Scrutton, Land in Fetters, 51 *seq.*, 54 *seq.* Maine, Early History of Institutions, 188 *seq.*, has given us an explanation of the origin of gavelkind. See also as to this and borough-English, Hearn, Aryan Household, 82, 83; Scrutton, Land in Fetters, 60 *seq.*; Denman Ross, Early History of Landholding among the Germans, 104; Bastian, Rechtsv., p. 185.

[2] Scrutton, Land in Fetters, 63 *seq.*; Hanssen, Agrarhistorische

In early days, possibly after the tribal group had lost its earlier forms and the household developed a modern phase of family tie and kindred, we must look for the *successores, yrfe,* heirs and successors, among those who were best adapted or remained to represent the family property.[1] At first chiefship was the character of the holding of the successor;[2] showing its derivation from warlike customs and tribal discipline. Mr. Hearn says "he succeeded to an office, and not to an estate." As the family narrowed down to blood relations, the notion of heirship assumed its modern aspect. Whereas, prior to this, even in Roman times, the estate is the basis of relationship and right of heirship, giving color and substance to it,[3] and is spoken of as a corporate thing or *universitas,* in the later form consanguinity is a controlling factor. As already stated, the unification and cohesion of people into larger political masses leads to the eventual group bound together by blood-relationship. We see this modern phenomenon in its blossom in Rome, while still the notion of succession retains much of its tribal character.[4] Blood-relationship, strictly so called, came into existence at that stage of social development which rendered possible an appreciation of family ties and degrees of consanguinity. Pontifical influences and ingenuity in ancient and modern form contributed no little to produce this result and give rise to that abhorrence of incest which plays so

---

Abhandlüngen, Vol. II.; Felix, Entw. des Eigenthums, Vol. II. That a similar statement holds true of early Roman law, see Corssen, Beiträge zur italischen Sprachkunde, p. 207, on the derivation of "lex."

[1] See Scrutton, *supra,* Chap. I.; Zoepfl, D. R. G., Vol. III., §§112, 113; Hearn, Aryan Household, Chap. VII., §3, Chap. III., §6.

[2] Hearn, *loc. cit.*

[3] See Zoepfl, D. R. G., Vol. III., §§113, 111; Holmes, Common Law, Lec. X.

[4] Upon some such theory is probably to be explained its continuance in Palestine long after priests and their moral influence had come into existence. A son procreated by incest or adultery was legitimate, even in the post-exilic period. S. Mayer, Rechte der. Israeliten, Römer u. Athener, Vol. II., p. 463.

conspicuous a part in the creation of these ties and this blood-relationship. Yet, in all likelihood, the family tie and the practice of exogamy together may have contributed in the production of the result, for it is not likely that the masses would be influenced in their daily life by clerical persuasion to such an extent as to change their habits of life, if those habits themselves had not conspired largely to produce the same result.[1]

Evidences of the early succession were that the ancestor could not disinherit his successor, the successor had to take unless he abandoned the group,[2] the successor was liable to the full extent of his inheritance for the debts and delicts of his predecesssor;[3] no descendant of the heir could take, but the succession, if he was dead, would go to one of the group who stood in the same degree to the predecessor.[4] The development of the family group along the line of consanguinity and the gradual increase in the alienability of property have given rise to different tables of degrees of kinship and to dispositions by will and deed or other conveyance. The fact that priestly influence has been the early intellectual creator of formulæ and inventions to carry out objective reforms and changes has tended to give a form and coloring to many devises known in the history of law which would otherwise probably not have existed. The modern doctrines of administration and distribution find difficulties growing out of this condition of things. One of these in English law, under acts relating to administration of the estates of deceased persons, is that an administrator who has committed waste is not liable to his successor for wasted assets, but only

---

[1] Zoepfl, D. R. G., Vol. III., §113, VII.; Scrutton, Land in Fetters, 4 *seq.*; Ross, Early Hist. of Landholding among the Germans, 54 *seq.*; Amos, Civil Law, 319; Hearn, Aryan Household, Chap. III., §5.

[2] Zoepfl, D. R. G., Vol. III., §113, VIII.; Amos, Civil Law, 328, 330; Hearn, Aryan Household, Chap. III., §6.

[3] Zoepfl, D. R. G., Vol. III., §113, IX.; Amos, Civil Law, 332.

[4] Zoepfl, D. R. G., Vol. III., §113, X.; Ross, Early Hist. of Landholding among the Germans, 48.

for assets *in specie.*[1] Now since creditors large and small, and quite numerous, are not infrequently interested, in addition to heirs or those who claim to be heirs, it very often becomes a difficult matter to say who shall bring the suit for the recovery of wasted assets, even after their value has been ascertained. The estate of a deceased person is still a *corpus* so long as it remains in administration, but only so long as it remains intact. After it is dissipated it seems to require the skill of the best intellectual ingenuity to work out satisfactory results. It would have probably been far better to treat such an estate as a *corpus* even as to that portion which has been wasted, and to allow the successor of a defaulting administrator to recover for the diminution thus arising.

The place of family spoken of by Aristotle, and referred to in the first chapter of this book in the development of constitutional law, is illustrated by this chapter. We note how vague all general affirmations of family influence in the creation of jurisprudence are, and yet we observe its changing phases coming up out of the wrecks and ruins of the past to give or help give a basis for a broader, national, constitutional life, in our most modern sense.

SECTION III.—IN THE LAW OF OBLIGATIONS.

An obligation may grow out of a misfeasance or a nonfeasance or a contract. Delicts and contracts produce obligations. An obligation rests upon all human beings in a greater or lesser degree to perform duties to mankind, to kindred and to the state. Such is its present broad signification, acquired from Roman sources.[2] In its beginning it represented much less. We now consider its signification

---

[1] Williams on Executors, Vol. I., marg. pp. 822–827; Beall *v.* New Mexico, 16 Wallace Rep. 540; State, for use, etc. *v.* Rottaken, 34 Ark. 148 *seq.* An administrator cannot set aside conveyances made by decedents in fraud of creditors. Wait, Fraudulent Conveyances and Creditors' Bills, §112.

[2] Ihering, Geist, etc., Book III., Part I., §54, p. 183.

broad enough to embrace all of those duties resting upon human beings which the law requires them to fulfill. Such might be its legal signification now. It was thus defined in Roman law: "Obligatio est juris vinculum, quo necessitate adstringimur alicujus solvendae rei, secundum nostrae civitatis jura."[1] It appears to have been a *legal* bond, that tied the obliged person down to something; he was necessitated to do it. The definition merely summed up, in a general form, what in detail occurred, and had occurred time out of memory, long before, in the Roman world.

These duties had expanded as the social groups formed and enlarged. The *stipulatio* might represent eventually the conspicuous form of *obligatio*, and *depositum, pignus, mutuum, commodatum, mandatum, emptio-venditio,* might represent classifications of contractual obligation as the community assumed that larger sphere which goes with increase and consolidation of population. Yet the basis upon which all rested comprised the relations which existed between individuals, or individuals and collective groups, respecting a greater or less control over another's actions, with reference to that other's sphere of activity, either with or without regard to the use, enjoyment or possession of some other external thing.[2]

No doubt in the earliest stages no abstract notion of duty or obligation existed. The things that were done, habit or spontaneity brought about, or were enforced by superior power. Deprivation of a possession might lead to forcible redress and recaption, or some other mode of revenge which animals visit on offenders.[3] Ties of birth gave possibility to

---

[1] Inst. 3, 13, Pr. Maine, Ancient Law, Chap. IX. See, however, Puchta, Institutionen, §262 *seq.*; Amos, Civil Law, Part II., Chap. III., §1.

[2] Savigny, Heutigen römischen Rechts, Vol. I., 339; Ihering, Zweck im Recht, Vol. I., 156 *seq.*, 270 *seq.*

[3] Compare Maine, Early Hist. of Institutions, Lecture IX.; Post, Ursprung des Rechts, p. 110; same, Bausteine, §§71, 148, 149; Inst. III., xiii., 2; Maine, Ancient Law, Chap. IX.; Spencer, Principles of Sociology, Vol. II., Part V., Chap. XIV., §533; same, Justice, Chap. XV.; Hunter, Roman Law, 352 *seq.*; Ihering, Geist, etc., Part III., Subd. I (3d ed.), 210.

the transfer of possession for temporary or permanent purposes; a thing might be exacted from him who had to be coerced or guarded against; and so *mutuum* and *pignus* might become possible eventualities. So general a phenomenon as is represented by obligation lies in a universal custom or habit, whose beginnings are apt to go back to those earliest forms of activity from which society emerged.

It seems to me that when external tribunals came to enforce the performance of duties, that is the redress of wrongs, they were impelled by a prevalent feeling—the outcome of the life of the mass—that the status had been changed, whereby some one was deprived of what was part of his integrity as a member of the group. Thus the aspect of dominion over some physical object would enlarge to embrace that of which the dominion had been temporarily lost, and self-help by the wronged one or compensation by way of transfer of some other object, or security to make good his claim on the part of the wrongdoer, would result.[1] Here are embryonic beginnings of a *quid pro quo*.

The earliest modes of redress implied the idea of recaption or of remedying a trespass by more or less forcible means.[3] Upon this, later forms of actions were developments. In all forms of action of early stages the aim seems to be to restore the prior status.[4] The development of procedure introduced the classifications of obligations which are peculiar to later systems of jurisprudence.[5] They become more clearly defined

[1] See chapter on Procedure. See also Law Quarterly Review, Vol. III., 166 *seq.*; Holmes, Common Law, Lec. VII.; Law Quarterly Rev., Vol. I., 162; Pollock on Torts, 1–3; Post, Bausteine, etc., §§148, 149.

[2] But see Schrader, Handelsgeschichte u. Warenkunde, 9 *seq.*; Leist, Graeco-Ital. R. G., Book II., Chap. II., §31, and p. 265.

[3] Pollock on Torts, 1, 2 and 3, and Appendix A, note by F. W. Maitland; Holmes, Common Law, Lecs. III., V., VII.; Leist, Graeco-Ital. R. G., Book II., Chap. III. and succeeding chapters.

[4] Maine, Ancient Law, concluding part of Chap. V.; Post, Bausteine, etc., §§40, 47, 71; same author, Ursprung des Rechts, Chap. XIII.

[5] Pollock on Torts, 2, 467, note by F. W. Maitland. Sir Frederick Pollock (Oxford Lectures and Essays, p. 61) and Leist (Graeco-Ital.

and more numerous as the courts and lawyers assume more definite and extensive functions. In this way is to be explained the classification of delicts and contractual obligations, and of the manifold heads of each. The process of development takes up the changing views and usages of the community, and may color them, render them perhaps more difficult to comprehend and less adapted to real needs than if this agency were less active. And to meet the evil, new forms and fictions may have to be devised by bench and bar so that the law may be consistent. But I do not share the view of Ihering that this is a meritorious activity of bench and bar, whereby the law is maintained as a conservative and perennial benefactor. The evil of such a course lies originally in a want of appreciation or observance of the drift of the community. The Roman system of procedure was as largely open to objections on account of its technicalities and detail as was the common-law procedure of England.[1]

This classificatory influence was conspicuous in Roman law, in giving more definiteness to the notion of the *quid pro quo* which constituted the *causa* of contracts in the days of Justinian; and it was likewise conspicuous in creating the notion of consideration which forms the criterion of English and American contracts. But I do not concur in the statement that courts originated the conception of consideration[4] or of *causa*. The earliest forms of exchange, and the earliest

R. G., §§60-62) base the origin of contractual law upon early treaties between tribes. No doubt these helped to create the ultimate contractual characteristics, but they were not the sole elements.

[1] Compare Keller, Der römische Civil-Process, etc., with Stephen on Pleading.

[2] Compare Puchta, Institutionen, §271 *seq.*; Savigny, Heutigen röm. Rechts, Vol. III., 360 & n.; Vol. IV., 225, Vol. V., 526. Holland, Elements of Jurisprudence, 182.

[3] Law Quarterly Review, Vol. III., 166 *seq.*; Holmes, Common Law, Lec. VII.; Pollock on Torts, App. A.

[4] Holmes, Common Law, Lec. VII.; Salmond, Law Q. Rev., Vol. III., 166 *seq.*

forms of redress for property taken, contain in solution the idea implied in consideration. And they may be an outcome of original gifts made to appease, and for which gifts were made in return.[1] Neither can I share the view of Mr. Hare that "consideration" is the criterion which distinguishes English legal notions of contract from that of Rome.[2] Meeting of minds is as much an element in English as in Roman law, and Roman law[3] gave almost the same effect to the notion of a *quid pro quo* as does English jurisprudence.[4]

There are in every system of developed jurisprudence numerous forms of contracts, such as written and verbal, express or implied or constructive contracts, contracts relating to personal property and to land, bailments of all kinds including pledges, mortgages, agency, partnership, sale, assignment, etc. These are the headings for branches of that class of obligations, and contain the essential elements of the contract. They do not represent deductions logically made from a general postulate; they are the slow work of developing industrial social activity. The summation which is now the definition of contract was long unknown in early jurisprudence,[5] and does not in all things find an echo in Roman jurisprudence. The field of torts ramified in a similar way. The earliest form of redress was self-help for injury done to the person, or some possession taken which was regarded as of value.[6] The word tort is

---

[1] Schrader, Handelsgeschichte u. Warenkunde, 9 *seq.* Compare Leist, Graeco-Ital. R. G., §34.

[2] Hare, Contracts, Chap. VII. Compare Pollock, Contracts, 151; also Law Q. Rev., Vol. III., 166.

[3] Holland, Elements of Jurisprudence, 174; Wharton, Contracts, §4, *seq.* Rewards offered are binding, Pollock on Contracts (Wald's ed.), 13, 20. Contracts by correspondence, *ibid.* 14. Acceptance must be communicated, 38 Mich. 692; Anson, Contracts, Part II., Chap. I., §7.

[4] Puchta, Institutionen, §272; Holland, Elements of Jurisprudence, 182. Compare Law Quarterly Review, Vol. III., 166, and Anson, Contracts, Part II., Chap. II.; with Hare, Contracts, Chap. VII.; Holmes, Common Law, Lec. VII.

[5] Pollock on Torts, 14, 15; Ihering, Zweck im Recht, Vol. I., 270 *seq.*

[6] See next chapter. Cf. Pollock on Torts, 2, 467, note by Mr. F. W. Maitland.

probably "nothing but the French equivalent of our English word *wrong*. In common speech everything is a wrong, or wrongful, which is thought to do violence to any right."[1]

All contracts aim at objects, not at mental conditions. The law takes no notice of mere mental operations apart from a physical expression of them.[2] It is a trite law that the thought of man is not triable, for even the devil does not know what the thought of man is.[3] The end in view must be of some utility; it must not aim at physical impossibilities. And though immoral contracts are vitiated, and these involve elements not depending for their distinguishing features on physical factors, still there is a large play of such factors here, and confessedly of social factors, for morals themselves are largely *rules of action* which the growth of society has left as a heritage.[4] If a contract is always an agreement it is such because that is frequently deduced from the acts of the parties.[5] *Credere* in its broadest signification was understood by Roman jurists to denote the transfer of a thing with the attendant obligation on the part of the receiver to return it.[6] Creditor was he who gave some thing, debitor he who received a thing.[7] When *the thing*

---

[1] Pollock on Torts, 1, 2.

[2] Ahearn *v.* Ayers, 38 Mich. 692; Pollock on Contracts (Wald's ed.), 2, note *a*.

[3] Brian, Ch. J., 17 Edw. IV., T. Pasch. Case 2, quoted in Brogdan *v.* Met. Ry. Co., 2 App. Cas. 662, 692.

[4] Spencer's Data of Ethics; Stephen, Science of Ethics; Maudsley, Physiology and Pathology of the Mind; same author, Body and Will; Bain, Senses and the Intellect; same author, The Emotions and the Will; Ribot, Diseases of Memory; same author, Diseases of the Will; Sully, Illusions; Luys, Brain and its Functions; Lewes, Problems of Life and Mind; Romanes, Mental Evolution in Animals; Fowler, Progressive Morality; Pollock, Essays in Jurisprudence and Ethics, Chap. XI.; Ihering, Zweck im Recht, Chap. IX.; Cope, Origin of the Fittest, 450 *seq.*

[5] Such was the mode of its origin. Zweck im Recht, Vol. I., 270.

[6] Zweck im Recht, Vol. I., 157.

[7] *Ibid.* 158, 271. Compare Schrader, Handelsgeschichte u. Warenkunde, 9 *seq.*

came to represent a right of ownership without dominion over or possession of the object, it likewise resulted that abstraction would put a duty on a debtor of returning an equivalent instead of the thing itself. The creation of money, coin, or a circulating medium tended to produce the duty of making return in this representative of value.[1] Agency is an enlargement of that form of representation which found expression first in procurators to represent those who had no right to appear for themselves in the tribunals. The baron, or master, was the first form of this kind of representative. A cognitor might come to represent another. A surety or warrantor for or to another was frequently obliged in early days to answer for his principal or warrantee.[2] The early town or village communities had to answer for the wrongs done by members of the groups.[3] A combination that owned property in common and accumulated property for common gain, especially when commercial purposes were in view, became designated as a partnership, joint stock company, or a corporation, in English or American law; *societas* in Roman law.[4] In the absence of other evidence a partnership might be considered as organized for commercial purposes.[5]

Nowadays contracts in manifold ways disclose their physical bases. The consideration usually involves a physical gain or disadvantage. The carrier's contract is for transportation of commodities, and requires delivery unless excused by physical events. Words are inadequate to relieve the carrier from the consequences of his own negligence. All bailments are based upon the custody by the bailee of objects of value. In sales or transfers of property

---

[1] Zweck im Recht, Vol. I., 158 *seq.*

[2] Siegel, Geschichte des deutschen Gerichtsverfahrens, Beilage I.; Essays in Anglo-Saxon Law, 191, 218, 253, 254.

[3] Rogge, Ueber das Gerichtswesen der Germanen, §6; Post, Bausteine, §§148, 149; Leist, Graeco-Ital. R. G., §§9, 10; same, Röm. Societas, 15; Post, African Jurisprudenz, §§26, 27.

[4] On the history of the *societas* see Leist, Zur Geschichte der römischen Societas.

[5] Dig. 17, 2, 7.

the tradition of objects of value is involved. In insurance contracts the phenomena of fire, water and death are assured against, and pecuniary compensation for loss is expected. Here no language is adequate to convert an agent of an insurance company into the agent of an insured person. In the language of the Supreme Court of Illinois, "there is no magic power residing in the words of [a] stipulation to convert the real into the unreal."[1] The objects and duties contemplated by agencies, partnerships, corporations are usually material in their nature, except where the object is moral or religious improvement. Partnerships and corporations are forms of contract that involve, as has been seen, the physical aggregation of more than one individual; and this phenomenon of physical aggregation, as already said in a former chapter, has contributed to give character to these special forms. Work and labor largely form the basis of contractual obligation, and the tests of inefficient work are most frequently of a material nature. In determining the scope of a contract it is admissible to introduce evidence of "every material fact that will enable the court to identify the person or thing mentioned in the instrument, and to place the court, whose province it is to declare the meaning of the word of the instrument, as near as may be in the situation of the parties to it."[2]

Contractual capacity depends upon such physical phenomena as a healthy brain, a sane mind; upon sex, as to whether the person be a wife; upon age, as to whether he be a minor. Necessity begets capacity in cases of minority, where the preservation of life and physical comfort are involved, and physical criteria determine what are necessaries within this rule.

In modern English and American law a tort is "an act or omission [not being merely the breach of duty arising out of

---

[1] Commercial Ins. Co. *v.* Ives, 56 Ill. 402. See also Bacon, Benefit Societies and Life Insurance, §221.

[2] Elphinstone, Rules for the Interpretation of Deeds, 50 *seq.*

a personal relation, or undertaken by contract] which is related to harm suffered by a determinate person."[1] It may grow out of an act, not justified by law, which does harm to another or his property, or in failing, when duty required, to prevent that which harms another or his property.[2] In other words, action and inaction entail harmful results which the courts now seek to rectify, in lieu of the practice of self-help or private revenge, which might otherwise prevail. The mode of redress or of relief is by pecuniary fines or compensation. Circumstances of aggravation disclosing a mental factor, such as spite or vindictiveness, entail more serious results, in the shape of larger compensation and, perhaps, imprisonment. One can see here without further elaboration how fundamental are physical and social factors in the development and existence of the law of torts. Mention has already been made of the part that water and air play in the creation of laws. And as aggregates of individuals form in municipal centers, the agency of these elements in the creation of legal regimen expands. This physical phenomenon has also been mentioned already. Nuisances are torts embracing a wide field, growing in extent with the development of new inventions and new industrial centers. Slander and libel embrace tortious infractions of law, which have been modified by the need of communication through commercial agencies respecting the condition of merchants and bankers.[3] .

The need of dwelling on physical and social factors in the creation of the law of obligations is revealed every day of our lives. Indeed they cannot be lost sight of; they form constant criteria. But they are apt to be improperly ignored in the creation of those laws which tend to render the mechanic negligent, under the protection of mechanic's lien laws, and in the creation of usury and sumptuary laws, and laws contemplating a patriarchal regimen on the part of the state.[4]

---

[1] Pollock on Torts, 19. [2] *Ibid.*

[3] Errant, Law of Commercial Agencies.

[4] See on this subject Spencer, Man versus the State.

SECTION IV.—IN THE LAW OF PROCEDURE.

The law of procedure is now classed as adjective law,[1] as distinguished from rules of action which relate to substantive rights.[2] But the classification cannot claim to be based on universally valid distinctions. Courts in the United States have not hesitated to declare enactments of legislative bodies unconstitutional where they seriously interfered with remedies previously existing,[3] claiming that they impaired the substantial obligations of contracts, or tended to deprive persons of their vested rights. Adjective law, in virtue of the use of that term, would seem, according to modern conception, to occupy a subordinate place.[4] And yet in early days it was notoriously otherwise. So great is the ascendancy of the law of actions in the infancy of courts of justice, that substantive law has at first the look of being gradually secreted in the interstices of procedure; and the early lawyers can only see the law through the envelope of its technical forms.[5] The earliest known codes give the first, if not the predominant, place to the modes or methods of bringing parties into court.[6] And Sir Henry Maine contends that the authority of the court of justice overshadowed all other ideas and considerations in the minds of early code-makers.[7] And that

---

[1] Holland, Elements of Jurisprudence, Chap. XV.; Austin, Jurisprudence, §§853, 1032, 1034; Amos, Science of Jurisprudence, 283.

[2] See the authorities cited in the preceding note.

[3] See, however, Austin and Amos, *supra*. Remedies have at times been invested by courts with the character of property. (See Hare, American Constitutional Law, Vol. II., Lectures 37, 38.) And courts have given decisions the character of legislation. Gelpche *v.* Dubuque, 1 Wallace, 175, 206; Havemeyer *v.* Iowa Co., 3 Wallace, 294; Olcott *v.* Supervisors, etc., 16 Wallace, 678; Harris *v.* Jex, 55 N. Y. 421.

[4] Maine, Early Law and Custom, 389.

[5] *Ibid.*

[6] *Id.* 366 *seq.*; Hammond, Introduction to Sanders' Justinian; and see authorities *infra*.

[7] Early Law and Custom, 383 *seq.*; Ancient Law, 4.

view is the prevalent one.[1] This authority was attributable to a disposition that grew up to settle disputes by other means than self-help[2]—a disposition necessitated by the superior power or prowess of the offender and his associates, and facilitated by that pressure which an aggregate mass of human beings may exercise upon an arbitrary and offending leader or leaders of the mass.[3] It would be contributed to by the desire of chiefs to make control over the tribe or tribes easier,[4] and it would be an outcome of military and priestly regimen seeking to obtain control over the discordant elements of the mass.[5]

Self-help is the first, as it is the most natural, form of redress known to beings who have made no self-conscious strides in social regimen. It is a form of redress known to animals, and is likely to continue long after social factors

---

[1] "Der Process selbst gehört zu den frühst entwickelten Rechtsinstitutionen. Zu einer Zeit, da die materiellen Rechtsbegriffe erst in sehr schwachen Umrissen für uns sichtbar werden, begegnet uns der Process bereits in ausgebildeter und präcisirter Gestalt und bildet einen der ältesten Gegenstände der Gesetzgebung." Ihering, Geist des römischen Rechts, dritter Theil, §50, p. 17; Clark, Practical Jurisprudence, 21, 42 *seq.*; Pollock, Torts, 21; Woolsey, Political Science, Vol. II., §230; Spencer, Principles of Sociology, §522; Leist, Graeco-Ital. R. G., Book I., Chap. III., §22, pp. 133–36; also §§65, 66.

[2] Siegel, Geschichte des deutschen Gerichtsverfahrens, §§1–8; Leist, Graeco-Ital. R. G., §46. Also Book III., Chap. II.

[3] Siegel, *supra*, §1.

[4] Siegel, *supra*. Leist attributes a good deal to the *Erinyes*, the anger of the slain and its appeasement, in achieving a social control over remedial procedure. See preceding reference in notes 1 and 2. But *quere* whether the process of growth was not at first the reverse of what Leist imagines. See also Coulanges, next note.

[5] Spencer, Principles of Sociology, Vol. II., Part V., Chap. XIII. De Coulanges thinks that the priestly influence was permanent and was imbedded in that worship of ancestors upon which ancient society was founded. Ancient City, Book III., Chap. XI. He says: "Law and religion were but one . . . no man invented them." The laws "presented themselves without being sought." "They were the direct and necessary consequences of belief; they were religion itself applied to the relations of men among themselves." See also Leist, Graeco-Ital. R. G., Book II., Chap. III., and Book III., Chaps. I. and II.

have replaced it in developing details with social forms of redress. Just as the art of naming may be practiced without a self-conscious realization of the relation between the human being and the objects he surveys,[1] as this may grow upon him by slow increment of experience, so may the impulse to self-help long exist and develop before any self-conscious formulation of *meum* and *tuum* or remedial right exists. Self-help is a product of that inherent self-preservative impulse which induces the animal to defend its own existence; it is a form of it, broadening, under gregarious influences, the feeling of self-preservation; and its development goes on in social life, so that eventually the notion of self-preservation may embrace the preservation of self and kindred and much of that with which the self has surrounded itself. Therefore,[2] in our very modern law, a man may under certain circumstances slay another in defense of his family, his house and household goods.[3]

There are law-writers who contend that the notion of right is innate to the earliest being,[4] upon the same principle that the ethical philosopher claims the same thing.[5] Such a

---

[1] As to which see Romanes, Mental Evolution in Man, Chapters V. to IX. inclusive.

[2] *Cf.* Bishop, Crim. Law, Vol. I., Chap. LVI., for further instances. Holland, Elements of Jurisprudence, 215, where he states that a new right may be realizable by the regulated self-help of the injured person, as when he is allowed to push a trespasser out of his field, or to pull down a wall which has been built in his path. *Ibid.* 165, 272. Nations exercise the right of self-help, such as reprisal. The notion of the sanctity of the house is found at an early stage of political life. Leist, Graeco-Ital. R. G., §38, p. 247. Hearn, Aryan Household, p. 222.

[3] *Cf.* preceding note.

[4] Ihering, Geist des römischen Rechts, Vol. I., §X.; Kant, Philosophy of Law; Fichte, Science of Rights; Stirling, Lectures on the Philosophy of Law; Miller, Lectures on the Philosophy of Law, Lect. I.

[5] *Cf.* Lecky, History of European Morals, Vol. I., Chap. I.; Porter, Human Intellect; Green, Prolegomena to Ethics; Martineau, Types of Ethical Theory, Vol. II.; Courtney, Constructive Ethics; Kant, Kritic der practischen Vernunft; Fichte, Science of Thought. But see *contra*, Leslie Stephen, Science of Ethics; Spencer, Data of Ethics; Sidgwick, Method of Ethics; Fowler, Principles of Morals, Vol. II.; Bain, Moral

notion, however, loses sight of the fact that law, like knowledge, progresses by a gradually extending synthesis.[1] A Scotch jural philosopher, who is Kantian in his belief, in speaking of the relation of the individual to the universe, combats such a notion as the innateness of legal right when he says: "In the age of infancy [man] is subject to physical law. His obedience to custom is almost a nervous involuntary reaction."[2] And as the views of the evolutionist may be reconciled with those of the intuitionist, in ethics, by predicating of mind a capacity for developing in the course of ages, and social historical continuity, under favorable conditions, a comprehensive and deep moral sense or sentiment, so may these views be reconciled with mine in assuming the eventual rise of a disposition to observe jural rules of action.

A condition of human kind in which self-help is the sole form of redress must be coequal to that of the brute. May the group be of a peaceful disposition or otherwise, self-help for a deprivation of what the individual possesses, whether life, freedom or objects, must, if the sole remedy, lead to anarchy—anarchy in which the law of survival decides in favor of the most powerful. In the earliest known form of political society self-help has in a measure become superseded by more orderly modes of redress. Since self-help depends upon the ability and inclination of the wronged one to obtain redress, and the strength of his following, a form of compensation, by way of arbitrament, voluntarily resorted to or coerced by the chief of the whole clan or tribe, would be instrumental in establishing a primitive form of ordered remedial procedure. Another step would be when self-help, though still permitted, is supervised and restrained by a more effective authority. The ultimate course of developing social

---

Science; Maudsley, Physiology and Pathology of the Mind; same, Body and Will; G. H. Lewes, Study of Psychology; same, Physical Basis of Mind; Bain, Senses and the Intellect; same, Emotions and the Will; Ribot, Diseases of Memory; same, Diseases of the Will; Luys, The Brain.

[1] Miller, Philosophy of Law, 43.

[2] *Ibid.*, 367.

organization has been to narrow the license of the individual in favor of social powers and rights; to narrow the right of self-help in favor of an orderly course of remedial procedure in courts. Military discipline, in the rudest political groups, makes for such a form of discipline.[1] If we look to savage tribes we see justice administered in a primitive gathering of armed men which is at once a council of war, a rude political assembly, and a judicial body. Among the Hottentots the whole kraal with the chief sit in the open fields in a circle; all matters are determined by a majority. If the culprit is convicted, and he is adjudged guilty of death, sentence is executed on the spot. The chief is the first executioner, he striking the first blow, and is followed by the others. Such a form of administering justice is to be found, with variations of detail, among many tribes. Relics of it are found among the Greeks in Homeric days, where justice was administered in the midst of the assembled agora. Among the tribes of Europe justice was administered by the whole tribe, in the open air, and relics of their administration continued until the ramified control peculiar to national development gradually superseded it.

When the impulses of self-preservation, including the defense of sustenance, mates and sometimes progeny, came into collision with the needs or corporate feeling of the aggregate into which the individual existence of the members of the tribe or herd was merged, it *necessarily* yielded to the latter. And in this way a corporate form of redress would come to supersede in a measure the more animal and unreasoning mode of redress by private vengeance or caption. The forms in which the corporate control took shape varied perhaps in details. It would not, if aroused to action, tolerate a breach of those forms of enjoyment and possession

---

[1] That this was the case among the earliest Greeks and Italians see Leist, Graeco-Ital. R. G., §43 *seq.*; among the early Germans, Siegel, Geschichte des deutschen Gerichtsverfahrens, *passim*; Essays in Anglo-Saxon Law, 183 *seq.*; and among Semitic peoples; Smith, Religion of he Semites, 397–400.

that had become invested with customary incidents of long standing. The tribe would endeavor to maintain its own integrity by resisting pressure from without, and by setting beyond the pale of its protection members who fled or resisted it. A military regimen begot subordination and discipline, under some head or chief; the needs of a military life would supersede individual claims. The expansion of groups that became possible with enlarged military needs and experience occasioned a limitation of individual license, so that the unregulated and anarchic mode of redress by self-help became more and more superseded by the larger discipline of the social body, however rude or immature, in which the individual was merged. The belief in ghosts or spirits of departed heroes (later also domestic *manes*) tended, in conjunction with the peculiar fancy which infantile minds disclose, to create a faith that enabled the leader or leaders of tribes or lesser groups to invest with a kind of sacredness such control and administration as there was.

In any event, early in the career of mankind that which the early being is found to hold in awe is the court or tribunal which exercises dominion over the affairs of his *social* life and duties. And death is for the most part a penalty which he recognizes and accepts for disobedience. And though it does not occur at first, yet, after a while, the arbitrary reprisal whereby is sought to be recovered the thing taken away, yields to the social penalty for thievery and desecration of the family group, or, as discipline becomes more effectual, to compensation by way of penalty or satisfaction.

In the days of Charlemagne, when the less organized tribal groups were more or less controlled by a national form of administration, and the perdurable process of merger into a larger national unity had begun, governmental control through courts had superseded self-help in many matters. It is true that the administration of justice was still ineffective and unorganized, and that self-help still largely prevailed. Yet there were local gatherings for purposes of administering justice of the different segregated groups, and even larger meetings embracing wider areas; also there was a royal or kingly control; all of which contributed to substitute the king's peace for the tribe's peace, and governmental relief either by capital punishment, compensation in the shape of *weregeld* or in other forms, or restitution of property or its equivalent, for self-help.[1]

The organization of a central administrative body tended eventually over a greater or less stretch of territory, everywhere where it came to pass, to supersede the rough-and-ready forms of redress of the nomad, or the better regulated modes of procedure of herdsmen and primitive husbandmen. The exorcisers of spirits, the priests, are the most influential framers of regulated modes of procedure, as they are the reformers of unregulated language and the promoters of such limited arts as there may be in the early stages of man's progress. These intermediaries between the gross idolaters among early mankind and the supernatural, obtain a control over the primitive mind which goes as far as the power of any chieftain may aspire to, and through them the court or tribunal may become respected and followed; but the tribunal itself was a thing of slow and painful and erratic growth, only emerging into light as it was forced into prominence by military growth or by pressing pastoral or agricultural interests, or as it was called into existence and a larger life by the expansion of the family group and the extension of the *patria potestas*. Simultaneously with such a growth was the expansion in numbers of household gods, and gods of the larger unity—which larger unity, though based on households, likewise promoted their growth; and this unification eventuated in a pontifical extension over the priestly and,

---

[1] A similar development, with of course differences of details, is noticeable among the ancient Greeks and Italians. Leist, Graeco-Ital. R. G., §43 *seq.* And among African tribes, so far as relates to the earlier stages, Post, African Jurisprudenz, Vol. 2, Parts VI. and VII. See also Pollock, Essays, "The King's Peace."

through the priests, over the judicial affairs of that unity. A quite similar expansion of court procedure is traceable in ancient Greece and in medieval Europe through the pontifical class.[1] It produced a casuistical system which facilitated governmental control; but it was in conflict with those customs of the people which their pursuits from time immemorial had been creating and building up, whether in the closer and larger corporate aggregate, or among the more diffused non-urban population. On this account the system of procedure occupies a lesser place in the development of jurisprudence than do the expanding rules of substantive law—substantive law which stands for legal conduct as distinguished from merely moral conduct. While procedure was among the most noteworthy contributing agencies of law, especially in the days when substantive law was recognized most definitely in connection with the disposition to obtain redress—to effectuate the feelings incidental to use, enjoyment and possession, and the rupture of those feelings by deprivation—it ceased to play the like conspicuous part as societies grew to civilization and maturity. Eventually the rules of mine and thine obtained a force and recognition by usage and habit and example, as ethical rules do.

Even more decidedly, because they builded on *data* that touched the needs and interests of mankind more—upon a scale which the somewhat sterile forms of procedure could not be expected to obtain. And when these substantive rules and customs became displaced by the casuistical conceptions of priestly inventors, the rules and forms of procedure were rendered even less prolific of change and increment than before. The substantive law, embracing thereunder the remedial rights (save the forms of procedure) which one is entitled to, covers a much wider field in jurisprudence than mere procedure.

However complex and scholastic in form the procedure

---

[1] *Cf.* Keller, Röm. Process; Year Books of 32 and 33 Edw. I., edited by Alf. J. Harwood, Preface xi., *seq.*; Leist, Graeco-Ital. R. G., Book II., Chap. III., Book III., Chap. II.

might become, judging by the history of Roman and English jurisprudence, it was bound to yield to practical life and movement, one of the principal effects of which has been to counteract and destroy the artificial and formal, though astute, creations of casuistical thinkers and believers. Industrial activity in commerce, in husbandry, in obtaining the means of subsistence and wealth, has driven the tribunals of the land to recognize the validity of arbitration tribunals which before were not accorded the same recognition; it gave a place and power to the jury, especially under Lord Mansfield, which radically enlarged the influence of mercantile customs; it induced the eventual abandonment of the artificial creations of the past, for a more simple and practical system of procedure. It is revolutionizing the work of the lawyers in the pursuit of redress. It has operated to ameliorate the law of imprisonment for debt, the law relating to married women, the law relating to exempt property, so that now, at least in the United States, the largest function of the lawyer consists in making judgments productive. Industrial life has tended to enlarge the recourse to attachments, creditors' bills, injunctions, receivers. When railroad properties are involved, the functions of courts have been carried so far as to involve the issuance of receivers' certificates in large sums for construction and other purposes. The doctrine of courts that their receivers cannot be interfered with by other courts found vigorous opposition, as the danger to practical interests thus entailed became conspicuous,[1] until Congress intervened by positive enactment and provided a remedy.[2] The appointment of receivers of railroads leading to the evil that large masses of meritorious claimants were inequitably deprived of large rights, produced an exceptional doctrine in favor of such claimants,[3] that seems to have departed from previous doctrines preservative of the rights of mortgagees.

---

[1] See Dow *v.* M. & L. R. R. R., 20 Fed. Rep. 266; Am. Law Review, Vol. XIX., 400 *seq.*

[2] Acts of 1888 (50th Congress), Chap. 866, Secs. 2, 3.

[3] American Law Review, Vol. XIX., 400 *seq.*

The passion for recovery of things of value which underlies procedure and sustains it, though it forced adjective law into new and more serviceable forms, did not prevent the tendency toward the casuistical expansion of those forms and incidental doctrines which eventuated in another and not less elaborate system of unfamiliar detail to the layman than before. The tendency to multiplication of forms is manifest as well in legislative rules[1] as in court and church service. The development of forms necessarily ensues where a profession exists to apply them; necessarily exists, too, because the promotion of order and discipline in remedial justice requires forms. The utility of forms of procedure in the growth of law is affirmed by Ihering to be conspicuously illustrated in Roman jurisprudence, and he asserts that it lost its scientific character as the slow changes inaugurated by the courts and lawyers in Rome were superseded by the naturally too radical legislation of reformers.[2] Yet it is noteworthy that despite Ihering's assertion, legislation has increased in volume and has become indispensable to make German remedial law conform less to Roman standards and more to the needs of German communities. The forms are the subordinate part of remedial law; the principles which underlie these forms are of primary importance—that is, a qualified tribunal, a fair examination, a speedy trial, a proper application of the rules of substantive law, and the enforcement of the judgment of the court as far as practicable—principles, in short, calculated to satisfy, as far as legitimate and practicable, the *passion* for recovery of things of value.

The law of evidence is the creature of experience rather than logic,[3] and in studying the history of it one cannot escape the necessity of tracing that experience.[4] Evidence is

---

See Woodrow Wilson, Congressional Government.

[2] Geist des römischen Rechts, §48 *seq.*

[3] That formal logic is untrustworthy as a working system for affairs of experience, see Sedgwick, Fallacies; Spencer, Principles of Psychology, Vol. II., Part VI., especially Chap. VIII.; also Part VIII., Chap. III.

[4] James B. Thayer, Presumption and the Law of Evidence, Harvard Law Review, Vol. III., 146.

any matter of fact which is furnished to a legal tribunal otherwise than by reasoning, as the basis of influence in ascertaining some other matter of fact. There is no law of reasoning other than what is found in the "laws of thought."[1] We have, in our inherited system of municipal laws, what is peculiar to English-speaking people—a law of evidence. In its main features it is unknown upon the continent of Europe. It developed in England because they had the jury in England, or rather because in England they did not give up the jury. On the Continent they had the jury seven and eight hundred years ago, but they lost it.[2] Evidence of intention not culminating in acts is of no value. Physical phenomena form the groundwork of evidential values in courts of law—*i. e.* matters of fact.

The judges of courts and the other constituent parts of judicial tribunals likewise reflect the growth of society. They have come to take a co-ordinate place in the body politic alongside of the legislative and executive departments of government. Originally they formed a part of the legislative and executive body. The earliest judge is a priest or a head man of a given tribe. He is not the exponent or interpreter of enactments, but he enforces the customs which the life of his and the tribe's surroundings has made possible. When a country becomes peopled with various groups following war, herding or husbandry, the chief and priest become separated. The one takes up war and government as a pastime, the other takes up the spiritual functions. But the rules of spiritual welfare become an ameliorating influence which adds to and colors the other practical usages. The warrior chief and his associates summon him to decide the issues of *meum* and *tuum*, where the more arbitrary will of a despotic mind is restrained from forcible caption or seizure. And in time, as the communities cement together by the construction of roads, intercourse, traffic, and spread of more enlightened and cosmopolitan usages, the warrior chief be-

[1] Spencer, Psychology, *ubi supra.*

[2] Thayer, *ubi supra.*

comes a nation's king, his council becomes a legislative and executive body, and the judicial body obtains a place apart. The priests monopolize the functions of judges, until the practical needs of the political unit become antagonistic to the purely theoretical, casuistical and spiritual ideas and forms of thinking of priestcraft. The courts obtain their modern form more and more as they yield to the demands for practical enforcement of rights and duties—rights and duties as they have become recognized in the industrial and commercial world; meaning by that world also all those forms of domestic relationship and incidental rights and duties which continued to exist. In this development the jury, grand-jury, the constable, sheriff, bailiff, marshal, chancellor, as well as the judge or justiciar or arbitrator, have played a part, and each has a history of its own. They all begin their career back in the days of tribal life, except perhaps the chancellor, whose earliest functions were those of scribe and who was of priestly cast.[1] Earliest tribes had no scribe.

The maxims of judicial administration, such as that judges shall be unbiased and not related to the parties, and that justice shall be freely and fairly administered without fear, favor or affection, had no place in tribal life.[2] These represent the final verdict of developing society, brought about by painful experience. The jury, now selected because of their unfamiliarity with the facts, are still selected from the vicinage, thus testifying to their original function of neighbors, lookers-on and witnesses. They are still selected for

---

[1] Stubbs, Cons. Hist. of England, Vol. I., par. 121; Waitz, Deutsche Verf. Geschichte, Vol. II., pp. 409, 410, 411 *seq.*; Gneist, Hist. English Constitution, Vol. I., 267, 268 and notes; Kerly, History of Equity, Chap. II. See further on this subject the next succeeding chapter.

[2] A glance at Hesiod, Works and Days (see Ancient Classics for English Readers, 367), will show the causes for complaint on this score in his day. See also Aristotle, Politics, Book VI., Chap. V.; Felix, Einfluss der Sitten u. Gebräuche, etc., pp. 31, 47, 110; Tacitus, Annales, II., 34; IV., 31; XIV., 28.

their neighborly feelings in the hope, very frequently realized, that thus the rigid and orderly rule of the law may be evaded and nullified. Judges too are not always true to the maxims thus enunciated; and a too comprehensive exercise of the franchise threatens to make judges who are too subservient to the *popular* voice.

The course of judicial administration has on this account been marked by eccentric growths and contradictory classifications. At no time in its history has the bar been able at all times to predict a certain result in mooted cases. The character of the judge plays a significant part in the practical administration of justice. Much depends upon his sympathies, his familiarity with needs and abuses, and upon his mental range. Such men as Papinian, Hardwicke,. Mansfield and Marshall make an epoch by the superiority of their mental reach and judicial prescience.[1]

---

[1] The application of substantive law by courts is shown in the philosophy of the doctrine of precedent, upon which subject something has been said in the first chapter of this work.

CHAPTER IV.

THE EVIDENCES OF PHYSICAL AND SOCIAL FACTORS IN CONSTITUTIONAL LAW.

The patriotic inhabitant of the United States who imagines that constitutional history is strictly applicable alone to his country, lives in ignorance of the claims of writers of other countries who have shown its application there. And it is in disregard of this circumstance that the lawyer in the United States so frequently views the constitution of the Federal Government as he would a charter.[1]

Constitutions, like laws, it is said "are not made, they grow."[2] Modern writers on the history of constitutions, whether of Germany or France or England, trace up the ultimate institutions and organic political organization of their respective countries from the establishment of the first settlements; as far as practicable from the earliest period.

They embrace in their inquiry not only the growth of imperial rule and legislative power, but they likewise embrace within the field of inquiry the development of the early barbarian and the succeeding village groups, towns, cities, classes, orders. They reveal the gradual process of expansion and change so far as it bore upon the unfolding of primitive local groupings into large territorial aggregates, as

---

[1] Von Holst, Constitutional History of the U. S., Vol. I., 64–70; Hannis Taylor, Origin and Growth of the English Constitution, Vol. I., 60. But see as to this the next chapter.

[2] Sir James Mackintosh. See Hannis Taylor, Origin and Growth of the English Constitution, Vol. I., 60. That this is applicable to the constitution of the United States, see, besides what follows, Bryce, American Commonwealth, Vol. I., Chap. XXXI.; Bliss, Sovereignty, 179; Texas *v.* White, 7 Wall. 700; Miller, Constitution, pp. 104, 105, 106; Chapter I., *ante*; Chase, J. *in re* Ware *v.* Hylton, 3 Dallas, 232.

preserved and maintained by an elaborate system of government.[1] And, following in their train, will be found writers upon the history of American constitutions who have pursued a similar course.[2] Just as a proper understanding of language takes note of the earliest roots from which language grew, so should a proper understanding of the history of constitutions depend upon a knowledge of the details of growth of local subdivisions of the country; for these helped to create it.

Constitutions are not all written, nor are they all of modern date, for we learn of a Mosaic Constitution, a Persian Constitution, an Egyptian Constitution, a Lycurgan Constitution, a Solonian Constitution, a Roman Constitution.[3] A constitution could hardly exist among a community

---

[1] Waitz, Deutsche Verfassungsgeschichte; Maurer, Mark-, Hof-, Dorf- und Stadt-Verfassung; Schwebel, Deutsches Bürgerthum; Arnold, Deutsche Freistädte; same, Geschichte des Eigenthums in deutschen Städten; Heusler, Ursprung deutscher Stadtverfassung; Stubbs, Constitutional History of England; Gneist, Constitutional History of England; Freeman, Growth of the English Constitution; Maine, Early Law and Custom, and Early History of Institutions; Green, Making of England, and Norman Conquest; Freeman, Norman Conquest; Biener, Das englische Geschwornen-Gericht; Siegel, Geschichte des deutschen Gerichts-Verfahrens; Freeman, English Towns and Districts; Stephen, Hist. of Criminal Law in England; Stubbs, Select Charters, etc.; Kitchen, Court Leet and Court Baron; Scruggs, Practice of Courts Leet; Laveleye, Primitive Property, etc.

[2] Howard, Local Constitutional History of the United States; Hannis Taylor, Origin and Growth of the Eng. Constitution; Robinson, Institutions, Vol. I.; Historical Studies issued by the Johns Hopkins University; Fiske, American Political Ideas; same, Beginnings of New England; same, Critical Period of American History; Hare, American Constitutional Law, first chapters; Woolsey, Political Science, Part III., Chap. X.

[3] S. Mayer, Rechte der Israeliten, Römer und Athener, Book II.; Schoeman, Athenian Constitutional History; Kuhn, Entstehung der Städte der Alten; Freeman, Comparative Politics, Lectures 3, 4 and 5; Marquardt, Römische Staats-Verwaltung; Curtius, History of Greece, Vol. I., Book II., Chaps. I. & II.; same, Vol. II., Book II., Chap. V, 176 *seq.*; Rawlinson, Hist. of Ancient Egypt, Vol. I., Chap. XI.; same, Seven Great Ancient Monarchies, Vol. II., Fifth Monarchy, Chap. III. For evidences of institutional life in Africa and among other tribes see Post, African Jurisprudenz, Part II.; same, Bausteine, §§103–129.

totally unorganized. It stands for some form of political organization, but it need not be finished and permanent; it is a creature of change and development.[1] The elements of constitutional law relate to the framework of government, and embrace the principles of usages which are expressed in the administrative functions of the governmental power or powers; they will likewise embrace, since these cannot altogether be left out of sight even in the rudest form of government, the social relations of the governed individuals. These elements vary in different periods and localities and under differing circumstances. Even the constitutions of the states of the American Union, notwithstanding the great similarity of their organic conditions, are not alike.[2]

The sacredness of a man's house will find its producing causes deep in the early practice of mankind; for practice was the basis of early social consciousness, as it is largely even at this day;[3] just as the symbols and languages of our day contain evidences innumerable of centuries of actual practice and usage.

As we saw in our first chapter, Aristotle based the state upon the family. He contended for an intermediate stage, in the course of political formative energy, between the family and the city—*γένος*.[4] This family life was not, as has been shown, a copy of modern family life, it was rather a savage or barbarian group-life in constitution; that is, it depended as much upon association[5] as upon descent, and if

---

[1] See Post, Bausteine für eine allgemeine Rechtswissenschaft, *loc. cit.*; Dicey, Law of the Constitution, Chapter II. Reclus, in the appendices to his great work on the Earth and its Inhabitants, reveals the constitutions of all modern peoples, from the savages of Africa to those of civilized and enlightened nations.

[2] Poore, Charters and Constitutions.

[3] Fustel de Coulanges, Ancient City, Books I., II.; Hearn, Aryan Household, Chaps. I. to IV.; Leist, Graeco-Ital. R. G., pp. 247, 492, 493; Meier and Schöman, Att. Process, Vol. II., 784, 785 (marg. p. 588).

[4] Politics, I., 25. See *ante* Chap. I.

[5] Starcke, Primitive Family, Chap. VIII.; Gomme, Village Community, 39 *seq.*; Chap. III., Sec. II., *ante*.

it held together was a group which held together for mutual aid, and it may be at a later stage to keep up the worship of *manes.*[1] The form it took in its expansion into a larger clan or tribe depended upon whether it inhabited mountains or plain, whether it pursued a predatory, a herdsman's or a husbandman's occupation. When it assumed that of the more settled occupations it had connected itself with land and a form of residence.[2] The *genos* of Aristotle, the *gens* of Rome, the *mark* or *gemeinde* of the Teutonic people, the Irish *clan*, and the village community of the East, may be regarded as essentially the same thing, at least to the extent that each depended upon a settled place of rendezvous or abode.[3] *Genos* and *gens* show a blood-kinship which lies at the root of the association.[4] The mutual obligations of clansmen were sometimes of the closest kind; every clansman was bound to assist and support, in all his difficulties, every other clansman. The relics of this are apparent in later times, in the duty the clan or village community or township owed to its members to defend them, pay their fine, help them to procure redress, and the like.[5] If one kinsman wronged another the remedy had to be sought in the domestic tribunal. If a member was killed by a stranger the clan took vengeance upon him.[6] When compensation was made by *weregild* or

---

[1] Hearn, Aryan Household, Chaps. III., IV., V., VI. Fustel de Coulanges, Ancient City, Books I., II. Coulanges, however, gives this early association too elaborate a constitution and a too developed cult.

[2] Leist, Graeco-Ital. Rechtsgeschichte, Book I., Chap. III.; Freeman, Comparative Politics, Lec. III.; Laveleye, Primitive Property; Hearn, *supra*; Maine, Village Communities in the East and West; same, Early Hist. of Institutions; same, Early Law and Custom; Gomme, The Village Community, Chaps. I. and II.

[3] Leist and Freeman, last citation. See also Kuhn, Entstehung der Städte der Alten, and the other authorities referred to in the last preceding note.

[4] See authorities cited in last preceding note, Platner, Beiträge zur Kenntniss des attischen Rechts, Chaps. IV., V.; and Chap. II., Sec. II.; also Chap. III., Sec. II. What is meant in earliest days by blood-kinship is shown by Smith, Kinship in Arabia, Chaps. I., II., and VII.

[5] Hearn, Aryan Household, Chap. V., §6. [6] *Ibid.*

otherwise it was made to the kinsmen.[1] In the Anglo-Saxon community, as in all early societies, the degree of security and distinction which each member enjoyed depended chiefly upon the number, wealth and power of his kindred, and there was little temptation to any one to separate from what has been called the family. But if the *tie* of kinship created rights, it also involved obligations which might become burdensome. As civilization advanced and members of the *maegth* became wealthy and powerful, or attained a higher position, a tendency appeared on the part of these to ignore their poorer kinsmen. Afterwards it came to the point that a freeman did not need to pay the *weregild* with a slave, or with one who for any cause had forfeited his freedom. The kinsmen lost their share in the *weregild*. And the widening of territorial control tended to destroy this clan integrity still more.[2] At Athens and at Rome the *gentes* were gathered together in a higher union, that of the *curia* or the *kome*, or later *phratria*. This stage corresponds with that of the *Höfe* of Germany, in all probability.[4] In Athens and Rome they yielded to the hegemony of some mother *gens*, or to some village community which had obtained the hegemony by ancestral priority, force or priestly coöperation.[5] That was likewise true of Germanic tribes.[6] A *phratria* was at first a brotherhood, an association of individuals clustered around a central figure

---

[1] *Ibid.* See also Essays in Anglo-Saxon Law (The Anglo-Saxon Family Law).

[2] Essays in Anglo-Saxon Law, 139. Compare Seebohm, The English Village Community; Maine, Early Law and Custom.

[3] Leist, *loc. cit.*; Freeman, Comparative Politics, Lect. III.; Kuhn, Entstehung der Städte der Alten; Platner, Beiträge zur Kenntniss des attischen Rechts, Chap. V.; de Coulanges, Ancient City, Book III.; Marquardt, Römische Staats-Verwaltung, 2d ed., Vol. I., Chap. I.

[4] Landau, Die Territorien, Part II., 103 *seq.*

[5] Compare Kuhn, Entstehung, etc.; Freeman, *passim*; Fustel de Coulanges, Ancient City, Book III. It may be that ultimate inquiry will show the same with regard to all early peoples. See Gomme, The Village Community; Kuhn, Röm. Stadt-Verf., Vol. II., last two chapters.

[6] Landau, Die Territorien, 313 *seq.*

or pair, said to form the basis of the tribe; in fact, the tribe is another name for it, frequently in a more developed form.[1] This did not form the basis of an early state until landholding came into vogue. *Demos*, landholding, was the original prerequisite.[2] The *phratria* in its later form or *curia* had a *curion*, a *phratriarch*, who presided at sacrifices and was an enlarged type of the head of the so-called household group.[3] The god of the later *phratria* was the eponymous hero.[4] *König* (king), from the Icelandic *kong*, *kon* and *koning*, signified originally any recognized leader or chief.[5] The derivation of chieftainship was the same everywhere; in modern Europe it culminated in kingdoms and imperial rule, in ancient Greece it never came to this.[6]

Thus in the ancient world as in the modern world the course of things was a growth from the primitive condition of nomadic and savage life, when the modern family had not, could not yet have been formed, when the basis of association was largely contiguity consequent upon a gregarious habit or instinct, which adherence to a parent or parents might foster, to be enlarged by adoption or by the enlargement resulting from procreation. Andrew Lang, a careful student of the myths of savage and ancient peoples all over the globe,

---

[1] Leist, *loc. cit.*; Freeman, Comparative Politics, Lect. III., 104. See Platner, Beiträge zur Kenntniss des attischen Rechts, Chaps. IV. and V.

[2] Kuhn, Die Entstehung der Städte der Alten, p. 11, note 6; Freeman, Comp. Politics, 87; J. H. U. Series, Vol. IX., pp. 327, 328.

[3] Fustel de Coulanges, Ancient City, Book III., Chap. I. The *phratria* was at first a domestic institution (if the term *domestic* is appropriate for this early period), while the *kome* and *polis* were political in their nature. Aristotle does not mention *phratria* as a political institution of primitive days. Politics, Book I., Chap. II. In confirmation of this view, see Platner, Beiträge, etc., Chap. V., and Leist, Zur Gesch. der römischen Societas; see also Leist, Graeco-Ital. R. G., Bock I., Chap. III., §§25, 26. (But see Schrader, Sprachv. u. Urg., pp. 574, 575.)

[4] Coulanges, Ancient City, *loc. cit.* See on ancestor worship in general, Spencer, Principles of Sociology, Vol. I., Part I., Chap. XX.

[5] Leist, Graeco-Ital. R. G., Book I., Chap. III., 105; Landau, Die Territorien, 313; Schrader, Sprachv. u. Urg. 584, note.

[6] Freeman, Comp. Politics, Lect. IV. See *infra*.

has found traces of savage life in ancient civilization. Though he thinks that in Homer's time the Greeks were practically civilized, he finds many evidences in their surviving relics of human sacrifice, mysteries, magic, religious customs and law of homicide, of savage origin. The existence of totemism among them is shown by numerous examples. "The Thessalians revered storks, the Thebans weasels, and the myth ran that the weasel had in some way aided Alcmena when in labor with Heracles. In another form of the myth the weasel was the foster-mother of the hero. Other Thessalians, the Myrmidons, claimed descent from the ant." He calls attention to the religious respect paid to mice in the temple of Apollo Smintheus, in the Troad, Rhodes, Gela, Lesbos and Crete, and that a local tribe was alluded to as *mice* by the oracle. The people of Delphi adored the wolf. And similar phenomena are shown to exist in Roman antiquities. In connection with the same set of ideas it is pointed out that several γένη, or stocks, had eponymous heroes, in whose names the names of the ancestral beasts survived. In Attica the Crioeis have their hero (Crio, "ram"), the Butadæ have Butas ("bullman"), the Aegidæ have Aegus ("goat"), and the Cynadæ, Cynus ("dog").[1] The belief in the common, confused equality of men, goods, plants, beasts, rivers, is common and fundamental in savagery. The activity of beasts in the myths of Greece springs from the same source as the similar activity of beasts in the myths of the Iroquois or Kaffirs.[2]

How could a primeval wilderness become the seat of a settled community in early days? If no immigration brought into the country civilization, it must needs have developed from among its own denizens, indigenous to the soil, the germs and riper fruit of civilized aggregation. How could that come? Clearly not until the surroundings had

---

[1] Lang, Myth, Ritual and Religion, Vol. I., Chap. IX.; Vol. II., Chap. XVII.

[2] *Id.* Vol. I., pp. 80, 81. See also Post, Bausteine, etc., Vol. II., p. 22; Smith, Kinship in Arabia, Chap. VII.

made landholding a recognized thing.[1] Besides that, it required the occupation of the country by many groups; it required, too, such pursuit of different occupations as would render aggregation in larger bodies possible, such as a pastoral, an agricultural and a seafaring life may represent; and it required a sufficient military organization to frustrate inimical groups or bodies. Such elements were found among the most advanced tribes of American Indians when the white man came to American shores. If, as Lang says, in Homer's time civilization already existed, the people must have gotten beyond the stage of Indian barbarism which the white man saw among the most developed tribes; they must have gotten beyond the cluster of huts or wigwams which marked the seat of Indian villages in those days. And such was no doubt the case. At that time the aspects of tribal life reflected in the *gens* (the early *kin* as explained by W. Robertson Smith[2]) had changed, become amplified in the shape of groups of villages connected by a *sacrificial* cult.[3] *Komai* or *demoi* were parts of such an aggregate in Homeric days. They were the federated village groups, whose occupations had merged them, like the early settled communities in Switzerland, in a social unit, in reference to which the habitations, lands, products, village *manes*, were common property, and which developed upon a common principle quite opposed to individual right.[4] In the period of the *kome* (village) formation, prior to the advent of the *metrokome* or the *polis*, we look in vain for an idea of those individual rights of property, security and protection which are said, in our constitutions, to be inalienable rights of man. We have seen

---

[1] *Cf.* Réclus, Earth and its Inhabitants, Africa, Vol. I., *passim*.

[2] Kinship in Arabia, Chaps. II., III., IV.

[3] On the sacrificial cult of Semitic peoples, consult Wellhausen, History of Israel, Chapter II., and Smith, Religion of the Semites, chapters on Sacrifice.

[4] As to the limited extent to which self-help had been superseded by priestly intervention in Homer's time, see Leist, Graeco-Ital. R. G., Book II., Chap. III., §46 *seq.*

that at this stage of social growth justice was obtained by the group to which the individual belonged, rather than by him; that the group was looked to for redress; a redress obtained through vengeance, weregeld, surrender of the offender, or by battle. The group followed as compurgators when wager by battle became superseded by a larger discipline, as we saw in an early chapter.[1]

When the *komai* or *demoi*, which were tied together for sacrificial purposes, developed a character as market places, as places of defence, as fishing resorts or harbors of refuge, or fording places, they obtained a feature which would in course of time, in connection with the natural increase and development which all enduring communities show, bring into existence a city (πόλις). The course of growth was by the joining or combining together of different groups, still for an indefinite period preserving their clan-like formation

---

[1] A very modern relic of this joint liability is to be seen in those New England States in which individual members of towns are subjected to liability, under execution against the town, for indebtedness of the town. And this without a hearing. See Eames *v.* Savage, 77 Maine, 212, 214; Hare, American Constitutional Law, Vol. II., 880, note. It was there said: "The practice of bringing suits against the political division of municipal organization, and collecting the judgment from the individuals composing it, is believed to have existed in England and to have been brought thence to New England. Actions against the Hundred were known as far back as Edward I." (Stat. 13 Edw. I., C. 2; 3 Comyns Dig., Hundred, C. 2). Mark the reason: "As 'the hundred' had no property except that of the individuals, the judgments must have been collected from the individuals." We stated the course of change from collective to individual property in another connection. It is obvious that this liability is not necessarily dependent on the fact stated by the court in the above cited case. The court's reasoning is not in this respect sustained by history. The liability of the hundred or the town depended upon collective liability; and this assumed the real proprietary to be the collective mass. That was the development of that course of expansion which is from household group upward in widening dimensions, until the organization of many villages and hundreds becomes practicable. See further *infra* in this chapter.

On collective property in antiquity, see also Laveleye, Primitive Property, Chap. X.

independent of each other.[1] The household group did not merge for a long time into the larger unity.[2] In ancient Athens every Athenian formed a portion of several distinct societies at the same time; he was a member of a household (merging into a family, possibly), of a phratry or enlarged family group, of a *kome* or *demos*, and of the *polis*.[3] That which always bound them the most closely together was the need of self-defence and fear of the gods. They carried the eponym of the clan or gens which had the largest possessions. Eventually classes came to be formed within the city, as its walls came to be built and extended and its localities defined, such as the *eupatridae* or well-born, *geomori* or husbandmen, and *demiurgi* or handicraftsmen.[4] The king of Athens in its first period dwelt in the citadel of Cecrops, where he held his seat of government, and the market place was the place for holding judicial process.[5] Solon's laws were the vain attempt of a most advanced observer and thinker for those days, similar phenomena of which may be seen from time to time among barbarous hordes; they left no enduring trace. Yet they reflected the expansion of the city, and show us the existence of trade, the beginning of coinage of money, and other evidences of a higher political life, such as the establishment of a fixed tribunal, the attempted establishment of a liberty of disposition of property, educational institutions after a form, etc.[6] Under the tyrant Pisistratus (it required the discipline of a tyrant to compel such results) Athens experienced an essential change. "Originally town and citadel had been one, and everything

---

[1] Kuhn, Die Entstehung der Städte der Alten; Curtius, History of Greece, Vol. I., Book II., Chap. II.

[2] Coulanges, Ancient City, Book III., Chap. III.; Platner, Beiträge, etc.

[3] Compare Coulanges, Platner, Beiträge; Freeman, Comp. Politics, Lect. III.; Kuhn, Die Entstehung der Städte der Alten; same, Römische Stadtverfassung, Vol. I. Kuhn, in the work last cited, illustrates the early identification of the individual with his group, by tracing up the doctrine of *munera*.

[4] Curtius, *supra*, 325.

[5] *Id.* 326.

[6] *Id.* 350 *seq.* *Cf.* Schrader, Handelsgeschichte u. Warenkunde.

which helped to give coherence to the city had been united on the rock of the Acropolis. . . . The market of [the] old town or city . . [was] situated where the ascent led up from the town to the citadel. Here on a broad incline the roads meet which lead from the sea and from the land. Hither the peasants on market days brought their wares for sale; here the old citizens assembled, and on a terrace hard by [the pnyx] held their public councils. But in proportion as Athens became the heart of the whole country, and as the sources of gain increased, a more numerous influx of population took place from the country districts. These rural districts became suburbs, and these suburbs necessarily formed a contrast to ancient Athens. . . . The most important of these suburban districts was the Ceramicus, the name of which was derived from the potters."[1] In this district the progressive and revolutionary factors were generated which successfully overthrew the exclusive exercise of municipal prerogatives by the old citizens or *eupatridae.* The growth of the city was attended with a development of non-urban and suburban vicinities, after the form of those village communities which were then still in existence; from which communities handicraftsmen came with wares. Thus gilds of handicraftsmen had become possible, and the agricultural community had begun to develop other industries.[2] A substantially similar course of development may be predicated of all ancient cities, including Rome;[3] it is also in the main true of the cities of Germany and France and England which did not start from Roman foundations or in later modern times.[4]

---

[1] Curtius, 385, 386.

[2] Compare Curtius, Vol. I., Book II., Chap. II., and Coulanges, Ancient City, Book IV., Chap. VII.

[3] Ancient City, *supra*; Marquardt, Römische Staatsverwaltung; Mommsen, History of Rome; Kuhn, Römische Stadtverfassung, Vol. I.

[4] See Maurer, Geschichte der Hof-, Dorf- und Stadt-Verfassung; Arnold, Verfassungsgeschichte der deutschen Freistädte. See also Gengler, Deutsche Stadtrechte; Gomme, The Village Community, pp. 208–230; Stubbs, Const. Hist. of England, Vol. I., 404, 405.

In the earliest periods of human kind we see human beings living in groups as already indicated. In the early history of communities undergoing a growth from the primitive stage, we shall see no community populating the land as a pastoral or agricultural people which does not live in the village or even a more developed form. In the Peloponnesus and elsewhere in Greece in earliest days there was no population outside of such communities;[1] and that is true of other people at a similar stage of growth.[2] So the early Germans and the Britons, who antedated Roman rule, had no population except of this nature, though it is said the Germans had no cities.[3] They had not yet become sufficiently advanced to form such cohesive and developed aggregations as cities; they lacked the roads, the agricultural knowledge and industrial occupations to achieve this. Eventually they formed cities, and not after Roman models either.[4] In the growth of medieval cities we see substantially the same process of aggregation, the same predominance of old inhabitants of influence as the ruling power, their gradual overthrow by the expansion of handicrafts and gilds, together with an expansion of the city's limits, a development of its architecture, its arts, its police, and its money

---

[1] Hermann, Griechischen Antiquitäten, Vol. I., §11, p. 83; Kuhn, Die Entstehung der Städte der Alten, p. 8; Engels, Ursprung der Familie, des Privat-Eigenthums und des Staats, Chapters IV. and V.

[2] W. Robertson Smith says of the Aryans and Semites, "In both races the first steps of social and religious development took place in small communities, which at the dawn of history exhibited a political system based on the principle of kinship, and were mainly held together by the tie of blood," etc., Religion of the Semites, p. 33.

[3] Tacitus, Germania, 16; Maurer, Mark-, Hof-, Dorf- u. Stadt-Verfassungsgeschichte; Waitz, D. V. G., Vol. I., p. 111; Heusler, Ursprung deutscher Stadtverfassung, 245 *seq.*; Arnold, Geschichte des Eigenthums, pp. 1, 2; Freeman, Comp. Politics, 130; Williams, Communes of Lombardy, J. H. H. Series, Vol. IX., p. 248.

[4] Arnold, Verfassungsgeschichte der deutschen Freistädten; Arnold, Geschichte des Eigenthums, pp. 1, 2; Freeman, Comp. Politics, 130; Williams, Communes of Lombardy, J. H. H. Series, Vol. IX., p. 248; Kuhn, Römische Stadtsverfassung, Vol. II., 407 *seq.*

and the roads converging there. There are still many relics of the earlier forms from which the city was originally derived left after the city has assumed a unified, consolidated existence, with mayor, *Rath* or board of aldermen and other officers—names which had their origin (before city life could have been thought of) among the groups that had so far developed a regimen and a productive power, had so far developed their landholding and their military constitution, as to have an overlord and a retinue to look after his interests and a number of serfs to supply his wants. The country around receives an impetus from the city organization.

In the names of words we can obtain an insight into the progress from primitive groups to city life. Take the suffix *ton*, the primary meaning of which is, it is said by good authority, to be sought in the Gothic *tains*, the old Norse *teinn*, and the Frisian *tene*, all of which mean a twig. It denoted a place surrounded by a hedge or rudely protected by a palisade. Originally it meant only a single croft, homestead or farm. In Scotland the solitary farmstead is still called a *toun*. In most cases the *ton* became the nucleus of a village; then the villages grew into the town. Frequently the town (for instance, London town) grew into a city.[1] It likewise continued to signify a more loosely aggregated and extended people than is ordinarily implied in city organization, as the townships of Massachusetts compared with the city of Boston, of which more will be said presently. The Anglo-Saxon *weorthig*, English *worth*, has a meaning analogous to *ton*, denoting a place warded or protected, probably an enclosed homestead for the churls, subordinate to the *ton*.

[1] The above portion of this paragraph is taken from Taylor, Words and Places, 79 *seq.* See also Maurer, Mark-, Hof-, Dorf- u. Stadt-Verfassungsgeschichte; Howard, Local Constitutional Hist. of the U. S., Chap. I.; The Germanic Origin of New England Towns, by Herbert B. Adams, in Vol. I. of Johns Hopkins Historical Studies; Gomme, The Village Community, pp. 208-230.

It constituted a suffix in the names of Bosworth, Tamworth, Kenilworth, Walworth, etc.[1] *Ham* and *heim,* two words whose primitive constitution was the household group or primitive association, have furnished suffixes to many existing villages, towns and cities of England and Germany. Their primitive meaning has survived in *home,*[2] showing how the constitution of the household changed with the expansion of the community, dropping those characteristics which did not depend upon consanguinity, and retaining the blood-relationship. *Ing* is said to have had the same place in early England that *mac* had in Scotland, *o* in Ireland, *ap* in Wales, or *beni* among the Arabs; it was the usual Anglo-Saxon patronymic, a clan name, and it found its way with the growth of the objects it represented into cities, such as Buck*ing*ham, Kens*ing*ton.[3] Such adventurers as Grim, Orm, Hacon or Asgar left their names in Grimsby, Ormsby, Haconby, Asgarby.[4]

Amphictyonies, or festival associations, are claimed by Curtius to be coeval with Greek history; to constitute even the first expressions of a common national history. Before the existence of these associations there existed nothing but single tribes, "each of which went its own way, adhering to its own peculiar code of manners, and worshipping before its own altars, to the exclusion of all worshippers of a foreign race."[5] They became conspicuous in the early period of Greek history, when by migration and settlement one group or tribe or people succeeded another; when, by federation, before some common sanctuary, a large enough collection of groups had ensued to give currency to a god common to such groups. There were amphictyonies at different stages of Greek history which embraced consecutively larger areas

---

[1] Taylor, Words and Places, 80. [2] *Ibid.*

[3] Taylor, Words and Places, 83. [4] *Ibid.*

[5] History of Greece, Vol. I., Chap. IV., 123. See also Freeman, Comp. Politics, Lect. III., 88; Hermann, Griechische Antiquitäten, Vol. I., §12.

and interests, and the temple at Delphi emphasized, as it grew, this expansion. That they occasioned the Olympian calendar, the games, the dramatic arts, and promoted poesy and the arts cognate to temple service, is unquestionable. But they did not expend their influence solely in this way, for they became the forerunners of the leagues of cities which outlasted the influence of the Delphian priesthood.[1] An amphictyony was but a copy of what existed in the *kome*, developed upon a larger scale. Both led to if they were not based upon the hegemony of one group, clan, tribe or community over others—a *synoikismos*, as that of Sparta and Athens.[2] Similar phenomena exist elsewhere among other peoples at similar stages of development.

The spread and presence of population entailed in the ancient world the establishment of offshoots or colonies. The headship in leagues of cities might for a time thus be promoted in favor of the mother city, but it would be more likely to cease as the child developed those more advanced elements which it had received from the prior experience of its parent. Eventually the leadership of some military genius would expand the dominion and rule of a single city or people. This is true of any people not possessing the characteristics of a developed *national* existence. It represents in its highest stage, as in Rome, an artificial bond imposed by some central power, dependent on leadership.

A peculiarity of ancient rule is the expansion of leadership in some one community, which obtained its most conspicuous illustration in the establishment of Roman dominion. It came from the East, and had begun to develop on Roman soil before it had obtained its limit in Greece. It may have

---

[1] There are strong general analogies between the course of development here spoken of regarding Greek growth and Semitic growth. *Cf.* Wellhausen, History of Israel; Smith, Religion of the Semites.

[2] Kuhn, Entstehung der Städte der Alten; same, Römische Stadtverf., Vol. II.; Leist, Graeco-Ital. R. G., Book I., Chap. III.; Hermann, Griechische Antiq., Vol. I., §11, p. 82; Schrader, Sprachv. u. Urg., p. 582.

had a less marked development in those Asiatic lands in which the conditions of climate and topography facilitated the rise of a single household above the balance of the given group,—clan or tribal aggregate,—as of the Achamenidæ in Persian history.

The leagues of cities in medieval days did not resemble those of the ancient cities. Though all were formed for the purpose of mutual protection, the basis of ancient leagues was sacrificial cult and war, while that of the more modern cities was commerce and the promotion of industrial arts. The basis of formation of the cities had obviously changed. The modern city was a product of military, clerical and kingly factors, it is true, but industrial and commercial development gave that coloring to it which made it wealthy, lasting, influential; and it was distinguished from the ancient city not in being a growth, but in being a growth from conditions which rendered its rise and continuance in the main indispensable. The populating of territory had preceded or been coeval with it, and the rise of handicrafts and barter had facilitated it. The banding together of large areas of territory under princely sway, of which more will be said presently, rendered the medieval city a mere element in the growth of dukedoms or kingdoms. No doubt more roads and better transportation, and a greater demand for roads and better transportation, led to the close intermingling and consolidation of the parts of the lord's dominions. These differences between the ancient cities and medieval municipalities were increased by differences of organization. The ancient city was more or less the seat of government for territory extending beyond it. Its policy was rather to build up administrative functions for territory and rule beyond the somewhat bounded locality of its inhabitants.[1] The weakness of ancient cities appeared in the character of loose municipal organization they dis-

[1] In this connection an excellent paper by William Klapp Williams, upon "The Communes of Lombardy" (in Johns Hopkins Historical Series, Vol. IX., p. 233), should be consulted.

played, and the lack of some organic power capable of keeping them alive and in harmonious intercourse. There was an absence of gradual development and too much of sudden and eccentric expansion in given localities, due to the promotion of warlike enterprises. Yet we can see many indications of individual capacity and energy then existing, quite equaling anything our modern age has produced; philosophers, sculptors, architects, artisans, poets, orators, dramatists, generals, then existed who exhibited a capacity capable of producing all that modern geniuses in similar fields have produced under favorable environment. Rome especially awakens our interest in the scope and extent of her development and dominion.

When Rome attained the zenith of her power she stood on the banks of the Tiber the leader, the dictator, of a vast territorial empire, reaching from the heart of Asia to the Atlantic shores, and from the equator to the North Sea. Her influence had gone far beyond her city walls. She dictated the policy of innumerable communities, to some of which she accorded equal municipal privileges to those enjoyed by herself, even to the right of connubial relations with her own citizens; to others she accorded commercial privileges, and some she destroyed. She built up with the expansion of her territory, by military prowess, a comprehensive provincial administration which bears the strongest evidence of ripe experience and study—all tributary to her, all accountable to her. Her power of control was seconded by a supervision which she retained by the periodical change of provincial administrators. She developed an elaborate system of finance and military organization. Her roads were safe and phenomenally good and reached the utmost confines of her dominion. She developed schools of practical philosophy, literature, jurisprudence, that kept pace with her spread of dominion; but she fell to pieces, leaving only vestiges of her power, in virtue of the antagonistic elements which she expanded within her dominion and the enfeeblement of her own citizenship. To her dominion the influence of medieval cities cannot compare. Agencies had arisen which precluded the possibility of imperial dominion for any of them. Rome was an outcome of surrounding growth, it is true, but she was more. She undertook to impose her civilization and superior advancement upon elements which were not adapted to receive them; she kept them attached to her and retained her own power until the whole organism became permeated by disintegrative elements. Then she dropped to pieces, not through any single cataclysm, but by perceptible stages,[1] embracing many generations and centuries.

She fell to pieces, leaving many evidences of her influence among the peoples who carried human history up to the highest stage of modern statecraft and civilization. She visibly affected Europe in the military, city and juridical phenomena she left behind. The Church itself utilized her knowledge of control and administration to attain for a time a widespread power. But the elements of enduring life continued their process of slow development, only imperceptibly affected by Roman power and influence. Such was the verdict which the stealthy and silent forces of social growth accorded to that imperial dominion in which territorial solidarity was practically unknown, in which the methods of control were devised to secure submission to the autocracy of the imperial city. It was a lesson that was not learned by Charlemagne, with all his ability, the dismembered parts of whose imperial dominions after his death gave protest to the artificial consolidation which he had attempted. It was lost in another way upon the framers of the constitution which French statesmanship adopted to stay the course of sanguinary revolution.

Thus far we have traced the institutions of early city life as they grew up. Many of the factors which produced them

---

[1] *Cf.* Gibbon, Decline and Fall of the Roman Empire. See Marquardt, Römische Staatsverwaltung; Mommsen, History of Rome and Roman Provinces; Kuhn, Römische Stadtverfassung.

found expression in other ways. Many other factors which tended to produce institutions varying from that produced by city life were affected by it; some were an outcome therefrom. In early days capture was the basis of a great spread of serfdom. In addition to this, the wild power of some head or chief would tend to produce that kind of unrestrained control over the weak and unresisting ones, such as the children and the women, which is another name for serfdom. Early Asiatic and European communities exhibit the existence of serfdom upon an extended scale. "Slavery has been the common law of all times and places till, within a few centuries past, it has, among most of the nations of the western Aryan stock, either died out or been formally abolished."[1] According to Mr. Spencer, women constituted the earliest slave-class.[2] The cultivation of the soil being a toilsome occupation, when early communities are found in which agriculture is at all developed it is carried on by the serfs.[3] The pursuit of agriculture was not voluntarily resorted to;[4] and the needs in this regard, as communities grew, entailed a resort upon an increased scale to serfdom.[5] The warrior chiefs and their followers were the masters; the women, the captives, etc., did the menial, predial and other work, including the herding of the flocks.[6] That an absence of autocratic regimen upon an elaborate or extended scale rendered the discipline over the earlier serfs less onerous is probable; they were counted in the household association, joined in the same devotions, shared the same sacrificial meal, were laid in the common tomb. The distinction between them and the blood relations, promoted by priestly encouragement of family relationship,

---

[1] Freeman, Comp. Politics, Lect. VI., 248. See also S. Mayer, Recht der Israeliten, Römer und Athener, Vol. II., §130 *seq.*; Wallace, Russia, Chap. XXIX.; Felix, Einfluss der Sitten u. Gebräuche, etc., 250 *seq.*, 326.

[2] Spencer, Principles of Sociology, Vol. I., Part III., §326.

[3] Maine, Early History of Institutions, 150, 151.

[4] Wallace, Russia, 335.

[5] Maine, *ubi supra;* Wallace, *supra.*

[6] See Maurer, Mark-, Hof- und Dorf-Verfassungsgeschichte.

tended to become more distinct as the elements of political existence took on more definite and multifarious forms, and tended in an increasing measure to render practicable the establishment of large territorial empires.[1] That the serf's position is most favorable where the pressure of a developed imperial or state power does not operate to render the status of the slave more severe, is indicated by the circumstance of his position in the early groups being equal to that of the mother and children, and is confirmed by the increasing onerousness of his position up to a certain point in large political jurisdictions.[2] In the days of the Persian invasion under Xerxes the relation of serfs to families in Greece is said by Curtius to have been easy: "Fostered by a community of manners and religion, . . . the relation between masters and slaves was regarded as mutually advantageous and in accordance with nature. *Nor was it possible to conceive of the existence of a Greek community without this basis.*" They performed all subordinate household duties, they tilled the land, attended to kitchen and cattle, they served their masters as handicraftsmen and laborers.[3] Their position in Palestine was not more onerous.[4] But at least in Athens, at this time, essential differences could be noted between their privileges and those of the blood relations.[5] In Rome, in its earlier days of imperial rule, the condition of the serf had become more severe as far as his duties were concerned. His status was controlled by his master; he obtained very little recognition by the government.[6] But when the effects of the introduction of large foreign elements, including the improvement in the condition of the serfs, gave that disintegrative impulse to Roman dominion already referred to, discipline gave way to

---

[1] See Hearn, Aryan Household, Chap. IV., §6; Chap. XV., §5.

[2] *Id.* Chap. XV., §5; Curtius, History of Greece, Vol. II., 286 *seq.*

[3] Curtius, Hist. of Greece, Book III., Chap. I., 286, 287. See S. Mayer, Rechte der Israeliten, Römer u. Athener, Vol. II., §132.

[4] S. Mayer, *ubi supra.*

[5] S. Mayer, *supra.* *Cf.* Vol. I., §75; and Vol. II., §132.

[6] See S. Mayer, *supra;* Hearn, Aryan Household, Chap. XV., §5.

the sentiment of higher feeling produced by the commerce and intellectual development which the expansion of Roman dominion had superinduced, his condition became ameliorated, and he received more and more recognition from the government.[1] Now the family relations had become marked off; the slave or serf was no longer the equal of the child.[2] In the time of Justinian the family had developed into an association depending upon marriage and involving the creation of *agnatic* as well as *cognatic* kindred.[3] The ramifying occupations of such a mass of population as was embraced within the pale of Roman dominion, dealing with commerce, finance, large landholdings not based on household or tribal grouping, but creative of large possessions in single hands by the exercise of superior financial skill or through military influence, all tended to change the *status* of serfdom from a household or tribal feature into a political *status;* or, as it is sometimes said, all tended toward public recognition of *status*. It eventuated in a recognition of some property rights respecting the serf's acquisitions under certain circumstances.[4] In the later history of mankind, as illustrated in the Southern States of the North American Federal Union, the position of serfs was due to agricultural conditions which started from individual needs, but received State recognition and control. There never was any similarity between the family relations and the condition of the serf among them. This is the latest stage prior to the extinction of predial servitude. It is another evidence that real family life as we understand it is a comparatively modern product.[5]

Serfdom, widely prevalent, is a characteristic of early stages of development, created most probably by the pursuit of

---

[1] *Cf.* Zrodolowski, Das Römische Privatrecht, Vol. I., §§25–28; Puchta, Institutionen, Vol. II., §§211, 212, 213; Amos, Civil Law, Part II., Chap. IV., §1.

[2] Amos, *supra*, §2 *seq.*

[3] Amos, *ubi supra*; Leist, Graeco-Ital. Rechtsg., Book I., Chaps. I. and II.

[4] Zrodolowski, *ubi supra*; Puchta, *ubi supra*; Amos, *ubi supra*.

[5] *Cf.* Laveleye, Primitive Property, Chap. XIII.

war, and lasting through the stages of pastoral and agricultural growth up to our modern date, *coloring all forms and modes of institutional growth.* A pervading type of *status*, it has played a conspicuous part in every phase of early political development, and is found wanting only in that earliest matriarchal condition which antedated the rise of political forms.

With the progress of slavery reflected in the history of Anglo-Saxon times[1] and among the Germanic peoples;[2] with the evolution of these peoples from early HOUSEHOLD[3] to POLITICAL *status* (as may easily be conjectured), went a movement of social forms and forces in other directions. We have seen, briefly outlined, the outcome in municipal organizations. We may also observe the play of such forms and forces in the growth of kingship and a nobility, in the concentration of dominion over territories and subject population, in ascending gradations.

The tribal chief, the *cyning*[4] or *konung*,[5] furnishes us with the illustration of a chieftainship which ultimately embraced the territory of France; so that of Britain, Austria, Prussia, etc. Its etymology is not to be sought in the mere chronicles of names, but in the social throes which converted a sparsely settled and barbarous wilderness into a beautifully cultivated land teeming with population, industrial arts, cities, etc. The histories of different countries give varying accounts of the vicissitudes attending the process of aggregation and consolidation and centralization of power which elevated a tribal dignitary, having small superiority over his associates, into a

---

[1] *Cf.* Seebohm, The English Village Community.

[2] *Cf.* Zoepfl, Deutsche Rechtsgeschichte, Vol. II., §24 *seq.*; Maurer, Hofverfassung, Vol. I., §§3–9; *Id.* Vol. II., §191 *seq.*

[3] The term *household* is used to represent the early kinship group and its developments.

[4] Freeman, Comp. Politics, Lect. IV.

[5] Landau, Territorien, Chap. V., 312 *seq.* The etymology of king is said to be dubious; Gneist, Hist. of Eng. Cons., Vol. I., 17, note. But see Isaac Taylor, The Origin of the Aryans, 193; Grimm, Rechts Alterthümer, 229; Schrader, Sprachv. u. Urg., 583, 584 and note.

more or less autocratic ruler over individuals and urban and non-urban communities, over industrial interests of enormous influence, over nobles of varying grades, some at times rivaling the king in power. In France and England the extension of his power meant the welding together of antagonistic rulers of lesser dominions by force of arms and, more especially, by the aid of those more irresistible forces which the development of agricultural and industrial communities in country and city life superinduced. The merger kept pace with a loss of dominion in the lesser nobility; with the welding together of these dominions into a territorial unit for imperial purposes. The earl, *graf* or count became the subject of the king, and with that his courts yielded a superior place to the king's courts. The *king's peace* came after a while to pervade the political body, displacing the arbitrary caprice or the ordered protection of the lesser lord.[1] As the concentration of power went on, aided by the habits and occupations and relationships among the masses, which rendered intercourse more and more expedient, upon an enlarging scale, over wider expanses of territory, the disposition toward unification increased. The ultimate empire or kingdom contained the evidences of this merger. The shire or county was originally the jurisdiction of a noble, a king in all but name. The component parts of which it was composed—manors, parishes, townships, hundreds—originally represented independent groupings having their own customs and observances and their own courts. They all came later than the earliest savage groupings; though savage groupings were the germ from which they evolved.[2]

The manors are, no doubt, the relics of that earliest form of landholding which has already been mentioned. They imply, of course, much more than this earliest form, but they represented the expansion of that early grouping by association which ultimately yielded to the control of a leader, and

---

[1] Pollock, Oxford Lectures, etc., Lec. III.

[2] Howard, Local Constitutional History of the United States, 5.

culminated in the formation of landed possessions controlled by a baron or the equivalent, and inhabited by cultivators, some of whom had comparative freedom and rendered little—and that little, certain—service, and by others more immediately belonging to his own following, who rendered menial or unlimited service.[1] Most likely the freer holders had previously constituted a separate and independent landholding element that had grown up from an independent group.[2] The ultimate constitution of the manor exhibits the holding of courts-baron and courts-leet, in the similitude of the courts of the kingdom.[3] Here presentment was made of the offenses cognizable before the manorial courts and lesser disputes were settled.[4] The free inhabitants in courts-leet inquired into encroachments on highways by ditching, enclosure, putting dunghills or carrion thereon, etc.; of eavesdroppers, barrators, unlicensed ale-houses, gaming-houses, bakers, pound-breach, rescue, game, constables, etc. They were directed to present such other offenses as they had personal cognizance of.[5] In courts-baron they presented informations regarding deaths of tenants, services withdrawn, lands concealed, escheats, commons, mortmain, who was tenant, waste, trespasses, pound-breach, encroachments, common inclosed, evidences belonging to the lord concealed, etc.,[6] showing a development from the mark community[7]—a com-

---

[1] Seebohm, The English Village Community; Gomme, Village Community, Chap. III., pp. 54 *seq.*; Scrutton, Commons and Common Fields; Landau, Die Territorien, Chap. II.; Gneist, Hist. of the Eng. Cons., Vol. I., 147.

[2] Landau, Die Territorien, Chap. II.

[3] Kitchin, On Courts-Leet; Sir Will Scroggs, Practice of Courts-Leet and Courts-Baron.

[4] In England the oath of the jury was, *mutatis mutandis*, like that in the king's courts; that is, those which superseded the earlier earls' courts, courts of Oyer and Terminer; Scroggs, 4, 5. In the court-baron, as well as the court-leet, the jury made presentment; *ib.*, 24.

[5] Scroggs, 8 to 11.

[6] *Id.*, 24 *seq.*

[7] Maurer, Markenverfassung, §§101, 102.

munity analogous to the tribal condition, as illustrated in the pages of Seebohm's excellent production on the English Village Community.[1] It has been called a group of clansmen.[2] The seventh century West-Saxon "tun" or "ham" "was in reality a *manor* in the Norman sense of the term—an estate with a village community in villenage upon it under a lord's jurisdiction."[3]

Here we see the spectacle of *demos* coming up, as it were, from the land, from the soil. We see it struggle into the condition of yeomanry.. We observe it gain momentum, through the rise of municipal centers out of the midst of the village life, by the very aggregation of that life. We note the consequent growth of barter and the spread of commerce, and the expansion of thought and court procedure, learning and literature through priestly influence; and as these break down the conservation of the village group, destroy its communal rights and disintegrate the little groups in the formation of national unity, the king grows before our eyes and the land loses its antagonistic divisions; courts *in eyre* become the resort of the larger suitors, and the manor courts become the *modus operandi* for enforcing the multitudinous customs of the landholder. The commerce that the Hanseatic League represents, recognized by the potentates of the land, swells the sum of contractual transactions, and courts of *pipowder* give justice to suitors while "the dust is still on their feet."[4] Hanseatic or commercial

---

[1] Seebohm, Eng. Village Community, Chap. IX.

[2] Howard, Local Cons. Hist. U. S., 10 *seq.*

[3] Seebohm, *ubi supra,* 147; *cf.* Gomme, The Village Community, Chap. III.

[4] Scrutton says "the court of *pipowders* in 1478 was a court that sat from hour to hour administering justice to dealers in times of fairs; according to Coke, it was to secure 'speedy justice for advancement of trade,' and there might be such a court by custom without either fair or market." Roman Law and the Law of England, Part II., Chap. XIV. He also mentions other merchants' courts, where justice was speedily administered, and by which contracts among merchants were speedily enforced, such as courts of the mayor of the staple, similar courts being

courts likewise add to the expression of commercial customs. The manor eventually becomes reduced in importance as family and individual importance increases. The growth of the community involves the spread of individualism. *Freedom is the outcome of political growth.*

The manor found its way into American political life with the advent of the colonists,[1] but it had ceased to contain bondsmen at that date. The indefinite service of villenage became reduced to a definite service, the holdings developed into fixed rights of tenure, mostly copyholds, with fixed hereditary succession, rights of common, etc., showing the outcome of developed landholding.

Another form in which the early community enlarged and grew was the township, a term which in the western portion of the United States stands for congressional divisions of territory, divided into sections and arranged for the convenience of ascertaining and describing localities, thus illustrating the most efficient and reliable method of dividing territory for purposes of landholding ever devised. The term now also stands for political subdivisions of counties having a greater or less extensive power of self-government.[2] Its origin has been traced to the clan or household. The name shows its continuity with the earliest landholding community; it came from *zaun, tun, hedge.*[3] Suffixes like *ing*, as already shown, are relics of this early holding. After a community of this nature had developed an independent jurisdiction it became known as a *tunscipe*, that is, the circle or jurisdiction of the *tungemot.* Grimm looks upon the early use of the term as synonymous with *praedium*, villa.

---

held at Bruges, Antwerp, etc. *Ibid.* For ancient type of merchant courts and remedies, *cf.* Meier and Schömann, Att. Process, pp. 636, 637; see also p. 72; Leist, Graeco-Ital. R. G., pp. 154, 507, 552.

[1] Old Maryland Manors, First Historical Series Johns Hopkins University Studies, Art. VII. See also same Series, 4th Vol., 16 *seq.*

[2] Howard, Local Const. Hist., etc., Chaps. II., III. and IV.

[3] Howard, *supra*, Chap. I., Sec. III.

Eventually he says it came to signify the later city.[1] The officers of the township were the *gerefa* or head man, the *bydel* or messenger, and the tithingman. In the free township these were chosen by the freemen, in the dependent township they were appointed by the lord.[2] The manor, it has been contended, was merely the township, territorially and personally under new judicial and economical conditions.[3] It was so, however, in this sense that both had expanded a new meaning. Littleton could say that every borough is a town.[4] By a grant of a town or village, manor land, pasture, meadow and other things might pass.[5] So by the term *manor* divers towns might pass.[6] Bracton distinguished between a "mansio" and a "villa," and said that a villa consisted of more than one *aedificium*.[7] A manor, *manorium*, he said, may comprise several adjoining buildings, or villas or hamlets adjacent to each other.[8]

Hundreds appear in the statutes of England as the regular sub-districts of the county only after the tenth century.[9] They represent, however, the old Germanic division of the military system, and antedate that period.[10] After settlement the name became applied to a district which had to provide a hundred men for the militia.[11] It is most likely that the signification of the term is a result of Roman importation, whose divisions of *centuries* were well known. The tribal constitution was antagonistic to numerical divisions, and the early employment of this term shows that it was employed

---

[1] Jacob Grimm, Deutsche Rechtsalterthümer, 534.

[2] Howard, *supra*, 21. [3] Howard, *supra*, 27.

[4] Litt., S. 171.

[5] Coke, Litt., 5a; Shepherd, Touchstone, 92a.

[6] Coke, Litt., 5a; 58a.

[7] Lib. IV., c. 31, fol. 211.

[8] *Ibid.*, fol. 212. See also Lib. V., c. 27, fol. 434.

[9] Gneist, History of the English Constitution, Vol. I., 47. See for the different opinions current regarding the meaning of the term, Howard, Local Const. Hist. U. S., Chap. V., Sec. II., 252 *seq.*

[10] Gneist, *supra*; Stubbs, Const. Hist. of Eng., Vol. I., §45.

[11] Gneist, *supra*.

without any definite regard to number.[1] It represented no doubt a jurisdictional unit, and in that respect is affiliated to the earliest village organization.[2] Stubbs says that the union of a number of townships for the purpose of judicial administration, peace and defense formed what is known as the hundred or *wapentake.*[3] It had its head, its *gemote.*[4] It had a constitution more nearly allied to a political form than either the *tun* or the manor. It was compared to the Roman *pagus* by Tacitus,[5] and it has been compared to the Greek *phratria.*[6] It never developed into a city, except in a form next to be considered. The Roman *pagus* comprised villages of rude abodes, with adjoining fields or pastures and a place of refuge in case of danger.[7] The original assemblages of the *pagi* were primitive, but as they spread out with increase of population by adoption or birth, and market days, sacrificial occasions or enlarged assemblages were introduced, they took on a more definite form, which produced eventually in Rome the city.[8] The growth of the city from this source in early Rome is shown by Marquardt. Within the

---

[1] See Waitz, Deutsche Verfassungsgeschichte, Vol. I., 148 *seq.*; Howard, Local Const. Hist., 254; Stubbs, Const. Hist. of Eng., Vol. I., §45.

[2] Howard, *supra*, 256.

[3] Const. Hist. of Eng., Vol. I., §45.

[4] Stubbs, *supra*, §§45, 46; Howard, *supra*, 258, 259.

[5] See Howard, 256.

[6] Howard, *supra*. But quaere?

[7] Marquardt, Römische Staatsverwaltung, Vol. I., 3, 4 *seq.* The oldest Italian people did not live in cities, but in tribal communities or *pagi* (*gauen*) in which the abodes and homesteads lay scattered; they were provided usually with a place of refuge and defense (*burg*) to which the inhabitants of such *pagi* would flee for safety; and the burg was also a place of safety for the sacred possessions and idols. Later on the place occupied by the commune was called *pagus*, and in time it became the center of a larger territorial and social unit. In earlier days this shifting commune was an integral part of a larger community (*civitas, populus*) which had its market, legislative, judicial and sacrificial gatherings. The places where these were held in many instances developed into cities, and superseded the *pagi* in the same locality. Marquardt, *loc. cit.* For further phases of development see *post*, p. 169. *Cf.* Duruy, Rome, Vol. II., Part I., p. 249.

[8] Marquardt, *supra*, 4, 5.

city's environs lay the *vici* and *castella*; a *vicus* comprises a complex of buildings, a street or quarter (like modern *wards*), and village groups without the the city's enclosure in which the houses, unlike the *pagus*, were heaped together.[1] Its inhabitants usually comprised owners of village land, communities whose domain was cultivated by peasants (*coloni*), slaves (*servi*) and manumitted persons. These village communities had their own temples and altars, a common ownership, adopted regulations in village assemblages, and elected leaders or heads (*magistri*) who saw that the customs of the village were observed. The *castella* or *castra* seem to have resembled these communities.[2] The hundred did not develop in this manner. It became a part of that more sparsely or less densely populated part of the land which became amenable to a larger discipline, such as the king or earl might exercise. It became lost in the county and national organization.

The "burh," "byrig," "borough," had its origin in the need of military protection. A hill with a rampart of earth or a strong wall, perhaps a palisade, was sufficient protection against the attacks of robber bands. Such protection was sought by the neighboring villagers, whether freeholders, tenants or serfs. They were likewise the resort of landless men, handicraftsmen and small tradespeople, who lived amongst the servants and followers of the landlords. The differences between the people thus crowded together entailed a larger and more detailed supervision through a *gerefa*.[3] There was, however, nothing in this approaching to the modern idea of a corporation, with a similar legal personality,

[1] Marquardt, *supra*, 8.

[2] *Ibid.* 9. See also Leist, Graeco-Ital. R. G., Book I., Chap. III., §24. The inquirer will find strong points of analogy between the early Greek and Latin forms mentioned by Leist in this Chapter III. and the early forms elsewhere prevailing in Europe at a similar stage of development.

[3] Gneist, History of the English Constitution, Vol. I., 53; Chalmers, Local Government, 64 *seq.* *Cf.* Schrader, Sprachv. u. Urg., p. 583; Leist, Graeco-Ital. R. G., §19.

a common seal, or its perpetual succession. "Even London, under its portreeve and bishop, the two officers who seemed to give it a unity and identity of its own, was only a bundle of communities, townships and parishes, each of which had its own constitution." As time went on they acquired further privileges from the overlord or king, of which the most important was the *firma burgi*, that is, the right to pay a fixed sum by way of compensation for taxes, and to assess and pay that sum themselves. The further growth of the towns into cities in England is shown by Stubbs and Chalmers.[1] Even after the cities were recognized as distinct unities, it was for a long time the same kind of unity as that of the county and hundred. They had their folk-moot, answering to the shire-moot; outside their ward-moot, answering to the hundred court; their hustings court. London, under the privileges conferred upon it, had a sheriff, a reeve (*gerefa*) of its own, and justiciar; its citizens were not to be called before any court outside of the city walls, were freed from danegeld, from scot and lot, from responsibility for the murder-fine and obligation to trial by battle, from toll, etc. Its citizens possessed their lands, the common lands, etc.[2] Kingly control prevented the cities from obtaining the same place they had obtained in Greek and Roman history, though at times, as among the municipalities in Italy,[3] and among the Hansa towns, such as Lübeck,[4] they attained a power equal to that of kingly rulers.

In the course of the development of shire and nation other

---

[1] Stubbs, Const. Hist. of Eng., Vol. I., 404; Chalmers, Local Government, 65 *seq.*

[2] Stubbs, *supra*, 405. For a similar course of development of Continental cities, see Maurer, Stadtverfassung; Arnold, Verfassungsgeschichte der deutschen Freistädte; same, Geschichte des Eigenthums in deutschen Städte; Gengler, Deutsche Stadtrechte; Heusler, Ursprung der deutschen Stadtverfassung; Woolsey, Political Science, Vol. I., §§152, 153.

[3] See Woolsey, Political Science, Vol. II., §§182, 183; Freeman, Comp. Politics, 131.

[4] See Helen Zimmern, The Hansa Towns, Period II., Chaps. I., II.; Schwebel, Deutsches Bürgerthum, p. 81.

local unities took form, such as tithings, parishes, etc., which need not be elaborated here. They bore the same evidences of social growth as other political forms within the county domain.[1] They also trace their analogies in early Greek and Roman history up to a certain point, that point which marks the distinction between the course of ancient and modern political development. It is a growth likewise making for individual freedom and fraternal association.

The county or shire has been in its beginnings compared to the Greek *phyle*,[2] the Latin *pagus*, the German *gau*, the Danish *syssel*, that is, the tribe looked upon as occupying a certain territory.[3] The history of development of all of them is alike to a certain point everywhere. In Rome, in early days, *pagus* had already come to signify a collection of houses and villages lying scattered over an expanse of territory of indefinite, though more or less limited range, which contained a burg (*arx, castellum*), to which the inhabitants fled for refuge, and which contained the idols of the *pagus*.[4] The place of refuge was also called *pagus*,[5] which was derived by the Latins from the Greek πηγή, village communities that have settled in the neighborhood of springs; by others, however, its origin was ascribed to communities of joint landownership.[6] Afterwards, with the lapse of time, changes came: the land became populated by larger communities and more numerous groups, and incidents of fellowship, fraternization and collective aggregation accumulated; so

---

[1] See Howard, Local Const. Hist., Chap. I., 23 to 49; Saxon Tithingmen in America, Johns Hopkins University Studies in History, Vol. I., Art. IV.; Stubbs, Const. Hist. of Eng., Vol. I., Chap. V.; The English Parish in America, Johns Hopkins University Studies in Hist., Vol. III., Art. IV.; Freeman, Comp. Politics, Note 72 to Lect. III.

[2] Howard, Local Const. Hist., Chap. VI., 289. *Phyle* instead of *phule* is the orthography of the German translators. Leist, Graeco-Ital. R. G., §18; Platner, Beiträge, Chaps. I., II. and III.

[3] Freeman, Comp. Politics, Lect. III., 118. *Cf.* Leist, Graeco-Ital. R. G., Book I., Chap. III.

[4] Marquardt, Römische Staatsverwaltung, Vol. I., 4.

[5] *Ibid.* [6] *Ibid.* See also p. 166 *ante*.

that in the days of the Emperors the *pagus* had become a geographical district, in which hamlets, manors and agricultural communities lay, but in which the common place of assemblage was preserved, in so far as that had not become an independent community, as a central village or hamlet, obtaining, as it grew in denseness and size, the character of a city.[1] The Continental *pagus, shire, gau,* or by whatever other name it may be called, was not a clearly defined jurisdiction so long as a kingly or national government had not yet developed. Even after it had developed, the district was slow in becoming definitive of a certain jurisdiction. And in its later day the jurisdiction was meagre, especially after the jurisdiction of its immediate ruler, the *comes* or *ealdorman*, had become superseded by the courts and the peace of the king.[2] In the works of one of the best historians of modern times,[3] the shire is shown to not be identical with the ealdorman's jurisdiction. It was, however, the province under the supervision of a shireman or reeve, whose presence gives "the clue to the real ground of the shire system." Though its main purposes were political, its original purpose was strictly financial. The king's reeve (*gerefa*), like the other reeves, was an agent through whom the king received what was owing to him. The reeve may have represented the immediate lord as well, but as a king's reeve he received a portion of the proceeds of the shire-court which fell to the Crown, "and, by a natural extension of this duty, the various sums payable within the limits of the shire, as customary dues, heriots, and the like." Each shire became obliged to "provide not only a stated number of men for the fyrd,[4] but a

[1] Marquardt, Römische Staatsverwaltung, Vol. I., 12, 13.

[2] *Cf.* Pollock, Oxford Lectures, etc., "King's Peace."

[3] Green, Conquest of England, 229.

[4] "The fyrd was . . . composed of the whole mass of free land-owners who formed the folk; and to the last it could only be summoned by the voice of the folk-moot." Conquest of England, 127. It was, when summoned, the early militia, and was the outcome of the duty to support the community

stated sum by way of compensation for the revenue which the king would have drawn from what had been folk-lands within its bounds, and at a later time a stated number of ships, or their equivalent in 'ship money'." The gathering of these sums was the duty of the shire-reeve. "His business ... was necessarily judicial as well as financial, for half of the work of a shire-court came to consist in the ascertainment, the assessment and the recovery of such royal dues, as well as fines and forfeitures owed to the Crown; and from presiding over the trial of this class of cases, the shire-reeve could not fail to pass, like the later Barons of the Exchequer, into the position of a standing judge of the court." The presence of the ealdorman and bishop was rare at the meetings of the shire-moot, and so the reeve became the presiding officer, and the court became the sheriff's court. The process of growth and change went on until, by the organization of a king's court, with itinerant judges to hold terms of court of *oyer* and *terminer* and general goal delivery, a system of *nisi prius* courts was evolved which superseded the county or sheriff's court in much of its jurisdiction, while that court obtained an essentially different jurisdiction.[1] Such a development substantially occurred elsewhere in continental Europe. And the county, thus started on its way, came to

---

and its lord by arms for defense, etc. See Stubbs, Const. Hist. of Eng., Index, *Trinoda Necessitas;* Gneist, Hist. of Eng. Const., Index, *Trinoda Necessitas;* Maurer, Hofverfassung, Vol. I., §143; Lappenberg, Anglo-Saxon Kings (Bohn), Vol. II., 398; Stubbs, Select Charters, pp. 153, 281, 343, 359, 370, 457, 469; Zoepfl, D. R. G., Vol. II., §36; Grimm, Deutsche Rechtsalterthümer, 295; Spencer, Principles of Sociology, Part IV., Chap. IV.; Part V., Chap. XVI.

[1] *Cf.* Howard, Const. Hist., etc., Part III.; Stubbs, Const. Hist. of Eng., Vol. I., §§126–129; Gneist, Hist. of the Eng. Const., Vol. I., 7, 43; Stephens, Hist. of the Criminal Law of Eng., Vol. I., Chap. IV.; Chalmers, Local Government, Chap. VI.; Maurer, Markenverfassung, §105 *seq.*; same, Hofverfassung, Vol. IV., §§656–719; Waitz, Deutsche Verfassungsgeschichte, Vol. I., Chap. XII.; Vol. II., Chap. VI.; Vol. IV., Chap. VIII.; Vol. V., Chap. III.; Vol. VII., Chaps. IX., X.; Zoepfl, Deutsche Rechtsgeschichte, Vol. II., §§37, 73*e*; Grimm, Deutsche Rechtsalterthümer, pp. 749 *seq.*

the United States: in the New England States yielding, in most of the jurisdiction it elsewhere obtained, to townships or other local communities; or, as is the case generally in the South and West, evolving into a definite territorial jurisdiction for the maintenance of law, order, roads, bridges, and property rights of minors, insane persons, the estates of deceased persons, etc. In the Middle States, constituting part of what, at the adoption of the Constitution, was known as the Northwest Territory, a mixed government divided between township and county exists.[1] The shire or *scir* became the *comté* (county) when the Normans came to England. It represented the outspreading of towns in England and also in Virginia and Massachusetts, and it involved the spread and increase of land and industrial groups or communities.[2] Beside this it represented the shaping of a local subdivision, constituting part of a larger governmental territorial whole, and its developed organization was not only for the purpose of subserving the interests of its territorial inhabitants, but was also instrumental in preserving and furthering the integrity of the superior political power. The decisions of the Supreme Court of the United States assume that the preservation of a republican form of government in the States (constituting part of that nation) involves the maintenance of local subdivisions.[3]

We have now obtained in outline a view of the expansion of the primal political constitution into a larger entity—an entity which in modern times, though it may vary in given areas such as are represented respectively by Great Britain, Switzerland, France, Germany, Russia, the United States,

---

[1] See Howard, Local Const. Hist., Part III.

[2] Howard, p. 312, and note 1; Johns Hopkins Historical Studies, Vol. III., 177, 368; Vol. II., Art. X., 437; Bryce, American Commonwealth, Vol. I., Chap. XLVIII.; Hannis Taylor, Origin and Growth of the English Constitution, Vol. I., Chap. III.

[3] As was said in Texas *v.* White, 7 Wall. 700. See what was said in Loan Ass'n *v.* Topeka, 20 Wall. 655, 663; State *v.* Denny, 21 N. E. Reporter, 274, 277.

etc., has become a more permanent and more cohesive and better organized political organism than existed in ancient times; and we are confronted with the need of explaining this remarkable difference.

The difference has been ascribed to the system of representation which, it is claimed, is peculiar to Germanic nations.[1] It must be conceded, however, that if, as is claimed, the "township" is the "primordial cell"[2] of our modern political structure, it was also such in the development of ancient political organisms. The conceptions of a city, state and a nation possess common elements developed up to a certain point; they possess similar phases of the earliest savage group, and that of the gens, the tribe, the township.[3] The earliest form of this government by representation is supposed to exist in the assemblage of the German mark. It, however, long antedated the period of the discovery of the mark.[4]

The assemblage of individuals for the disposition of such business as concerns the mass affected, is to be sought for in its earliest forms in that state of humankind nearest approaching the gregarious brute. If any things were then conned over and deliberated upon they were apt to be very few and very simple things, concerning more especially sensual desires, sustenance or protection of the mass, attended by the whole body, or the adult males of the body, in an informal and sudden manner, upon the spur of the occasion.[5] Later on the assembled individuals would fall more or less clearly into two divisions: the elder, the stronger, the more sagacious, who formed the smaller part and who carried on the discussion; and the younger, the weak, the dependent, the undis-

---

[1] Fiske, American Political Ideas, Chap. II., 70 *seq.*; same, Beginnings of N. E., 28; Green, Making of England, 170; Hosmer, Samuel Adams, Chap. XXIII.

[2] Hosmer, *loc. cit.* *Cf.* Green, Making of England, 175.

[3] Freeman, Comp. Politics, Lect. III., 134.

[4] *Cf.* Spencer, Principles of Sociology, Part V., Chap. IX.

[5] *Cf.* Spencer, Principles of Sociology, Vol. II., Part V., Chap. V.

tinguished, constituting the larger portion, became listeners.[1] In New Zealand, we are told, the government was conducted in accordance with public opinion expressed in general assemblages.[2] Among the Tahitians public assemblies were held, and the king could undertake no affair of national importance without consulting the landholders.[3]

Among the hill tribes of India, "assemblies of the whole tribe, or any of its subdivisions, are convened to determine questions of general importance."[4] Among the aborigines of Victoria, when a tribe plans revenge on another tribe supposed to have killed one of its members, "a council is called of all the old men of the tribe . . . the women form an outer circle around the men. . . . The chief (a native of influence) 'opens the council'."[5] Similar phenomena were found among the early Germans by Tacitus.[6] "No controlling force at first exists save that of the aggregate will as manifested in the assembled horde." Later, "leading parts in determining this aggregate will are *inevitably* taken by the few whose superiority is recognized."[7] Among these controlling few, some one—perhaps the head of the modern group, perhaps some other—eventually becomes predominant.[8]

Out of these early forms of government, if they may be called such; out of these spontaneous gatherings for mutual care and protection, at first little differing from that of gregarious herds of cattle,[9] evolved the representative form of government now extant.

From this developed the kingly, later the executive agency of government, and the legislative, the judicial.[10] And the English *witenagemot* evolved in the same way.[11] Green says

---

[1] *Cf.* Spencer, Principles of Sociology, Vol. II., Part V., Chap. V.
[2] *Ibid.* [3] *Ibid.* [4] *Ibid.* [5] *Ibid.*
[6] *Ibid.*; Tacitus, Germania, 11, 12. [7] *Ibid.* [8] *Ibid.*
[9] See Lindsay, Mind in the Lower Animals, Vol. I., Chap. XXI.; Romanes, Animal Intelligence, Index, "Coöperation."
[10] Spencer, Principles of Sociology, Vol. II., Part V., Chaps. VI. to XIII.
[11] Stubbs, Const. Hist. of Eng., Vol. I., Chap. XI., §123 *seq.*; Green, *infra*; same, Conquest of England, Chap. I., 35; Gneist, Hist. of the Eng. Const., Chaps. XVI., XVII.

that after the end of Roman rule in England, and with the settlement in that land of the Saxon conquerors, . . . "the form of the people was wholly military. The folk-moot was, in fact, the war host, the gathering of every freeman of the tribe in arms. The head of the folk, whether ealdorman or king, was the leader whom the host chose to command it. Its witenagemot, or meeting of wise men, was the host's council of war; the gathering of those ealdormen who had brought the men of their villages to the fields."[1] In this portrayal of what occurred in this later day, we note a development of what is founded in the circumstance of social aggregation in its most primitive form.

Let us observe this organon of government as it evolves. "Among the members of primitive groups, slightly unlike in various ways and degrees, there is sure to be some one who has a recognized superiority." This superiority is of several kinds, due to age, headship, prowess, etc. The headmen of the Khonds are usually descended from some daring adventurer, so are the chiefs of the highland tribes of Central Asia. The traditions of tribal life extant in more developed organizations, such as the Mexicans of the western hemisphere, as well as the early Greeks and other ancient monarchies, indicate the same thing.[2] The Norwegian sea-kings, as well as the German *principes* whom Tacitus spoke of, were alike the heads of groups or associations of early households, who had developed beyond the most primitive conditions, in consequence of the multiplication of numbers, the pursuit of sustenance, the defense of home and territory, and the following of war.[3] The English king came from the

[1] Green, Making of England, Chap. IV., 167.

[2] *Cf.* Spencer, Principles of Sociology, Part V., Chap. VI., §472; Freeman, Comp. Politics, Lect. IV.; Woolsey, Political Science, Vol. I., §142; Waitz, D. V. G., Vol. I., Chap. VIII.; Vol. II, Chap. II.; Stubbs, Const. Hist. of Eng., Vol. I. (see Index, "King"); Gneist, Hist. of the Eng. Const., Vol. I., Chaps. I. and II.; Landau, Die Territorien, 312 *seq.*; Leist, Graeco-Ital. R. G., Book I., §§22, 23.

[3] Landau, Die Territorien, 312, 313.

Anglo-Saxon *cyning*, who was analogous to the Icelandic *kong, kon, konung* (German *könig*),[1] and represented a person of a superior group or household.[2] In England and France the *cyning* became a national leader, a king; and in this way the assembly of which he was the leading element became of greater and of national importance. With the settlement of the Saxon conquerors upon the British Isle the king ceased to be a mere war leader, but tended to become a national *representative*. He represented in this national expansion the need which the various groups of conquering warriors felt and territorial demands showed forth of the need of a collective head. The rise and development of kingship thus "represents the national as distinguished from the tribal stage of political development."[4]

The assemblage of the early groups discharged all functions religious, judicial and legislative, as well as executive in their nature. The idea of separating them never formed an element of thought until the spread of population, and its aggregation into new and varied forms, exhibited on the one side local assemblages, and on the other side the independent activity of a larger, more central body. The disinclination to attend such assemblages is the characteristic of all people, ancient as well as modern. It is likely to be kept up only by those whose profit lies in keeping it up. The local assemblages retained their character because the local jurisdiction enforced attendance. The larger assemblage, created by the same agencies that rendered a large central assemblage possible, obtained a larger field as it expanded territorially. All this the consolidation already mentioned rendered in-

---

[1] Landau, Die Territorien, 312, 313; Grimm, Deutsche Rechtsalterthümer, 230.

[2] Landau, *loc. cit.*

[3] *Cf.* Waitz, Deutsche Verfassungsgeschichte; and Stubbs, Const. Hist. of Eng. See also Gneist, Hist. of the Eng. Const.; Green, Making of England, Chap. IV. Spencer, Principles of Sociology, demonstrates this fact.

[4] Freeman, Comp. Politics, Lect. IV., 165. *Cf.* Leist, Graeco-Ital. R. G., Book I., Chap. III., pp. 105, 106.

evitable in some form. And the judicial functions became relegated to a different and distinct body as this central assemblage became not only more extensive in numbers, but also as its duties became more expanded, ramified and onerous. Thus the judiciary of England, France and Germany, as well as other national growths at a similar stage of development, became an independent department of government, in which eventually the chief or king came to have no hand or jurisdiction. And the legislative functions likewise tended to become segregated, at last becoming merged, in Great Britain, in a body sitting in two chambers, both of which were essential to the discharge of its functions. It was, however, still more or less closely connected with the chieftainship or king, its duties being of that nature which rendered the king's coöperation and supervision of greater importance and more needful than it could be in the discharge of judicial functions.[1]

Much of this growth was not peculiar to modern nations;[2] nor is the idea of representation contained in it peculiar to modern peoples. The chief in earlier days was not infrequently elective.[3] The central assemblage, as it concentrated power in its hands, whether in the Palestinian *synhedrin*, the Spartan *gerusia*, the Greek *areopagus*, or Roman *senate*, was none the less representative because it could fill the ranks by co-optation among its own class.[4] The *rath* or *council* of medieval cities could do the same thing.[5] The practice of co-optation from one's own class comes from a very widespread and deeply-seated disposition, in virtue of

[1] See works of Stubbs, Gneist, Spencer, Freeman, Waitz, referred to in preceding notes.

[2] *Cf.* Spencer, Principles of Sociology, Vol. II., Part V., Chaps. VI.-XI.

[3] Spencer, Principles, etc., Vol. II., Part V., Chap. VI.; Woolsey, Political Science, Vol. I., §169, pp. 520–528.

[4] Mayer, Rechte der Israeliten, Röemer u. Athener, Book II., Chap. III.

[5] Arnold, Verfassungsgeschichte der deutschen Freistädte, Vol. I., p. 302; Heusler, Ursprung der deutschen Stadtverfassung, Chap. V.

which we continue and prolong a position in which we are enabled to exercise authority over others, and may be found illustrated in the disposition of leaders of political parties to maintain themselves in power.

The expansion of the better consolidated national organizations of modern times is marked by the tendency of the latter to retain an equilibrium between the various functions of the community. It may be in many respects marked by social cataclysms, such as the overthrow of free cities, or the oppression of the peasantry, or the humiliation of the nobility, or a French revolution, but its tendency is toward a harmonious solidarity. Evidences of this are contained in the simultaneous expansion of the manorial holdings, kingly power, and the functions of the central assembly. Further evidences of it are found in the tendency which the elements at the base of the government show to combine against excesses of the others—the king and the peasantry against nobles, nobles and the peasantry against the king, king and nobles against the peasantry.[1] Another evidence of this tendency to an equilibrium is afforded by the spread of commerce and the effect this has had in promoting city growth and country growth in connection with each other, and also national stability in relation to the internal parts as well as toward other nations. The pursuit of science has likewise afforded testimony of the same fact, and the best evidence thereof is contained in the complex yet harmonious workings of the English Constitution.[2] The clergy have, in consequence, been relegated to that appropriate place wherein they may promote, without the allurements and temptations of political place, the spiritual welfare of their disciples. And the best results have, no doubt, been attained in the United States of North America.[3]

---

[1] The histories of England, France, Germany, Russia, Rome, Greece, Palestine, Persia, etc., offer illustrations of this. See Draper's Intellectual Development of Europe; Buckle's History of Civilization in England.

[2] Gneist, Hist. of the Eng. Const., Chap. LVIII.

[3] See Fiske, American Political Ideas, Chap. III., but *cf.* Bryce, American Commonwealth, and Maine, Popular Government.

It is because these complex wholes are so much the creatures of growth, begotten by the interchanging influence of reciprocal or conflicting elements, that the definition of nation must be faulty.[1] Every important term which symbolizes the parts or functions of the political organism is indicative of growth; thus, as we have seen, king or chief contains evidences of it. So does the term *parliament.* "Describing the assembling of 'citizens at the sound of a great bell to concert together the means of their common defense,' Sismondi says, 'this meeting of all the men of the state capable of bearing arms was called a parliament'."[2] It was originally, therefore, the early war council.[3] We have seen the process of growth of the courts, with their judges, juries, etc., the customs and rules which accumulate with the spread of industrial, municipal and national life. The mayors, aldermen, and marshals of our towns and cities; the tithingmen, constables, etc., of our townships, counties, hundreds, parishes, cities, in the names thus given, symbolize the same process of growth.[4]

A constitution of such a national organon, comprehending

---

[1] *Cf.* Wharton, American Law, §374; Burgess, Political Science and Constitutional Law, Part I., Book I.; Bluntschli, Theory of the State, Book II., Chap. II.; Freeman, Comp. Politics, 81, 82; Woolsey, Political Science, §57; Waitz, D. V. G., Vol. I., p. 140, note 2; Amos, Science of Politics, 345, 358 and *passim*; same, Science of Law, 329; Supreme Court of the United States in the following cases: Cherokee Nation *v.* Georgia, 5 Peters, 15 *seq.*; Penhallow *v.* Doane's Admrs., 3 Dallas, 80, 81, Paterson, J.; *Ibid.*, 90, 91, 92, Iredell, J.; Ware *v.* Hylton, 3 Dall. 199; Hare, American Const. Law, Vol. I., 12, 13, 35; Legal-Tender Case, 110 U. S., 421, 435. See Note 1, Chap. V., *post.*

[2] Spencer, Principles of Sociology, Vol. II., Part V., §491. See Woolsey, Political Science, Vol. II., §183. Similar events will be found in early German history, Maurer, Hofverfassung, etc.

[3] Spencer, *supra*, §500; Woolsey, *supra*, pp. 360 *seq.*

[4] Howard, Local Constitutional History, etc.; Johns Hopkins University Studies, Vol. I., Article IV., VIII.; Maurer, Stadtverfassung, *passim*; Zoepfl, D. R. G., Vol. II., §§29, 38; Heusler, Stadtverf., p. 191; Waitz, D. V. G., Vol. II., 300; Grimm, Deutsche Rechtsalterthümer, 315, "Meier."

the more lasting phenomena which conspire to maintain order and government, is *par excellence* a thing of growth. It represents the more comprehensive usages and customs of the larger aggregate, as that aggregate finally culminated in a larger political territorial unit, and it is unthinkable without the prior and continuous contemporaneous growth of the parts of that unit. And this must be true whether the constitution is one which is written or is one lying in usage, as well one over a confederation of municipalities as one over a federation of states, or one over a people previously organized into states and still preserving their state organization. The reformers of France in vain endeavored to stay a mighty and awful upturning by written constitutions which they devised, as did Locke and Shaftesbury in vain endeavor to make a constitution for a much smaller community in the Carolinas—all to no purpose, because these paper constitutions did not correspond with the prior or contemporaneous elements of the social organism.

In the United States at the present day is exhibited one of the most extraordinary of political phenomena. A Federal Constitution, a charter not so much of individual rights as of governmental privileges, is conferred upon an agency which, though continually shifting in character and in its *personnel*, is still a continuous and powerful organization. It did not grow as human beings grow, by unfolding the physical germs which were implicit and potential in the body; but it evolved from the expansion of elements upon which it depended for life and strength. It was an agency supposed, intended by those who fashioned it, to be dependent upon the instrument which created it. It needed that to give it a form and character. But when it took lease of life thus invigorated, it instantaneously assumed a scope and purpose which the elements that made up the bone and sinew—the life current—of its existence fashioned in the mold which their development assumed and gave.

CHAPTER V.

EVIDENCES OF PHYSICAL AND SOCIAL GROWTH IN THE CONSTITUTION OF THE UNITED STATES.

The discussion thus far, especially that contained in the last preceding chapter, if it indicates anything, reveals the fact that the Constitution of the United States, like other constitutions, is a product of growth and represents the latest point which governmental political principles have attained. It represents the institutional life of the *nation*[1] so far as relates to governmental regimen. That institutional life did not entirely break all connection with European institutional life with the *Declaration of Independence.* The rules relating to property, contract, procedure and personal security still remained, and so did domestic as well as commercial and agricultural habits and customs of the people in other directions, which were as deeply ingrained. The integrity of State formations,[2] with all that this implied, as

[1] The question, frequently a bone of contention in the United States, as to whether the United States, under the Constitution of the United States, constitute a nation, seems to me hardly to justify it. The nation is made up of the people in it and their political agents, presented with a regimen which controls domestic and foreign affairs, according to well-ordered forms which the experience of the community has rendered possible. Respecting internal affairs, the administrative functions are divided between the Federal Government, State governments, counties, townships, school districts, cities, etc. Respecting external affairs, in its relation with other nations, the interests of this nation are in the control of the Federal Government. Wharton, American Law, §374; Chinese Exclusion Case, 130 U. S. 604, 605. And this statement holds good, even though the Federal Supreme Court in the Legal Tender Case (110 U. S. 449), spoke of "Congress, as the legislature of a sovereign *nation.*" Compare Texas *v.* White, 7 Wall. 700; Loan Ass'n *v.* Topeka, 20 Wall. 655, 663; and, especially, J. H. U. Series, Vol. VIII., pp. 7–77.

[2] Constitution of the United States, Art. IV., Sec. IV. In the light of this plain recognition, there is no basis for the position maintained by Dr. Von Holst and by Mr. Weeden, to the effect that the States had no existence anterior to the formation of the Constitution; that they were

illustrated in preceding chapters of this work, and the English common law,[1] became incorporated into the Constitution of the Federal Government, and thus crystallized into organic formulæ at the base of its organization, and formed, in connection with other provisions of that instrument, a basis of support in construing its provisions, save in those particulars in which the peculiar history of this country rendered those rules inapplicable.[2]

It is not the purpose of this book to enter upon a discussion of the history of this organic grant of powers. That has been well done already.[3] That history is undoubtedly familiar to all of those whose interest in this work will induce the reading of it; a history which reveals the play of circumstances.[4] Possessing by inheritance the undercurrent

---

only colonial members of a confederation, or what you will. Von Holst, Const. and Pol. Hist., Vol. I., Chap. I.; Weeden, Social and Econ. Hist. N. E., Vol. II., pp. 840, 866. *Cf.* J. H. U. Series, Vol. VIII., Art. I.; Vol. IX., pp. 83, 129, and *post*, pp. 193–195.

[1] *Cf.* Art. III., Sec. II.: "The judicial power shall extend to all cases in *law* and *equity*," etc. That is, English jurisprudence as illustrated in the administration of its tribunals. See Amendments I. to VII., inclusive. Amendment VII. says: "In suits at *common law*, where the value in controversy shall exceed twenty dollars, the right of trial by jury shall be preserved," etc.; Miller, Constitution, pp. 486, 489, 502.

[2] Compare Wharton, American Law, §§30, 114, 524; Dicey, Law of the Constitution, Part II., *The Rule of Law*.

[3] See list of authorities cited in Fiske, Civil Government, 275 *seq.* *Cf.* Bancroft, Formation of the Constitution; Von Holst, Constitutional and Political History of the United States; Fiske, Critical Period of American History; Nar. and Crit. Hist. of the U. S., Vol. VII., Chaps. III. and IV.; Story on the Constitution of the United States.

[4] The motto of the Johns Hopkins historical department upon its numerous publications is taken from Dr. E. A. Freeman, the historian: "History is past politics and politics present history." In *The Forum* for April, 1892, in an article entitled "Review of my Opinions" (p. 157), Dr. Freeman, in conclusion, says: "It is that chance proverb of mine which the historical students of Johns Hopkins have honored me by setting up over their library, it is by the application which I have made of it both to the events of the remotest times and to the events which I have seen happen in the course of sixty-nine years, that I would fain have my life and my writings judged."

of independent feeling which actuated the English yeoman and baron in securing the establishment of a limited monarchy with a parliament and the maintenance of local control in many matters of internal concern, Englishmen came to this shore and colonized this country.[1] They were followed by Dutch and Swedish colonists, who possessed or soon took up substantially similar local institutions and feeling. Out of the expansion of this feeling, and these local institutions, in ever-increasing areas of political organization, a feeling unlike the autocratic and aristocratic principles of Europe found expression in *continental* life. I use the term continental, because a continental feeling—not merely the spirit of the town-meeting or a commonwealth—was required to create a later *national* feeling.[2] When Washington took command of the Revolutionary volunteers at Cambridge he found them a mass of rough-and-ready and independent people, who had little respect and less servility for title and kingship;[3] they were elements from which came that American feeling which we see thus in the course of formation into national proportions. Aristocracy and kingship could no more thrive among such a bucolic and autonomous people, as they had obtained a lodging-place in Europe, than could vegetation in the everlasting sands of the Sahara desert; no more could they thrive among these than among the pioneers of our Western plains. Washington himself typified the finer phases of that American growth.[4] It was a growth

[1] See James K. Hosmer, Anglo-Saxon Freedom, Chap. VIII. The literature upon this subject may be ascertained by Vol. III. of Narrative and Critical History of the United States.

[2] That nations have a policy and morality of their own, see Taylor, Morality of Nations; Leslie Stephen, Science of Ethics, Chap. III., Secs. XVIII. to XXIII. inclusive. *Cf.* Weeden, Social and Econ. Hist. of N. E., Vol. II., last chapters of the work.

[3] *Cf.* Henry Cabot Lodge, George Washington, Vol. I., 134 to 138.

[4] Lodge, Life of Washington. *Cf.* The Beginnings of American Nationality, Johns Hopkins Historical Series, Vol. 8, Arts. I. and II.; Fiske, Critical Period of American History, 187; Weeden, Social and Econ. Hist. N. E., Vol. II., last two chapters; Ware *v.* Hylton, 3 Dallas, 222 *seq.*; Higginson *v.* Mein, 4 Cranch, 419.

bottomed, as national growth usually is, save where it is interfered with by factitious institutions, upon the experience of the people (the colonists) and their descendants.

The peculiarity of this evolution was that it finally culminated in a violent rupture with the older forms of government in Europe.[1]

Perhaps it is idle to discuss the question as to whether the American colonists would ever have fought for independence and severed their connection with the English Government under different circumstances than existed.[2] It cannot be entirely profitless to discuss this. If we may obtain a lesson from the French Revolution, which was brewing when ours was, and which came to a climax not long after ours, it becomes at once apparent that mere revolution and the mere setting up of written constitutions are of no avail, in the attempted establishment of forms of government such as ours, in uncongenial environments. The written constitution achieves nothing unless sustained by the continental or the national spirit. Thus we see how the rupture, ever widening between the colonies and the mother country as the continental spirit grew into national spirit, was eventually destined to become a national rupture, deep-grained enough to start and maintain a constitution. The mercantile policy of Great

---

[1] This movement repeated upon a larger and successful scale what was earlier attempted in the movement in England which ended in the Cromwellian rule; Hosmer, Anglo-Saxon Freedom, Chaps. IX. and X. When Napoleon Bonaparte parted with Louisiana to the United States he gave this remarkable testimony to his subjects in Louisiana, in his public declaration to them, of the value of this government: "May the Louisianians know that we separate ourselves from them with regret, and that we stipulate in their favor all that they can desire; and may they recollect that they have been Frenchmen, and that France, in giving them up, *has secured for them advantages which they never would have obtained under the government, however kind, of an European mother country.*" Fay Hempstead, Pictorial History of Arkansas, 119. This circumstance, if true, is not mentioned by Mr. Henry Adams, in his quite exhaustive discussion of the Louisiana Purchase, Vols. I. and II., Hist. of U. S. during the first administration of Thomas Jefferson.

[2] *Cf.* Hosmer, Anglo-Saxon Freedom, 220, 221.

Britain, which far outran in liberality the conservative policy of its aristocracy, was in essential antagonism to any process of national expansion in the United States of America.[1] The result of the growth of the colonies was that they wanted no king. They were willing to accept the good heritage, but the useless they had outgrown. They had no taste, as Continentals, who had roughed life through all the stages of independent political regimen, for king, nobility or feudality; and when national regimen became necessary they wanted to retain the guarantees of independence as far as practicable. It required all of that dismal experience which followed in the wake of independence, under the Continental Congress and Articles of Confederation, and the enormous influence of Washington, Franklin and others, to prevent them from retaining these guarantees in excess, to obtain the excellent result which was involved in the Constitution of the United States.

This leads me to refer to a point which needs treatment. It will probably be assumed that in my discussion of the underlying elements of our constitutional life I accord no place to individual initiative. Such is far from being my purpose. The mind of man coined the Constitution as it is written. It required this coinage before it could obtain currency. A series of beliefs or maxims which lie unexpressed in the consciousness of a people, and not yet realized in an enduring shape or established institutions, has a problematical value. Such beliefs or maxims attain the dignity and value of current coin by being put into a written form. The few maxims of government contained in the Constitution of the United States were well known to the States, and they had currency there. But the wider continental spirit had not attained the point assured by the adoption of the Constitution. The growth of that continental spirit along the lines of slow national development, in the direction of an established and stable government of

[1] See Hosmer, Anglo-Saxon Freedom, Chap. XIII.

co-ordinate departments and national powers, would have been required before the same result could have been attained without the aid of a constitution. It is needless to say that the time required for such a growth would have been indefinite and prolonged. Here the coinage of ripe and superior intellects came in, to breathe forth the unuttered and unformulated aspirations of the mass in an enduring form. And therefore this constitution is fully deserving of the eulogium passed upon it by the foremost minds of Europe.[1]

The course of growth which the American people, in their national form, discloses is marked by stages of development found in earlier peoples; not unlike the manner in which modern civilized individuals disclose in modified yet multiform ways the stages of earlier, less civilized existence. This has already been indicated in the last preceding chapter. The claim of the great historian Freeman, that the New England township of our colonial ancestors typified more closely the earlier *tunscipe* of Britain than does the relic of it left in England to-day,[2] is indicative of this tendency in social bodies, as in individuals, to reproduce, as they develop, earlier forms. It is hardly true that these forms will at the later day assume exactly the same outlines as they had in the earlier day, but there will be fundamental features of resemblance. Indeed, where social organization, on virgin soil,

---

[1] Gladstone, Maine, Bryce and others. See also De Tocqueville, Democracy in America. *Cf.* Bryce, American Commonwealth; Sir Henry S. Maine, Popular Government, Essay IV.; Hosmer, Anglo-Saxon Freedom, Chap. XV.; Fiske, Critical Period of American History, Chapter V., 223. "As the British Constitution is the most subtle organism which has proceeded from progressive history, so the American Constitution is the most wonderful work ever struck off at a given time by the brain and purpose of man." Fiske, *supra*, quoting Gladstone. See Gladstone's words again quoted in Miller, Constitution, p. 32 of the text and p. 66, *note*.

[2] American Inst. Hist., by Edw. A. Freeman, J. H. Hist. Series, Vol. I., 15. See Germanic Origin of the New England Towns, by Herbert B. Adams, *id.*, Art. II. "If you wish to see Old England you must go to New England"; Freeman. See also Hosmer, Anglo-Saxon Freedom, 113; Weeden, Social and Econ. Hist. N. E., *passim*.

reforms, and in a measure starts again the course of political government, some reversion to the earlier forms is spontaneous and inevitable.[1] When Europe became Romeless, it started again with the earlier local group as a basis, just as the colonists started with the earlier local group,[2] though, of course, there were current relics of the more developed conditions where their influence had penetrated deep enough.[3] This reversion was, therefore, a necessity before the later forms in American constitutional life were attainable.[4]

The claim, so justly made, that in the first period of colonial life on this continent the white man was essentially an Englishman, could only be modified gradually. His ideas were English in most of the fundamental matters of his political life—his town-life, his church-life, his life in the courts—and his legal views were and are still largely colored by English ideas. His Americanism rested upon an English foundation, just as Englishry, in the formative period of England's constitutional life, rested upon Germanic, or rather Saxon, foundations. Yet there is a difference; for while American constitution-makers began their work in a late day of English *national* integration, English constitution-makers began before any German *nation* had yet integrated.[5] These constitution-makers alike took up and

---

[1] *Cf.* Rudimentary Society among Boys, by John Johnson, Jr., J. H. Hist. Series, Vol. II., 501; Hosmer, Anglo-Saxon Freedom, 115.

[2] *Cf.* Waitz, Deutsche Verf.-Geschichte, Vol. I.; Stubbs, Const. Hist. of Eng., Vol. I.; Gneist, Eng. Const. Hist.; Green, Making of England; Gomme, The Village Community, Chap. III.; Seebohm, The English Village Community; Essays in Anglo-Saxon Law. But see Freeman, Chief Periods of European History, Lect. VI.

[3] It is well known that when civilized barbarians go back among their own people they revert back to the old conditions; and this is said even of civilized beings as such.

[4] Hosmer, Anglo-Saxon Freedom, Chapters VIII., XIII.; Fiske, Beginnings of New England, and Critical Period of American History; Am. Inst. Hist., by Edw. A. Freeman, Art. I., Vol. I., J. H. U. Series.

[5] I mean by *constitution-makers* the active elements among the people which primarily tended toward a constitutional political organism. *Cf.* Hosmer, Anglo-Saxon Freedom, Chap. XIII.

molded an all-pervading early form of political integration, whose existence could be traced, in more or less developed stages, in the forms of the primitive Aryan—before that spread of population ensued which gave us the ancient Greek, the Iranian, the Tuscan, the Roman, or any other of the early peoples who inhabited at one time or another Europe and Asia.[1] It was a form whose counterpart is confidently affirmed to find its copies among the barbarian and savage tribes of undeveloped countries in our day.[2]

The present most civilized and moral man is the best representative of centuries of progression and retrogression; he is, so to say, the product of the compromises of the ages past. So are our best, most advanced social forms. In keeping with this, the needs of human kind gave currency to developed ruling powers and the spread of a legal spirit over wide national and international domains; and these needs also evolved, out of indefinite want of organization, an increasing complexity in administrative governmental functions, and an increasing expansion of bureaucratic features. The United States—meaning thereby the people in their social pursuits, their local governmental forms, their commonwealths, and their composite national organism—as well present an example of this latest result of social and political evolution as any other country.

Outside of the preamble, the Constitution of the United States establishes a framework of government, consisting of the co-ordinate departments, each invested with a fair share

[1] See the last preceding chapter of this work. Also *cf.* Gomme, The Village Community, Chap. I.; Taylor, The Origin of the Aryans, 186; Schrader, Sprachvergleichung und Urgeschichte, 568 *seq.*; Post, Bausteine, etc.; same, Ursprung des Rechts; same, Die Geschlechtsgenossenschaft der Urzeit; Morgan, Ancient Society; Maine, Village Communities; Hearn, Aryan Household; Spencer, Prin. of Soc. (Political Institutions); Leist, Graeco-Ital. R. G.

[2] See *post*, and Spencer, preceding note; also see Lubbock, Prehistoric Times; Tylor, Anthropology, 219, 420.

of administrative powers, divided into classes peculiar to the purpose and object of each department. Treason, the privileges of citizenship, the powers and forms of organization of the States, and the effect of State records are in a greater or smaller measure defined therein. It contains provisions relating to the public debt, oath of office, religious tests, and the supremacy of the provisions of the instrument. A ratification of the Constitution is provided for. In a series of amendments provision is made against the abuse of governmental functions and for the protection of the citizen. The last five amendments relate to matters which grew up under the Constitution, indicative of startling defects therein—defects productive of evils which were thereby intended to be corrected.

The provisions relating to the framework of government are occupied first with the constitution and powers of the legislative department of the government. Waiving the question whether, appropriately, a bill of rights and the powers of the executive department in separate chapters or articles should not have first engaged the attention of the framers of the Constitution (in favor of which modern experience speaks in no uncertain tones), in other respects that instrument is less artificially constructed than more recent State constitutions.[1] For instance, the powers of Congress, as defined in Article I., Section VIII., are not all peculiar to Congress. They need the President's concurrence to make them effectual. Nor is the term *Congress* a happy one.[2] The Congress of the States prior to the adoption of the Constitution gave currency to the term. It had little appropriate application to the legislative body created by the article referred to. That body was in many respects a copy of the Parliament of England, except that its powers were narrowed to the purpose of its creation. The language employed to grant those

---

[1] *Cf.* Constitution of Pennsylvania or of Arkansas, now in force (1891), with the Federal Constitution. See Ben Perley Poore, Charters and Constitutions.

[2] Fiske, Civil Government, 203.

powers is full of pleonasms. As James Madison wrote to Joseph C. Cabell, under date of September 18, 1828, "The Constitution vests in Congress expressly 'the power to lay and collect taxes, duties and excises,' and 'the power to regulate trade.' That the former power, if not particularly expressed, would have been included in the latter, as one of the objects of a general power to regulate trade, is not necessarily impugned by its being so expressed. Examples of this sort cannot sometimes be easily avoided, and are to be seen elsewhere in the Constitution. Thus, the power 'to define and punish offenses against the law of nations' includes the power afterwards particularly expressed 'to make rules concerning captures, etc., from offending neutrals.' So, also, a power 'to coin money' would doubtless include that of 'regulating its value,' had not the latter power been expressly inserted. The term taxes, if standing alone, would certainly have included duties, imposts and excises. In another clause it is said 'no taxes or duties shall be laid on exports,' etc. Here the two terms are used as synonymous."[1]

"To regulate the value of coin"[2] would clearly imply the power given in the next clause[3] "to provide for the punishment of counterfeiting the securities and current coin of the United States." Indeed, many of the powers recited in detail are covered by other provisions, and if they had not been, would clearly have been embraced in the omnibus clause called the "general welfare," or elastic clause,[4] which recites that Congress shall have power "to make all laws which shall be necessary and proper for carrying into execution the foregoing powers and all other powers vested by this Constitution in the Government of the United States, or in any department or officer thereof."

That the use of superfluous phraseology did not enable the framers of the Constitution to cover all points was indicated

---

[1] *Cf.* A Short Tariff History of the United States, by David H. Mason.

[2] Art. I., Sec. VIII., 5. [3] *Ibid.* 6.

[4] *Ibid.* 18. See Fiske, Civil Government, 245, 259.

in the first administration of Washington—the first administration under it—when the question was as to whether Congress had power to create a *national* bank.[1] No phraseology therein contained, in terms, authorizes Congress to create a bank any more than it does the creation of lotteries; and, according to statutory rules of construction, the recital in detail of powers conferred excludes other instances.[2] The powers of the Federal Government have been forcibly expanded upon more than one occasion to adapt the instrument to the needs of the country.[3] And clauses which were intended to confer the power of protecting American industries by high tariff regulations have lost their original meaning.[4] Here are defects of language of great importance.

---

[1] Wharton, American Law, §417; McMaster, Hist. of the People of the U. S., Vol. II., 28 *seq.*; McCullough *v.* Maryland, 4 Wheaton, 316.

[2] This rule does not seem to be applied with the same strictness to constitutional provisions as to statutory enactments. *Cf.* Juilliard *v.* Greenman, 110 U. S. 421, 438, 439.

[3] Instance the purchase of Louisiana and Alaska, the issue of paper currency, the Emancipation Proclamation, the assumption of jurisdiction of the Supreme Court of the United States over the decisions of State Courts by writs of error under the provisions of the Act of Congress.

[4] Instance the "commerce clause." See Mason, A Short Tariff History of the United States. The Supreme Court of the United States bears out this construction of the commerce clause in many opinions. "It authorizes Congress to prescribe *the conditions upon which commerce in all its forms* shall be conducted between our citizens and the citizens or subjects of other countries"; Field, J., Mobile Co. *v.* Kimball, 102 U. S. 696. "The Act of Congress of August 3, 1882, 'to regulate immigration,' which imposes upon the owners of steam or sailing vessels who shall bring passengers from a foreign port into a port of the United States, a duty of fifty cents for every such passenger not a citizen of this country, is a valid exercise of the power to regulate commerce with foreign nations"; Head Money Cases, 112 U. S. 580; People *v.* Compagnie Générale Transatlantique, 107 U. S. 59. It has been held, in a number of cases, that the exaction of a tax or license fee on interstate commerce was a regulation of commerce committed exclusively to Congress under the commerce clause. See Welton *v.* Missouri, 91 U. S. 275, in which case Mr. Justice Field said: "The power to regulate conferred by that clause upon Congress is one without limitation; and to regulate commerce is to prescribe

Coupled with the powers of Congress are powers denied to the States.[1] These would seem to have been more appropriately referred to after the powers of all the departments of the Federal Government had been recited. The propriety of defining treason in an organic instrument, especially in connection with the constitution of the Supreme Court and the jurisdiction of that and lesser courts,[2] may well be questioned. If it was a needful provision it should have been incorporated in a bill of rights.

The failure to define citizenship in the United States was a grievous defect in the Constitution. This has now been supplied after a long and most sanguinary fratricidal war, fought, if ever wars were fought, for principle, and as doggedly and stubbornly and bravely as freemen ever fought on Marston Moor or around Boston. And the end of this late emendation has not come yet; for the blind zeal of the successful side carried them beyond the object of that war, to invest with the franchise and right to hold office a great mass of enfranchised slaves, thus exposing the Anglo-Saxons in many parts of the South to the greater fecundity, immorality, mendacity and simplicity of the negro race. Who knows but that thus a great historical mistake has been made; a crime of the century committed?

These matters inform us that the Constitution was, indeed, the artificial work of men—men who were fallible, and not without the disposition here and there to say too much, and

---

rules by which it shall be governed, that is, *the conditions upon which it shall be conducted; to determine how far it shall be free and untrammeled, how far it shall be burdened by duties and imposts, and how far it shall be prohibited.*" *Id.*, 279, 280; Robbins *v.* Shelby Co. Taxing Dist., 120 U. S. 489; Bowman *v.* R. R. Co., 125 U. S. 465; Leloup *v.* Port of Mobile, 127 U. S. 640, 648; Phila. Steamship Co. *v.* Pennsylvania, 122 U. S. 326; Asher *v.* Texas, 128 U. S. 129; Western Union Tel. Co. *v.* Alabama, 132 U. S. 472. The acts prohibiting Chinese immigration, as well as objectionable pauper immigration, derive their validity from the same clause. Chinese Exclusion Case, 130 U. S. 581, 589 *seq.* *Cf.* Miller, Const. of the U. S., Lect. IX.

[1] Art. I., Sec. X. [2] Art. III., Sec. III.

elsewhere to say too little; men, some of whom were surcharged with pedantry and the desire to air it; and others of whom were of diverse and antagonistic opinions deep-set and hard to change; and men, a very few of whom possessed that profound statesmanship which, built up from actual contact with the roughest and most startling experiences attending the budding forth of the new federal organism, saw the greater evils to be avoided—even though the remedy might come in an imperfect form, even though the phraseology of the organic instrument was illogical, redundant, and in some respects inadequate. It was sufficient for these that it gave to the federal organism independent powers derived from the people and not from the several States.[1]

The inadequate data which have come down to us indicate that the best part of what history told of past democracies, and of the blessings of the English bi-cameral system, was known to the men who framed the Constitution.[2] That bi-cameral system had found adoption among a number of the States, and was not a new thing. One writer, qualified to speak, has told us that all of the States, except Pennsylvania, Vermont, and for a while Georgia, had the bi-cameral system; that the name "Senate" was used for the upper house in Maryland, Massachusetts, New York, North Carolina, New Hampshire and South Carolina; that the name "House of Representatives" for the lower house was in use in Massachusetts, New Hampshire, South Carolina, Pennsylvania and Vermont.[3] It was to be expected that the home words for the two chambers would be the choice for designating the two chambers composing the federal legislative body rather than the English designations. We have already seen how

---

[1] *Cf.* Fiske, Critical Period of American History, 236 *seq.*; Hosmer, Anglo-Saxon Freedom, 234; Wharton, American Law, §§370, 371; Hannis Taylor, Origin and Growth of the English Constitution, 65.

[2] Bryce, American Commonwealth, Chap. III.; Fiske, Critical Period, etc., 290, 291.

[3] Mr. Alexander Johnston, New Princeton Review, September, 1887. *Cf.* Ben Perley Poore, Charters and Constitutions.

the use of the word "Parliament" was eschewed. And as the terms were borrowed to give names to the two chambers, so were the composition and practice of the two bodies modeled after State exemplars, with such exceptions as were induced by the wider area and the different bases of representation applicable to the Federal Government as distinguished from the bases of State legislative representation. In determining the basis of representation in the Federal House of Representatives, the slave element produced grave complications.

The President was copied from the Governors of the States. The name itself had been in use in Delaware, New Hampshire, Pennsylvania and South Carolina. Every State prescribed a form of oath for its officers. Pennsylvania furnished the form of oath for the President. New York furnished an exact prototype of the office of Vice-President in its Lieutenant-Governorship. The provisions for the recognition of interstate citizenship and for the rendition of fugitive slaves and criminals were suggested by the eighth article of the New England Confederation of 1643 and the fourth article of the Confederation. The first eight amendments are in substance a reiteration of the English Bill of Rights.[1] The ninth, tenth and eleventh amendments were felt to be necessary to guard against too extended an application of Federal powers at the expense of the States and the people.

Mr. Johnston says that the most solid work done by the framers of the Constitution was in giving powers to Congress and the establishment of a Federal judiciary. And yet the same phenomenon is presenting itself here which is the case in Great Britain—experience is slowly but surely merging larger power in the lower house at the expense of the upper house and the Executive.[2] And the judiciary have not yet

[1] For a struggle for similar principles in the reign of Charles I., see Hosmer, Anglo-Saxon Freedom, Chapters IX. and X.

[2] *Cf.* Woodrow Wilson, Congressional Government; Bryce, American Commonwealth, Chapters XIII. to XXI., inclusive.

obtained the full jurisdiction contemplated by the Constitution, showing that the popular confidence is not and never has been given to it in the measure contemplated by the framers of the Constitution.[1]

The Constitution was in form neither an entirely original nor a perfect creation—no more so than a contract upon such a large subject would be; both, following in the line of more or less previous experience, would exhibit the use of superabundant phraseology in proportion to the abundance of caution possessed. Yet, in the discussions shown in Elliott's Debates, in the writings of Mr. Madison and Mr. Bancroft's second volume on the Formation of the Constitution, it does not appear to have been always felt that the provisions suggested were already in use among the States. The primary thought seems to have been to secure a more perfect and stronger Federal power which should not be dependent upon the States, should therefore have sufficient taxing power of its own, and should have the power of protecting the commerce and fostering the industries of the United States. Such was, primarily, the motive, produced by the threatened dissolution of the Confederation, which led to the Commercial Convention at Annapolis, and, eventually, the Constitutional Convention at Philadelphia. It needs to be remembered that the Constitutional Convention usurped powers not accorded to it in its organization, and that the idea of a Constitution forced itself into prominence as the deliberations proceeded; a technical breach of the trust confided to the members of this convention, which was concurred in by Washington and Franklin. But the factors of national organization thus impelled them. And the debates of the convention, if fully reported to us, would still leave unreported that undercurrent of experience whose

[1] And the judicial power, and mode of exercise of that power, are simply a wider application of English methods. *Cf.* Willoughby, Constitution of the United States; Dicey, Law of the Constitution, Part I., Chap. III., 154, 155; Bryce, Am. Com., Vol. I., Chap. XXIII., 252, 253; Maine, Popular Government, Essay IV., 218 *seq.*

familiarity with charter and constitutional framework and principles constituted the most substantial element in securing the successful framing of the organic act.[1]

To me it seems, gathering up some views from this detail of the texture and formation of the Constitution, that the work of framing it was the product of circumstances. These circumstances were the inadequacies of State control over *continental* affairs—the need of some *continental* organic political agency independent of the States, so that *continental* harmony and unity would have a chance to blossom to fruition and become permanent. Independent power and resources given to some continental organic political unit *necessitated* the construction of a framework of government, while previous experience and conservative habits *necessitated* the formation of that framework largely on lines of thought which had become fixed in the life of the people. A bicameral system, with an executive head and cabinet, and three co-ordinate departments of government, had been experienced to be up to that time the safest, or at any rate the best known and most desirable incidents of government. These things having been established, the rest of the work was to reduce these necessities to form, to fill in the needful details and set the government going. Incidentally, as the States had brought great trouble on themselves by the unlimited issue of irredeemable paper, these were prohibited from doing the same again; and the power to coin money was put in the hands of Congress, so that a uniform coinage and standard of value should be introduced. The States were also prohibited from continuing the ruinous policy of impairing the obligation of contracts, an outcome of the vicissitudes and emergencies which induced the issue of irredeemable paper. Congress was invested with power to regulate foreign and interstate commerce, and, as a part of the exercise of this power, to protect and foster *American* industries.

---

[1] *Cf.* Miller, Const. of the U. S., Lect. IX., pp. 433–446.

It does not admit of question but that the framers of the Constitution had an eye to the future when they adopted it. All that has been said of the objects of its formation indicates that. But the prescience was vague and indeterminate, and has not come down to us in a way which justifies us in according to men any profound insight into the future of the country as that future came about. George Washington, the presiding officer of that body, and, upon the whole, the best judge of the actual trend of events in the country in his day, never gave currency to any thoughts which went beyond the future peopling of the territory lying between the Atlantic seaboard and the Mississippi. Before the Constitution had started on its journey through the States, when the question was as to its adoption, the first ten amendments, which did not occur to the framers of it, were urged and insisted upon by the people. And from time to time since, notwithstanding the liberal stretching to which construction has subjected the language of the organic act, the need of further amendments has been felt, and they have been adopted.

A German writer has said that the people of this country have *canonized* the Constitution of the United States; that we have accorded to it a sacredness which interferes with the appropriate and harmonious expansion of the government; and that thus has been occasioned a series of secondary rules and canons which as much make up its body of law as the organic provisions themselves—rules and canons which depend upon that broad field of implied powers whose limit is undefinable.[1] How, with the confessed faults it exhibited, due to the inevitable fallibility of its framers and the poverty of language, it could fail to require in time the harmonizing influence of construction, it would be difficult to conceive. And how an organic law could have endured, and become respected and adhered to, without making it the conserva-

[1] Von Holst, Constitutional History of the United States, Vol. I., Chap. II. See also Hannis Taylor, Origin and Growth of the English Constitution, 60.

tive basis for construction to play upon and about, it is also difficult to understand. The so-called canonization of the Constitution consists in giving emphasis to its provisions, and in adhering with a reasonable degree of firmness to its provisions. Any other course would have wiped it out and utterly destroyed its influence for usefulness; for in the contempt and disregard we feel for language in any document is involved its ultimate powerlessness and uselessness. If anything beyond growth and change of fundamental ideas and aspirations has alienated the affection of the people from the sacred text of Holy Scriptures, it has been the destructive criticism to which that work has been subjected. The Constitution, under the disintegrating agency of a similar process, would undergo a similar process of dissolution. That so-called canonization, rather that conservative process of constitutional preservation, stands always in marked contrast to the theoretical constitutions of so-called philosophic framers of new governments, whose systems, like that of Sieyès, when put to the test of popular construction, tumble to pieces. Von Holst himself shows that the term canonization is improper, for, as he proceeds in his voluminous, interesting and instructive history, he shows how the provisions of the Constitution and its true intent were nullified and narrowed down by the slave power, which sought to narrow the sphere of action of the Constitution in favor of State power and jurisdiction.[1] We have seen how the Presidents, Congress and the Supreme Court have expanded its provisions from time to time, and how the people by amendment have filled up defects therein. The Constitution in its earlier stage was far from being canonized; it was then looked upon with suspicion and distrust by many, including some of the most prominent statesmen of the day. And that distrust eventually gave rise to an anti-Federalist party, headed by Thomas Jefferson, which for nearly half a century

[1] Von Holst's principal refrain is with reference to the slave power and its consequences.

kept control of the government, and which bids fair to do the like again. The affection of the people then, it was fully agreed upon all sides, was rather with the local State jurisdictions than the more distant Federal Government. Not only was the formation of an anti-Federalist party, even against Washington, a strong indication of the absence of the canonizing agency in the respect and veneration due the Constitution, but whenever special State interests were involved, the disposition to resort to nullification resolutions was another indication of the same sort. To the Supreme Court of the United States, whose mode of judging and determining constitutional and other questions, has been by adhering to precedent and established canons of construction, and to the custom of the American bar and people to adhere to a similar ordered legal development, may be attributed the maintenance and respect entertained for that organic law.[1]

I have thus, in meager outline, endeavored to account for the existence of the Constitution in this country, and the moving agencies in producing and maintaining it. We can see in its adoption and continuance the effect of ordered self-government, due to township, county, city and commonwealth administration, and to the influence of minds made patriotic by the pursuit of national ends. Under all outward manifestations, whether in the Constitutional Convention, in Congress, the Presidency, the Supreme Court, or among the people, we see the current of past experience, asserting itself in an adherence to inherited jurisprudence and to inherited governmental and other ideas, changed by the environment which evolved from independent colonists an independent complex national sovereignty. Just as that coinage of sentience and thought—language—contains the remains of past physical and intellectual action, so does the coinage of our Federal Constitution contain remains of the historical pro-

[1] The term "canonization," with its satirical implications, is apt to sway the adversely inclined against the Constitution, in favor of those socialistic and anarchistic dogmas which render such theories as Henry George and Edward Bellamy acceptable.

gress of the people;[1] that is, not a mere disorderly and unorganized mass of units, but a people with a highly developed number of local and State governments, a people with a cultivated political consciousness: a political consciousness which also implied the perception by men of their relations to one another in family and local political communities, of their power to shape their own political destinies within bounds.[2] We have seen, in the last preceding chapter, the course of development of the local subdivisions of the States of the Union:[3] a course of development, by the way, unlike the general course of development in ancient or earlier modern times, because it builded upon experience which had outgrown the mere expansion of local village-community life—a process of growth which characterized the *kome* (κώμη)[4], the *metrokome* (μητροκώμη), the *polis* (πόλις), the *metropolis* (μητρόπολις)[5] of ancient Greece and Rome. The awakening and formation of the federal spirit in this country was a form of political awakening, a throwing off of constitutional indifference characteristic of organic beings, upon national proportions, and was beyond the more premature, loose and earlier federations of Greek cities; just as it was the spread by contact and expansion of colonial centers in America which led to statehood. The evolution of the commonwealth of Connecticut from the previous general

---

[1] Hosmer, People and Politics, Book II., Chap. IV.; Hannis Taylor, Origin and Growth of the English Constitution, Introduction.

[2] Hosmer, *supra*, 133.

[3] *Cf.* Weeden, Social and Economic Hist. of New England, Vol. I., 49 *seq.*; Hosmer, Anglo-Saxon Freedom, pp. 112–123.

[4] *Cf.* Kuhn, Ueber die Entstehung der Staedte der Alten, Einleitung; Schrader, Sprachvergleichung u. Urgeschichte, 578; Aristotle, Politics, Book I., Chap. II. Aristotle defines a kome to be "a society of many families which was instituted for lasting and mutual advantage." It is a village in English form. It may be composed of emigrant members of one family, and the children and children's children. *Cf.* Kuhn.

[5] Kuhn, Städtische u. Bürgerliche Verfassung des römischen Rechts, Vol. I., 271; Marquardt, Röm. Stadtverwaltung, Vol. I., Chap. I.

government of town settlements[1] is not unlike the evolution of the ancient Greek *συνοικισμός* (*synoikismos*);[2] and in some details is a reproduction of a still earlier and, therefore, deeper organic political form.[3] But the analogies are only relative to the organic process of development; the relative place and meaning of the early form, in a political sense, has become colored in its latest phase by the incidents of English political and jural conceptions of a higher and national character. The colonists upon the New England shores of North America drifted, by the nature of their necessities, into local subdivisions, more and more controlled, as in Connecticut, by a *General Court*, as the territory became populated. And the *General Court* became, not unlike the early parliaments, or witenagemotes, split up into segregated functional groups, coördinated into executive, legislative and judicial departments. The essential difference between the Connecticut colonists and the early English, and the still earlier Greek, was that the colonists had evolved, after centuries of German and English development, a political capacity which, with expansion, and without too much federal influence, would be capable of appreciating and sustaining a national territorial unit of magnificent proportions, based on popular suffrage.[4] And the Constitution itself is an evidence of this capacity, for the reserved power of the people is expressly mentioned therein.[5] The preamble is also an evidence of it.[6]

---

[1] *Cf.* Johnston, Connecticut, Chaps. VI. to XII.; Andrews, The River Towns of Connecticut, Johns Hopkins Series, Vol. VII.

[2] Kuhn, Ueber die Entstehung, etc., 188 *seq.*; Schrader, 582.

[3] Post, Bausteine, etc., Book II., §§112, 113. See also Schrader, *supra.*

[4] See Maine, Popular Government, Essay IV.; Hosmer, Anglo-Saxon Freedom, Chap. XIII.

[5] Constitution, IX. and X. Amendments.

[6] Mr. Bryce (American Commonwealth, Vol. I., Part I., Chap. XXVI., p. 300), says: "The aim of the Constitution seems to be not so much to attain great common ends by securing a good government as to avert the evils which will flow, not merely from a bad government but from any government strong enough to threaten the pre-existing communities or

Though the framework of the Federal Government, when subjected to practical tests, has given rise to a good deal of friction and extravagant construction, occasioned by the necessities of our national economy,[1] yet, implied in the possibility and combined existence of the *Constitution*—which has substantially answered the purposes of an hundred years rule of democratic power—there is such an amount of political discipline as can only be accounted for by the training which the English-speaking people from an early period have gone through,—a training colored and matured and purified by the self-dependent life which colonization of America involved. The term *constitution* itself, more than the indefinite influence of *logos,* was, in this connection, a happy inspiration, induced by the consciousness that "articles of confederation" would never answer the purpose; an inspiration which may well claim uniqueness, since it produced the newest and best signification which the word had yet attained; an enlarged valuation of the word which substituted the ordered political experience and knowledge of a self-governing people for the arbitrary expressions of the *imperator.*[2] This new valuation of the word has gone broadcast over the world, giving definiteness to the institutional characteristics of barbarian as well as more developed political entities.[3]

---

the individual citizen." In saying this he loses sight of the fact that the Constitution was adopted to attain durable and urgent common ends of overruling importance. See Bancroft, Formation of the Constitution; Fiske, Critical Period of American History.

[1] Bryce, American Commonwealth, Vol. I., 301.

[2] *Cf.* Miller, Const. of the U. S., 63, 70, 71 notes.

[3] See Post, Bausteine für eine allg. Rechtswissenschaft, Book II., §§103 *seq.*; same, African Jurisprudenz, Vol. II., Part II.; Spencer, Principles of Sociology, Part V.; S. Mayer, Rechte der Israeliten, Roemer u. Athener, Vol. I., Book II.; Von Maurer, Mark-, Hof-, Dorf- u. Stadt-Verfassungsgeschichte; Howard, Local Constitutional History of the U. S.; Stubbs, Const. Hist. of Eng., Vol. I.; Maine, Early Hist. of Inst.; Woolsey, Political Science, Vol. I., Part III.; Freeman, Comp. Politics; same, Origin and Growth of the Eng. Const.; Boeckh, Athenian Constitution; Waitz, Deutsche Verf.-Geschichte; Freeman, Hist. of

To it we may safely ascribe that ultimate canonization, as Von Holst improperly called it, which kept it safely alive amidst the throes of extraordinary civil commotion, spread over a half century in its rise and culmination. The term itself—since the term itself and the fact it stands for assume the existence of that national unity which every statehood must possess to be respected among nations; since these designate the unity which expresses the *national* aspirations of the people in an ordered and definite form—must likewise stand, *ex necessitate rei*, for that sum of properties, as Leslie Stephens calls it,[1] which a national unity possesses and develops on its own account. Such properties, on their moral side, are not amenable to the standards of an intuitive ethical theory. The carrying on of war, the Indian policy, the dilatory payment of debts, the *diplomacy* peculiar to governmental regimen, are not fashioned after canons of intuitive ethical theory; they represent rather the traditions which seem best calculated to secure the largest national gain for the whole people, and unless sustained by ripe experience and conservative proceedings are calculated to produce much discord and evil. The venerated name of Washington was not proof against the charge of immorality in this regard.[2] And probably, if measured by the rules of ascetic or theoretical morality, the entire movement of rebellion (which culminated in the national unity here), with its violent measures on both sides, as well as the governmental discipline on a national scale which it engendered, were unjustifiable and reprehensible; just as the existence of slavery, and the subsequent abolition of it by war, and the destruction of homes and innocent men, women and children, were inex-

---

Federal Government; Putter, Historische Entwickelung der heutigen Staatsverfassung des deutschen Reichs; Gneist, Hist. of the Eng. Const.; Dicey, The Law of the Constitution; Anson, Law and Custom of the Constitution.

[1] Science of Ethics, Chap. III., Part II., Sec. XVII.; Taylor, Morality of Nations, Chap. IV.

[2] Lodge, Life of Washington, Vol. II., Chap. V.

cusable, according to the canons of an *innate* morality. The movement of the American people toward a national, constitutional existence, and those traditions of governmental regimen which went along with it and gave us the possibility and reality of an enduring and harmonious political national unity, were the increment left from individual and social turmoil and strife and unique physical surroundings (not possible to the Tauregs or Tibbus of the Sahara, or even to the people of England),[1] which carried in its train a vast, an incalculable quantity of immoral action when tested by the rules of intuitive morality.

A reference to the Federal Constitution would be, of course, incomplete which did not, however briefly, touch upon the institutions whose existence it emphasizes. Thus the separation of the fundamental governmental functions into three departments, according to the phase of activity in administration which these separately or collectively exercise, needs passing mention. Enough has already been said on the exercise of executive, legislative and judicial powers by different coördinate departments;[2] yet the functions thus separated were not divided up according to any theoretical scheme. They became divided in virtue of that process of segregation which social and political bodies in the course of development disclose. No nation has ever been free from this mode of growth; only the process of segregation has not been as definite and permanent as in England or the United States. The functions themselves are already seen in the earliest political forms. Executive, legislative and judicial functions are performed by the administrative bodies of the earliest tribes which have attained any political forms; only they are apt to be exercised by the members of the tribe or group

[1] See De Tocqueville, Democracy in America, Vol. I., 209.

[2] See Montesquieu, Spirit of Laws, Book XI., Chap. VI.; Bryce, American Commonwealth, Vol. I., Chaps. III. and IV. See also the last preceding chapter of the present work.

themselves. Whenever chieftainship became possible, the functions of the executive, at least, were apt to become segregated from the mass of administrative functions of the group, and the functions of judge became exercised whenever the chief exercised priestly power or influence. Chieftainship and priestly influence, if attaining to more than mere temporary leadership, were bound to eventually obtain the power and right of representation and dictation even in legislative matters; and therefore we may trace back to very early traditions the exercise of all of these three functions by representative bodies or agents. It is true they might not be such representatives in virtue of any conscious process of reasoning or initiative, nor upon any extensive scale, but they became such in virtue of the fundamental fact that they depended upon a governed unity, and upon the further fact that they discharged functions relating to that unit which otherwise must have been largely performed by it. There were always at the base of the governmental organon the members of a group or groups, more or less compound in character, increasing in numbers, variety and detail as the organon became larger and more varied in character.[1] It was in the volume and distribution of these coördinate functions that peoples in the past disclosed flagrant and disintegrating political defects. They succumbed in virtue of a faulty and self-destructive distribution of governmental functions. The lack of broad and enduring cohesive bodies, connected together by a national growth as fundamental in character as the local growths, or the too developed functions

---

[1] *Cf.* Spencer, Prin. of Soc., Vol. II., Part V.; Post, Bausteine, etc., §103 *seq.*; same, Ursprung des Rechts and Genossenverfassung; Waitz, Deutsche Verfassungsgeschichte; De Coulanges, Ancient City; Lewis Morgan, Ancient Society; Hearn, Aryan Household; Maine, Early Law and Customs; same, Early Hist. of Inst.; Lang, Myth, Ritual and Religion; Lubbock, Prehistoric Times; Lindsley, Mind in the Lower Animals, Vol. I., Chaps. XXI., XXII.; Green, Making of Eng., 166 *seq.*; Stubbs, Const. Hist. of Eng., Vol. I.; Gneist, Hist. of the Eng. Const.; Woolsey, Political Science, Part III.; S. Mayer, Rechte der Israeliten, Römer u. Athener, Vol. I., §33 *seq.*; Leist, Graeco-Ital. R. G.

of one administrative branch at the expense of another, at one time or another, explain the dissolution and disintegration of past and ancient political forms. Lack of circumstance or opportunity no doubt will account for much of this; will account for the decay of political organisms whose architectural remains surpass ours in magnificence and durability. The course of mankind represents the eventual rise of organons containing a better balanced distribution of administrative functions.[1] And even now it is not certain how far we have attained perfection in this regard—as little, indeed, as it is how far the civilized, settled and sheltered being has improved the physical constitution of man beyond that exhibited by the savage. We have already seen that the bi-cameral system is tending to disappear. And in view of the vagaries of a George and Bellamy, there is no telling what changes will have to be made to escape the consequences of a senile government. In any event, the drift of human events, amenable to a process of growth which sloughs off the worse for the better elements, is toward progress, and, accordingly, toward a better distributed and better regulated individual and social regimen; consequently there is justification for the idea that we have the best form of government yet extant. If this is so it is because our executive, legislative and judicial coördination is the product of centuries of social and political growth, taking root and bearing fruit in the most congenial soil and under the most favorable conditions. Without that our Constitution would have shared the fate of the theories of Locke and Shaftesbury and of Sieyès.

The subject of taxation is one which has bred a vast amount of oppression and discontent. Its history is marked by excesses on the part of rulers, and rebellious opposition where subjects had any voice in affairs. The bureaucratic tendencies which it bred, the espionage it induced, the obli-

---

[1] *Cf.* Hosmer, People and Politics; Bagehot, Physics and Politics; Amos, Science of Politics; Aristotle, Politics.

gations its enjoyment put upon rulers and their satellites to satisfy the murderous discontent of the masses, are depicted on the pages of history of every ancient nation which obtained a national or even a state character.

Taxation, like all organized social incidents, has broadened in its connotation and application, with the growth of mankind. Its signification is traceable down to the primitive gifts or tributes of peoples to their rulers or conquerors, of tribal associations to their chiefs. Its earliest form is probably the tribute which subjugated people gave, in kind, to their oppressors or conquerors.[1] Its necessity is apparent, in the absence of any other fund, or sufficient fund, for the maintenance of the state. While it does not bear the relation to mankind which language does, nor possess its psychologic value, it is a never-failing incident of political administration, even if archaic in form, except perhaps in the most primitive days. It is a characteristic of political organization at an early stage, and it did not come up as an invention, but developed as a necessary and spontaneous incident of political life. The forms it takes on are such as the surrounding circumstances, the traditions of the social form and the will of the mass, tend to effectuate.[2]

The power of taxation accorded to the Federal Government was given in such terms, and with a view to those forms which were best known to and had been in use in the Colonies; and the Colonies had inherited much of their knowledge and practice upon this point from England, where the knowledge had come up and expanded from the village forms of a later and non-migratory tribal life. The substitution of a money equivalent for services in kind, in the course of political development, corresponds with the rise of contractual transactions in lieu of mere sensual dealings by

---

[1] Spencer, Principles of Sociology, Vol. II., Part V., Chap. XVI.; Hallam, Middle Ages, Index, "Taxation."

[2] Take our modern "tariff laws." The term is traceable to the Arabic "ta'rîf." And the levy of duties thus emphasized finds its practice in the tribes of the Sahara, back in the earliest days.

means of barter and exchange; it corresponds with the replacement of the condition of status by that of contract; it corresponds with the rise of a common representative of value, instead of the thing *in specie*. It became a necessity in its modern forms as a condition of serf-like regimen became superseded by a freer, more independent and autonomous existence. And this independent, autonomous existence, spontaneously and unconsciously becoming prevalent, marked by changing vicissitudes and by the rise and fall of many peoples, was made conspicuous in our form of representative government.[1] Representation, which thus became a predominant characteristic of political progression, in symbols of value as well as in governmental agency, disclosed a wider application, a more extensive prevalence in the law of contract, and, incidentally, in those forms of agency with which the law deals. It found expression in duties, imposts, and other forms of taxation.

The occupation of war, as already mentioned, one of the most primitive of occupations—perhaps the first occupation, outside of sensual cohabitation and search for food, which engaged the attention of the earliest being[2]—is likewise lodged in the keeping of the Federal Government. The industrial movement has largely displaced the earlier prevalence of the practice of war. To war, and the coercion which tied a militant group together and bound it to a chief, we may trace the beginnings of political existence. Inasmuch as the power of government grows *as a force*, in spite of opposition, it must follow that militant life begot political forms. Here there is

---

[1] Puchta, in thus stating the position of many jurists, says that the fundamental characteristic of law is freedom of the individual; Institutionen, Vol. I., §2 *seq.*; but that this is dependent on social growth, and has a relative signification, in no way assuming independence of social development, is irrefutable. See Ihering, Geist des römischen Rechts, etc., Part II., §30 *seq.*; Spencer, Principles of Sociology; Amos, Science of Law; Austin, Province of Jurisprudence; Maine's Works; Pollock's Essays in Jurisprudence and Ethics; Stephens, Science of Ethics; Ihering, Zweck im Recht, *passim*. And see *post.*

[2] *Cf.* Chap. II., Sec. II., *ante.*

an early possibility of command, of the enforcement of a rule or a sanction; here may be found in germ legislative, executive and judicial representation, from which point the germ may grow to maturity under favorable conditions. But it is one of the remarkable phenomena of evolving social life that this *necessity*, in the beginning of political regimen, has come to be regarded as a retarding factor in our later social growth. Ethical doctrine unreservedly condemns it.

And yet there may be some reason for pausing before committing political life to the ethical canon which renders war criminal and useless. It is hardly likely that any administration would favor the entire abolition of all militancy, including naval institutions, especially as all nations are agreed upon keeping them up. It is a question whether this military force is not a prime and indispensable factor to counteract and keep down that anarchic element which dissatisfaction, poverty and theory combine to create. In the maintenance of military establishments the United States is assured an unmolested expansion. But the fact that this fundamental function has been taken away from the States and has been conferred upon the Federal organon, is one of the most pronounced *indicia* that war has ceased to be the fitful everyday pastime of individuals or groups within the organic whole, and that now it serves the useful purpose alone of maintaining national *integrity*. The States, however, may guard themselves against internal enemies, and enforce their laws, with the aid of the military forces, *by force of arms*, thus showing how military may accompany judicial coercion, how executive and judicial coercion may assume a militant aspect. In the main, however, from the smallest local subdivision up to the Federal organon, the government is based upon an industrial life.

Less fundamental, less primitive are those declarations of principles contained in the first eight amendments to the Constitution. Though they breathe the aspirations of mankind centuries ago, and find a more or less responsive echo among a cognate people upon the continent of Europe; though somewhat similar phases of popular feeling may be found in archaic political histories of Indo-Germanic peoples, yet they are the later results of political evolution. In the village-community period, or in the still more antique groups of the earliest savage, we look in vain for such declarations of principles; declarations which give expression to series of customs and inherited notions, around which definite conceptions and feelings had clustered. It took time before the abstractions thus formulated could become the occasion for strong emotional feeling; savages as little as animals could be trained to fight for an abstraction. These conceptions and feelings thus expressed had become a part of the natural emotion which personality engenders as it develops, but they were of social form. The declarations of principles referred to speak of personal freedom, sacredness of home, personal security, protection of property, and a popular form of adjudicating controversies, and imply a state of political existence beyond that of mere savage or barbarian. The sacredness of home is not a characteristic of savage peoples; and the protection of property alluded to is based on individual, not joint-tribal possessions. These possessions have made their painful, dreary and slow progress from the earliest forms of social grouping through feudal life and landholding, and barter and trade, and later, commerce and contract; and tribunals to enforce the results of barter, commerce and contracts have given them their most modern form. The rise and spread of city life have facilitated the spread of these industrial requirements. Personal security was attainable at an early period, but it was a security limited to the group of which the individual was a member; a security which depended largely upon the relative proximity of other inimical groups. But the security which is attended with regulated order, and which reaches over a definite expanse of territory, can only be predicated when a *king's peace* goes beyond tribal limits. The course of evolution is toward an ever wider expansion of the territory of regulated order and protection, divided up into national domains. But the freedom which is assured as the realm of guaranteed security expands, has varied at different times in the history of mankind, has varied among different peoples, has varied among the same people at different stages of social and political development.

The ancient Grecian was bound to a discharge of certain political functions to his *demos, kome* or *phratria*;[1] services which the Latins called *munera*, and which long military service or service in the Senate or other important ways and offices alone could relieve of.[2] As imperial rule superseded and replaced the rule of the *kome*, the *phratria*, and the city, the *munera* became replaced by severer exactions against the high and the low.[3] We see the struggle for freedom here quite unsuccessful. And yet the Roman jurisprudence discloses a consecutive improvement in favor of rights throughout its history. The freedom mankind now enjoys is peculiar to our present age. The freedom enjoyed in the United States is peculiar to that country. The freedom of mankind depends upon the cohesiveness of its various groups, the form of political government these groups have, the capacity the members of a political unity display for ordered self-government, and upon the current sentiments regarding sacredness of property and other possessions and contractual obligations, not to mention other social incidents. In this respect freedom discloses the same dependence upon man's development which progressive morality discloses.[4] Its course is not always upward and onward; the comparative peace and prosperity of one decade may

---

[1] Aristotle, Politics, Book III., Chaps. I., III.

[2] Kuhn, Römische Stadtverfassung, Vol. I.

[3] *Ibid.* Gibbon's Decline and Fall of the Roman Empire also illustrates this.

[4] Ihering, Zweck im Recht; Fowler, Progressive Morality; same, Principles of Morality; Stephen, Science of Ethics; Spencer, Data of Ethics; same, Justice.

become replaced by the next; the clash of classes may be attended by alternating successes and failures; the wealth of to-day may become replaced by the poverty of the next generation. The history of mankind is full of ups and downs, and all the ruins are not to be sought for in ancient times. Upon the whole, however, man's personality has widened, his sphere of usefulness has become more extended, his rights, privileges and opportunities and capacity for enjoyment have become enlarged. And with these, man's obligations, legal and ethical, have widened, enlarged and become more complicated.

The ethical philosopher is certain to err on one side or another, either by enforcing too lax or too rigorous a doctrine, who ignores the characteristics of given occurrences and the ethical need of the moment, in the complicated history of modern individuals living in and through a social organism, whose pressure upon them is from all sides and in multiform details.[1] The killing of individuals to save near kith and kin, or to save a nation, is not regarded as immoral; the falsifying of facts for the purpose of avoiding some greater evil has been held to be justifiable; the too persistent following of the path of glory, in the interest of national renown, has been condemned where it involves poverty and misery to wife and children; the too tender solicitude for the young, when it begets a pampered spirit, has been called unethical; the giving of largesses to the poor, the founding of poor-houses, foundling-hospitals, have been condemned in so far as they breed vagrancy and incontinence. Frequently a detailed inquiry is essential to ascertain the drift of an act, whether in the end it be good or bad. But the ready consciousness of right which the given social training begets solves the problem thus frequently presented quite quickly, much as instinct impels the animal along the right path. For in this, as in most things, individuals live a spontaneous,

[1] Leslie Stephen, Science of Ethics; Fowler, Progressive Morality; same, Principles of Morals; Taylor, Morality of Nations.

unconscious life, doing mechanically the things which a complicated web of circumstances is continually imposing upon them. And thus freedom is attained; freedom in the selection of alternatives, in the enjoyment of our possessions, in the pursuit of remedies for wrongs done, in the enjoyment of all the blessings which flow from our constitutional political complexus; freedom as home life, class life, church life, commercial life, city or country life, state and the nation's life, enable us to understand it.

The later phenomena which the other seven amendments of the Constitution give expression and currency to are peculiar to this country.

CONCLUSION.

Whatever resemblance there may be between this nation and other constitutional political organisms, none are like it in that growth which is implied in our social development from township and county to state and federal organisms. None are like it, upon the same scale of territorial magnitude, in that moderate and excellent spirit which, in the main, has preserved the country from the enforcement of extravagant theories, there being but one instance of such extravagance, that is, the conferring of the franchise upon a great mass of uneducated slaves. The heritage which was received, through English experience, from our forefathers—which on English soil developed a sturdy, independent yeomanry—in such a fruitful atmosphere as that of untamed, virgin America, was bound to create a self-dependent and honest population. The result thus obtained, forming the fundamental tone of our national consciousness, has colored all succeeding phases of our national population; and against it anarchists must inevitably beat themselves to death, until a farming population becomes crushed out by the city life and the city politics and the city morals of the nation. For, as in Rome, so here city life is the worst breeder of political and social contagion. The future, however, may show a cure for this.

This colonial spirit that, in the wilderness of America, hewed out our beginnings as a nation—bred and reared in the forest, on the farm and in adversity—while *aided* by the city life of our forefathers, created that national pulse and feeling, however obscured it may have become, which ended in a unique and quite undefinable sovereignty. It created a state feeling which manifested itself in the safeguards of state integrity which were incorporated in the Constitution. To the same spirit is attributable the solicitude displayed in the provisions of the Constitution against unseemly and arbitrary encroachment upon the customary and individual rights of the people. He who reads the history of colonial days must be struck with the earnestness, piety and capacity for autonomous government shown, in spite of the rudeness and lack of discipline frequently apparent. No other people were more careful in their conclusions, so swayed by intelligent understanding of their needs and situation. The example of French license and anarchy, of German docility, may be fittingly placed in contrast with American self-control, notwithstanding that the war of the Revolution of 1776 was attended with great vexations, incidental to the upturning of the established order in some details, and was fraught with trouble and weakness under the Articles of Confederation, and was provocative of much popular clamor and dissatisfaction. The nation was then in process of forming; it was not yet formed.

As a code formulates and makes clear the hidden principles of rule and law, and preserves them from a radical destruction and too uncertain destiny, so did the Constitution preserve and formulate enough of the national aspiration and feeling here to enable the national unity to obtain a more regular and stronger pulsation and a larger and more ordered influence. It is a product of the best and most orderly aspirations of the colonial life in this country. It is in this regard a unique and invaluable product. No better testimony could be obtained of the true character of the best and most intelligent manhood of our forefathers. While it was impossible of conception, except among a people who had advanced along the path of civilization and enlightenment to a place which implies the existence of humane laws bearing upon most of the relations of mankind in industrial and moral points of view, yet it was no mere code of laws. The framers thereof in framing it undertook to blend precedent with new and larger purposes. The success they achieved, under all the favorable environment, is marked by a century of uninterrupted and phenomenal growth.

It would be unfortunate if the tribunal to which has been delegated the duty of construing the Constitution had placed upon that instrument a narrow and strict construction, such as might be accorded to a statute in derogation of the common law or a contract. Fortunately a larger, more liberal rule has been employed.[1] "A constitution is an instrument of government, made and adopted by the people for practical purposes." . . . "It should be construed so as best to subserve the great objects for which it was made."[2] In this way the Federal power has not been emasculated or curtailed of essential powers which a narrower construction might have entailed. We have already discussed the subject of implied powers as held by the Supreme Court of the United States. Those implied powers have been held to authorize the establishment of a national bank, of issuing legal-tender paper currency, to authorize Congressional legislation relative to appeals from the decisions of State tribunals to the Supreme Court of the United States, the release of Federal judicial officers from imprisonment by State officers on charge of murder, under a writ of *habeas corpus*. The Federal courts, under their claim of independent existence, have felt authorized to pursue their quest after principles of equity, common law, commercial law, general law of contracts, general principles of construction, and so on, without reference to the rulings of State courts in the given State where the transaction occurred.[3]

It is quite comprehensible how this species of construction

---

[1] *Cf.* Wharton, American Law, §368 *seq.*

[2] Desty, Federal Constitution, 39; Juilliard *v.* Greenman, 110 U. S. 421, 438, 439; McCullough *v.* Maryland, 4 Wheat. 316, 405, 407.

[3] 16 Peters, 495; 2 Black, 418; 92 U. S., 501; 102 U. S., 14; 18 How., 517; 1 Wall., 83; 19 Wall., 666; 100 U. S., 239; 18 Wall., 546; 14 Wall., 661; 16 Peters, 1; 4 How., 353; 12 How., 139; 13 How., 268; 107 U. S., 102; *id.*, 529; 3 How., 464; 10 Wall., 497; 16 Wall., 678.

has benefited the nation as a whole. Any other course might have tended, especially in the first half century of the life of the Constitution, to cripple, if not to destroy many of the benefits of Federal control. In any event, the factors which produced the Constitution and which tended to keep it alive, operating even in the hands of strict constructionists, such as Jefferson and John Randolph (as when Jefferson, sustained by Randolph in the House of Representatives, created an embargo and purchased Louisiana; and, to add another instance, when Jackson nullified nullification), culminated in making a nation, somewhat in despite of the unelastic terms of the Constitution, showing that the nation's growth, upon the whole, is not upon lines previously outlined in any constitutional theory, unless that theory happens to fit in with the facts comprising such growth.

Here it is deemed best to close this introduction to the study of the Constitution. The author's object has been to make apparent, in outline, how true it is that our Federal Constitution, though unique and entitled to great admiration and obedience, though conceived and formulated in deference to experience and actual growth, is, like other, *unwritten*, constitutions, amenable to the undercurrent of national growth. If God's conception and creation—man—is amenable to such factors and laws, surely man's must be. The author's object has also been to obtain for the Constitution that large view which renders the Constitution a framework of government, coming up in the course of ages of social growth, to serve its purpose for good or for bad as its provisions shall be applied in consonance to social and physical factors in the social and political organism.

One thing I feel convinced of, that the petty schemes of such visionaries as Henry George and Edward Bellamy are not fashioned upon the proper scale of earthly movement, as herein indicated. The procession of social aggregates reveals a painful progress toward more perfect conditions, in spite of the decay of many nations. It illustrates the omnipotent workings of a mysterious Providence, whose scale of movement is not fashioned upon any plan heretofore discovered by such prophets as the two writers indicated. I prefer the course of the conservative statesman, seeking cautiously after remedies in the light of the country's history, having due regard to the lessons of the past. Political prophets are apt to be exalted too high in their own conceit to teach us the proper course. And I have faith in that mysterious destiny which in its own way is drifting us along toward higher conditions, for such is the lesson of history and past politics.

AUTHORITIES REFERRED TO IN THE BOOK.

Acts of Congress of the 50th Congress.

Adams (Henry). History of the United States, Vols. I. and II. (Scribner, New York, 1890.)

Alabama Supreme Court Reports, Volumes 53, 70, 80.

American Bar Association, Reports, Volume XI.

American Law Review, Volumes 16, 19; New Series, Volume I.

Amos (Sheldon). Roman Civil Law.

—— Science of Law (International Scientific Series).

—— Science of Politics " " "

—— Systematic View of the Science of Jurisprudence. (Longmans, London, 1872.)

Anson (Sir Wm. R.). Principles of the Law of Contracts (Aldrich's Edition). (Callaghan, Chicago, 1880.)

—— The Law and Custom of the Constitution. (Oxford, 1886, Clarendon Press.)

Aristotle. Politics.

Arkansas Supreme Court Reports, Volumes 2, 23, 26, 29, 33, 34, 38, 39, 47, 50.

Arnold (William). Geschichte des Eigenthums in deutschen Städten. (Basel, 1861.)

—— Verfassungsgeschichte der deutschen Freistädte. (Gotha, 1854.)

Austin (John). Jurisprudence (Campbell's Edition). (Cockroft, New York City, 1875.)

Backhofen (J. J.). Das Mutterrecht. (Stuttgart, 1861.)

Bacon (Frederick H.). Law of Benefit Societies and Life Insurance. (Thomas, St. Louis, 1888.)

Bain (Alexander). Emotions and the Will. (Appleton, New York, 1876.)

—— Moral Science. (Appleton, New York, 1882.)

—— Senses and the Intellect. (Appleton, New York, 1879.)

Bancroft (George). History of the United States. (Boston, 1879.)

—— Formation of the Constitution. (New York, 1883.)

Bates (Clement). Law of Partnership. (Flood, Chicago, 1888.)

Bellamy (Edward). Looking Backward.

Benjamin (Judah P.). Law of Sales (Corbin's Edition). (Linn, Jersey City, 1884.)

Biener (F. A.). Das englische Geschwornengericht. (Leipsic, 1852-1855.)

Bishop (Joel Prentiss). Criminal Law. (Little, Brown & Co., Boston, 1872.)

—— Law of Married Women. (L. B. & Co., 1875.)

—— Non-Contract Law. (Flood, Chicago, 1889.)

Blackstone (Sir Wm.). Commentaries on English Law, Book I.

Bliss (Philemon). Sovereignty. (Little, Brown & Co., Boston, 1885.)

Bluntschli (J. C.). Theory of the State. (Oxford, 1885.)

Bonwick (James). Daily Life and Origin of the Tasmanians. (London, 1870.)

Bracton (Henricus). De Legibus et Consuetudinibus Angliae.

Buckle (Henry T.). History of Civilization. (Appleton, New York, 1873.)

Burgess (John W.). Political Science and Constitutional Law. (Ginn, Boston and London, 1890.)

Burrell (Alexander N.). Law of Assignments for Creditors (Bishop's 3d Edition). (Baker, Voorhis & Co., New York, 1877.)

Caesar (Julius). De Bello Gallico.

California Supreme Court Reports, Volumes 3, 15, 43.

Chalmers (M. D.). Local Government. (English Citizen Series.)

Chitty (Joseph, Jr.). Law of Contracts (11th Am. Ed. by Perkins). (Hurd & Houghton, New York, 1874.)

Clark (E. C.). Practical Jurisprudence. (Cambridge University Press, 1883.)

Constitution of the United States.

Contemporary Review for 1881.

Cooley (Thomas M.). Law of Constitutional Limitations. (Little, Brown & Co., Boston, 1874.)

—— Law of Torts. (Callaghan, Chicago, 1880.)

Cope (E. D.) Origin of the Fittest. (Appleton, New York, 1887.)

Corssen (W.) Beiträge zur italischen Sprachkunde. (Teubner, Leipzig, 1876.)

Coulanges (Fustel de). Ancient City. (Trans. by Small.) (Lea & Shephard, Boston, 1889.)

Courtney (W. L.) Constructive Ethics. (London, 1886.)

Curtius (Ernst). History of Greece. (New York, 1886.)

Desty (Robert). Constitution of the United States. (Bancroft, San Francisco.)

—— Federal Procedure (6th Edition). (Bancroft, San Francisco.)

Dicey (A. V.). Introduction to the Study of the Law of the Constitution. (London, 1889.)

Digby (Sir Kenelm). History of the Law of Real Property. (Clarendon Press.)

Dos Passos (John R.). Law of Stockholders and Stock Exchanges. (Harper, New York, 1882.)

Duruy (Victor). History of Rome. (Jewett Publ. Co., Boston.)

Elphinstone (Howard Warburton). Rules for the Interpretation of Deeds. (Maxwell, London, 1885.)

Elton (Charles). Origins of English History. (Quaritch, London, 1882.)

Encyclopædia Britannica, Article 'Family.'

Endlich (G. A.). Interpretation of Statutes. (Linn, Jersey City, 1888.)

Engels (Friedrich). Der Ursprung der Familie, des Privateigenthums und des Staats. (Zürich, 1884.)

English Reports, Volume 2, Appeal Cases.

Errant (Joseph W.). Law Relating to Mercantile Agencies. (Johnsons, Philadelphia, 1889.)

Essays in Anglo-Saxon Law. (Little, Brown & Co., Boston, 1876.)

Fassel (Hirsch B.). Das mosäisch-rabbinische Civil-Recht. (Sommer, Wien, 1852.)

Federal Reporter, Volumes 1, 20, 28. (West Publishing Co., St. Paul, Minn.)

Felix (Ludwig). Der Einfluss der Natur auf die Entwickelung des Eigenthums. (Leipsic, 1883.)

—— Der Einfluss der Sitten und Gebraüche auf die Entwickelung des Eigenthums. (Leipsic, 1885.)

Fichte (J. G.). Science of Thought (Kroeger's Translation). (Lippincott, Philadelphia, 1869.)

Fiske (John). American Political Ideas. (Houghton, Mifflin & Co., Boston.)

—— Beginnings of New England. (Houghton, Mifflin & Co., Boston.)

—— Critical Period of American History. (Houghton, Mifflin & Co., Boston.)

—— Outlines of Cosmic Philosophy. (Houghton, Mifflin & Co., Boston.)

Florida Supreme Court Reports, Volume 20.

Fowler (Thomas). Progressive Morality. (Humboldt Library.)

—— Principles of Morality, Volume 2. (Oxford, Clarendon Press, 1889.)

Freeman (Edward A.). Chief Periods of European History. (Macmillan, London, 1886.)

—— Comparative Politics. (Macmillan, New York, 1874.)

—— English Towns and Districts. (Macmillan, London, 1883.)

—— Growth of the English Constitution. (Macmillan, London, 1876.)

Garlanda (F). Philosophy of Words. (New York, 1886.)

Gengler (H. G. Ph.). Deutsche Stadt-Rechte des Mittelalters. (Nürnberg, 1866.)

George (Henry). Progress and Poverty. (Appleton, New York, 1881.)

Gibbon (Edward). Decline and Fall of the Roman Empire (Milman's Edition). (Harper, New York, 1883.)

Goddard (John L.). Law of Easements (Bennet's Edition). (Houghton, Boston, 1880.)

Gommé (G. L.). The Village Community. (Contemporary Science Series.)

Gould (John M.). Law of Waters. (Callaghan, Chicago, 1883.)

Gneist (Rudolph). History of the English Constitution. (Putnam, New York City, 1886.)

Graham (William). Old and New Socialism. (International Scientific Series.)

Green's Brice on Ultra Vires. (Baker, New York City, 1880.)

Green (John Richard). Making of England. (Harper, New York, 1882.)

—— Norman Conqu.st. (Harper, New York, 1884.)

Green (T. H.). Prolegomena to Ethics. (Oxford, 1883.)

Griffis (William E.). The Mikado's Empire. (Harper, N. Y., 1883.)

Grimm (Jacob). Deutsche Rechtsalterthümer. (Göttingen, 1854.)

Hallam (Henry). Middle Ages. (New York, 1880.)

Hammond (William G.). Introduction to Sanders' Justinian.

Hanssen (George). Agrarhistorische Abhandlungen. (Vol. 1, Hirzel, Leipsic, 1880. Vol. 2, 1884.)

Hare (J. I.). American Constitutional Law. (Little, Brown & Co., Boston, 1889.)

—— Law of Contracts. (Little, Brown & Co., Boston.)

Harvard Law Review, Vol. 3, article by James B. Thayer.

Hearn (W. E.). Aryan Household. (Longmans, London, 1879.)

Heusler (Andreas). Der Ursprung der deutschen Stadtverfassung. (Böhlau, Weimar, 1872.)

Holland (Thomas Erskine). Elements of Jurisprudence. (Oxford, 1880.)

Holmes (O. W., Jr.). Common Law. (Little, Brown & Co., Boston, 1881.)

Holtzendorff. Encyclopædia, Systematischer Theil. (Leipsic, 1882.)

Hosmer (G. W.). People and Politics. (Osgood, Boston, 1883.)

Hosmer (James K.). Samuel Adams. (American Statesman Series.)

—— Anglo-Saxon Freedom. (Scribner, New York, 1890.)

House of Lords Cases, Volume 3.

Humphrey, Tennessee Supreme Court Reports, Volume 6.

Hunter (Wm. A.). Roman Law. (Maxwell, London, 1876.)

Ihering (Rudolph von). Besitzwille. (Fischer, Jena, 1889.)

—— Geist des römischen Rechts, etc. (Leipsic, Vol. 1, 1878, and Vol. 2, 1880, Vol. 3, 1877.)

—— Grund des Besitzschutzes. (Fischer, Jena, 1869.)

—— Zweck im Recht. (Leipsic, Vol. 1, 1884, Vol. 2, 1883.)

Iliad.

Illinois Supreme Court Reports, Volume 56.

Institutes of Justinian, Liber 2, Title 1.

Irish Reports, Common Law, Volume 2.

Jevons (W. Stanley). Money and the Medium of Exchange. (International Scientific Series.)

Johns Hopkins University Studies. Historical Series. Volumes 1 to 9 inclusive.

Johnston (Alexander). Connecticut. (American Commonwealth Series.)

Jones (Leonard A.). Law of Liens. (Houghton, Mifflin & Co., Boston, 1888.)

Kansas Supreme Court Reports, Volumes 20, 34.

Kant (Immanuel). Kritik der practischen Vernunft. (Leipsic, 1827.)

Keller (Ludwig von). Der römische Civil-Process und die Actionen (Wach Edition). (Tauchnitz, Leipsic, 1876.)

Kelley (John F.). Law of Contracts of Married Women. (Linn, Jersey City, 1882.)

Kitchin (John). Jurisdictions; or the Lawful Authority of Courts Leet, Courts Baron, etc. (Streater, London, 1663.)

Kuhn (Emil). Entstehung der Städte der Alten. (Leipsic, 1878.)

—— Städtische und bürgerliche Verfassung des römischen Reichs. (Leipsic, 1864.)

Lamprecht (Karl). Deutsche Geschichte, Vol. I. (Berlin, 1891.)

Landau (George). Die Territorien. (Perthes, Hamburg and Gotha, 1854.)

Lang (Andrew). Myth, Ritual and Religion.

Laveleye (Emile de). Primitive Property (Marriott's Edition). (Macmillan, London, 1878.)

Law Quarterly Review, Vols. 1, 3, 4, 5.

Lecky (W. E. H.). History of European Morals. (Appleton, New York, 1883.)

Leist (B. W.). Graeco-Italische Rechtsgeschichte. (Jena, 1884.)

—— Zur Geschichte des römischen Societas. (Jena, 1881.)

Lewes (George). Physical Basis of Mind. (Houghton, Osgood & Co., Boston.)

—— Problems of Life and Mind. (Houghton, Osgood & Co., Boston.)

—— Study of Psychology. (Houghton, Osgood & Co., Boston.)

Lewis (John). Law of Eminent Domain. (Callaghan, Chicago, 1888.)

Lieber (Francis). Civil Liberty and Self-Government. (Lippincott, Philadelphia, 1883.)

—— Hermeneutics (Hammond's Edition). (Thomas, St. Louis, Mo., 1880.)

Lindley (Sir Nathaniel). Law of Partnership (Ewell's Edition). (Callaghan, Chicago, 1881.)

Lindsay (W. Lauder). Mind in the Lower Animals. In Health, Vol. 1. (Appleton, New York, 1880.)

Littleton on Tenures (Coke's Commentary). (Philadelphia, 1853.)

Lubbock (Sir John). Ants, Bees and Wasps. (International Scientific Series.)

—— Prehistoric Times. (Appleton, New York, 1878.)

Luys (J.). The Brain and Its Functions. (International Scientific Series.)

Maine (Sir Henry S.). Ancient Law. (Scribner, New York; First Edition.)

—— Early History of Institutions. (Holt, New York, 1875.)

—— Early Law and Custom. (Holt, New York, 1883.)

—— Popular Government. (Holt, New York, 1886.)

—— Village Communities. (Murray, London, 1872.)

Maine Supreme Court Reports, Vol. 77.

Markby (William). Elements of Law. (Oxford, Clarendon Press, 1874.)

Marquardt (Joachim). Römische Staatsverwaltung. (Leipsic, Vol. 1, 1831; Vol. 2, 1884; Vol. 3, 1885.)

—— Privatleben der Roemer. (Hirzel, Leipzig, 1886.)

Marshall (W. E.). A Phrenologist among the Todas. (London, 1873.)

Martineau (James). Types of Ethical Theory. (Macmillan, 1886.)

Maryland Supreme Court Reports, Vol. 30.

Mason (David H.) A Short Tariff History of the United States. (Chicago, 1884.)

Maudsley (Henry). Body and Will. (Appleton, New York, 1884.)

—— Physiology and Pathology of the Mind. (Appleton, New York, 1876.)

Maurer (George L. von). Mark, Hof, Dorf und Stadt-vèrfassung. (Mark, 1886; Hof, Vols. 1 and 2, 1862, Vols. 3 and 4, 1863; Dorf, Vol. 1, 1865, Vol. 2, 1866; Stadt, Vol. 1, 1869, Vol. 2, 1870, Vol. 3, 1870, Vol. 4, 1871.)

May (H. W.). Law of Fraudulent Conveyances (Worthington's Edition). (Blackstone Pub. Company, Philadelphia, 1887.)

Mayer (Samuel). Rechte der Israeliten, Römer und Athener. (Leipsic, Vol. 1, 1862; Vol. 2, 1865.) Third volume not cited.

McLennan (John F.). Studies in Ancient History. (Qauritch, London, 1876.)

Meier and Schömann. Der Attische Process. (Calvary, Berlin, 1883-1887.)

Meitzen (August). Die Ausbreitung der Deutschen in Deutschland. (Jena, 1879.)

Michigan Supreme Court Reports, Vol. 38.

Miller (Samuel F.). Lectures on the Constitution of the United States. (Banks, New York, 1891.)

Miller (W. G.). Lectures on the Philosophy of Law. (London, 1884.)

Mills (Henry E.). Law of Eminent Domain. (Thomas, St. Louis, 1879.)

Mind, Vols. 8, 13.

Mississippi Supreme Court Reports, Vol. 63.

Mommsen (Theodore.) History of Rome.

Morgan (Lewis). Ancient Society. (Holt, New York, 1878.)

Narrative and Critical History of the United States, Vol. 4.

North Carolina Supreme Court Reports, Vol. 188. Devereux's Reports (same court), Vol. 2.

Northeastern Reporter, Vol. 12. (West Publishing Co., St. Paul.)

Northwestern Reporter, Vol. 34. (West Publishing Co., St. Paul.)

Odyssey.

Oregon Supreme Court Reports, Vol. 14.

Pacific Reporter, Vol. 13. (West Publishing Co., St. Paul.)

Palgrave (W. G.). Narrative of a Year's Journey through Central and Eastern Arabia. (London, 1866.)

Pennsylvania State Reports, Supreme Court, Vol. 87.

Perry (J. W.). Law of Trusts. (Little, Brown & Co., Boston, 1874.)

Petherick (J.). Egypt, the Soudan and Central Africa. (London, 1861.)

Pierce (Edward L.). Law of Railroads. (Little, Brown & Co., Boston, 1881.)

Platner (Edward). Beiträge zur Kenntniss des attischen Rechts. (Marburg, 1820.)

Political Science Quarterly Review, Vol. 3.

Pollock (Sir Frederick). Essays in Jurisprudence and Ethics. (Macmillan, London, 1882.)

—— Law of Contracts (Wald's Edition). (Clarke, Cincinnati, 1881.)

—— Law of Torts. (Blackstone Pub. Co., Philadelphia, 1887.)

—— Oxford Essays.

Poore (Ben Perley). Charters and Constitutions. (Government Printing Office, Washington, D. C.)

Porter (Noah). The Human Intellect.

Posnett (H. M.). Comparative Literature. (International Scientific Series.)

Post (Albert Herman). Bausteine für eine allgemeine Rechtswissenschaft. (Oldenburg, 1881.) Ursprung des Rechts. (Oldenburg, 1876.) African Jurisprudenz. (Oldenburg and Leipzig, 1887.)

Potter's Dwarris on Construction and Interpretation of Statutes. (Gould, Albany, N. Y., 1871.)

Puchta (G. F.). Cursus der Institutionen (Kruger's Edition). (Vol. 1, 1875; Vol. 2, 1881, Leipsic.)

Rawlinson (George). History of Ancient Egypt. (Estes & Lauriat, Boston, 1882.)

—— Seven Great Monarchies, Vol. 2. (Millar, New York, 1884.)

Réclus. Primitive Folk. (Contemporary Scientific Series, 1891.)

Réclus. Earth and its Inhabitants. Europe, Volume 1. (Appleton, New York, 1883.) Asia, Volume 1. (Appleton, New York, 1883.) Africa, Volume 1. (Appleton, New York, 1883.)

Ribot (Th.). Diseases of Memory. (International Scientific Series.)

—— Diseases of Will. (Humboldt Library Series, New York.)

Robinson (Conway). Institutions. (Richmond, Va.)

Roemer (Jean). Origins of the English Peoples and Languages. (Appleton, New York, 1888.)

Roescher (William). Political Economy. Translation by Lalor. (Callaghan, Chicago, 1882.)

Rogers (Thorold). Work and Wages. (Putnam, New York, 1884.)

Rogge (Karl A.). Ueber das Gerichtswesen der Germanen. (Halle, 1820.)

Romanes (George J.). Animal Intelligence. (International Scientific Series.)

—— Mental Evolution in Man. (Appleton, New York.)

Ross (Denman W.). Early History of Landholding among the Germans. (Soule, Boston, 1883.)

Sanders' Justinian (Hammond's Edition).

Savigny (Friedrich Carl von). Gesch. d. heutigen römischen Rechts, Volume 1. (Veit, Berlin, 1840.)

Schömann, (G. F.). Athenian Constitutional History (Bosanquet's Translation). (London, 1875.)

Schouler (James). Law of Personal Property. (Little, Brown & Co., Boston.)

—— Law of Husband and Wife. (Little, Brown & Co., Boston.)

Schrader (O.). Linguistisch-Historische Forschungen zur Handelsgeschichte und Warenkunde. (Jena, 1886.)

—— Sprachvergleichung und Urgeschichte. (Jena, 1890.)

Schwebel (Oskar). Deutsches Bürgerthum. (Berlin, 1883.)

Scroggs (Sir Wm.). Practice of Courts Leet and Courts Baron. (J. Nutt, Savoy, 1714.)

Scrutton (T. E.). Commons and Common Fields. (Cambridge Un. Press, 1887.)

—— Land in Fetters. (Cambridge Un. Press, 1886.)

—— Roman Law and the Law of England. (Cambridge Un. Press, 1885.)

Sedgwick (Theodore). Interpretation and Construction of Statutory Law and Constitutional Law. (Baker, New York, 1874.)

Seebohm (F.). The English Village Community. (Longmans, London, 1884.)

Shepherd's Touchstone.

Sidgwick (Henry). Method of Ethics. (Macmillan, London, 1877.)

Siegel (Heinrich). Geschichte des deutschen Gerichtsverfahrens. (Giessen, 1857.)

Smith (George H.). Right and Law. (Callaghan, Chicago, 1887.)

Smith (John W.). Mercantile Law. (Bancroft-Whitney, San Francisco.)

Smith (W. Robertson). The Religion of the Semites. (Appleton, New York, 1889.)

—— Kinship in Arabia. (Cambridge University Press, 1885.)

Spencer (Herbert). Data of Ethics. (Appleton, New York, 1880.)

—— Justice. (Appleton, New York, 1891.)

—— Man *v.* the State. (Appleton, New York, 1880.)

—— Essays, Moral, Political and Æsthetic. (Appleton, New York, 1884.)

—— Principles of Psychology. (Appleton, New York, 1878.)

—— Principles of Sociology. (Appleton, New York, Vol. 1, 1879, Vol. 2, 1883.)

Starcke (C. N.). Primitive Family. International Scientific Series.)

Stephen (Henry J.). Principles of Pleading (Tyler's Edition). (Morrison, Washington, 1882.)

Stephen (Sir James F.). History of Criminal Law in England. (Macmillan, London, 1883.)

Stephen (Leslie). Science of Ethics. (Smith, Elder & Co., London, 1882.)

Stubbs (William). Constitutional History of England. (Oxford Clarendon Press, Vol. 1, 1875.)

Sully (James). Illusions. (International Scientific Series.)

—— Sensation and Intuition. (Kegan Paul, London, 1880.)

Supreme Court of the United States, Reports. Dallas, Volume 2. Wheaton, Volume 6. Peters, Volume 2. Wallace, Volumes 4, 6, 7, 11, 16, 17, 20. United States, Volumes 101, 102, 117.

Tacitus. Germania.

Taylor (Hannis). Origin and Growth of the English Constitution. (Houghton, Mifflin & Co., Boston, 1889.)

Taylor (Hugh). The Morality of Nations. (Kegan Paul, London, 1888.)

Taylor (Isaac). The Alphabet. (Kegan Paul, London, 1883.)

—— The Origin of the Aryans. (Contemporary Science Series.)

—— Words and Places. (Macmillan, London, 1885.)

Taylor (Pitt). Law of Evidence. (Blackstone Pub. Co., Philadelphia.)

Texas Supreme Court Reports, Volumes 68, 70.

Tiedman (C. G.). Law of Real Property. (Thomas, St. Louis, 1884.)

Transactions of the Ethn ologicalSociety. (London.)

Tylor (E. B.). Anthropology. (Appleton, New York, 1881.)

United States Exploring Expedition, Report.

Von Holst (H.). Political and Constitutional History of the United States (Translation by John Lalor). (Callaghan, Chicago, beginning 1877.)

Wait (Frederick). Law of Fraudulent Conveyances and Creditors' Bills. (Baker, New York, 1884.)

Waitz (George). Deutsche Verfassungs-Geschichte, Volume 1, 1865. Volume 2, 1870. Volume 3, 1860. Volume 4, 1861. Volume 5, 1874. Volume 6, 1875. Volume 7, 1876. Volume 8, 1878.

Wallace (D. Mackenzie). Russia. (Holt, New York, 1878.)

Weeden (William B.). Economic and Social History of New England. (Houghton, Mifflin & Co., Boston, 1890.)

Wellhausen (Julius). History of Israel. (Black, Edinburgh.)

Wells (J. C.). Law of Res Adjudicata and Stare Decisis. (Mills, Des Moines, 1878.)

Westermarck (Edward). The History of Human Marriage, Part I. (Helsingfors, 1889.) This is now incorporated in a larger work upon the same subject, by the same author, published by Macmillan.

Wharton (Francis). Commentaries on American Law. (Kay, Philadelphia, 1884.)

—— Law of Evidence. (Kay, Philadelphia, 1877.)

Williams (Edward V.). Law of Executors. (Kay, Philadelphia, 1877.)

Wilson (Woodrow). Congressional Government. (Houghton, Boston, 1885.)

Wisconsin Supreme Court Reports, Volume 42.

Woolsey (Theodore). Political Science. (Scribner, New York, 1886.)

Wright (R. S.). Law of Criminal Conspiracies. (Blackstone Publishing Co., Philadelphia, 1887.)

Wundt (Wilhelm). Grundzüge der physiologischen Psychologie. (Engelmann, Leipsic, 1880.)

Year Books of 32 and 33 Edward I., edited by Alfred Harwood. (Longmans, London, 1864.)

Zimmern (Helen). The Hansa Towns. (Putnam, Story of Nations Series, N. Y.)

Zrodolowski (Ferdinand). Das römische Privatrecht. (Prague, 1877.)

INDEX.

A.

B.

C.

D.

E.

M.

N.

O.

Reprints of the Legal Classics Published by The Lawbook Exchange, Ltd.

☙Admiralty & Maritime Law ☙

Flanders, Henry. [1824-1911]. *A Treatise on Maritime Law.* Boston: Little, Brown and Company, 1852. xvi, 444 pp. Reprinted 1999 by The Lawbook Exchange, Ltd. ISBN 1-886363-72-2. Cloth. $75.

Kulsrud, Carl J. *Maritime Neutrality to 1780. A History of the Main Principles Governing Neutrality and Belligerency to 1780.* Boston: Little, Brown, and Company, 1936. x, 351 pp. LC 99-38825. ISBN 1-58477-027-9. Reprint available March 2000 by The Lawbook Exchange, Ltd. Cloth. New. $65.

Marsden. R.[eginald]. G.[odfrey], ed. *Documents Relating to Law and Custom of the Sea.* [n.p.]: The Navy Record Society, 1915-6. Two volumes. xxxiii, 561; xl, 457, [5] pp. Reprinted 1999 by The Lawbook Exchange, Ltd. LCCN 99-24138. ISBN 1-886363-96-X. Cloth. $175.

[Twiss, Sir Travers]. *The Black Book of the Admiralty, with an Appendix.* Monumenta Juridica. Edited by Sir Travers Twiss. Four volumes. 4, xciii, 491, [2]; 4, lxxxvii, 500, 31; 4, lxxxvi, 673, [1], 31; 4, clii, 559, 32 pp. LCCN 97-38809 ISBN 1-886363-39-0. 1871. Reprinted 1998 by The Lawbook Exchange, Ltd. Cloth. $495.

☙ Law & Literature ☙

Barton, Dunbar Plunket. *Shakespeare and the Law.* With a foreword by James M. Beck. Boston: Houghton Mifflin Company, 1929. xl, 167 pp. Reprint available October 1999 by The Lawbook Exchange, Ltd. LCCN 99-26602. ISBN 1-58477-000-7. Cloth. $60.

Darrow, Clarence. *A Persian Pearl. And Other Essays.* East Aurora, NY: The Roycroft Shop, 1899. 175 pp. Reprinted 1997 by The Lawbook Exchange, Ltd. ISBN 1-886363-27-7. Cloth. $50.

Darrow, Clarence S. *An Eye for an Eye.* New York: Fox Duffield & Company, 1905. 213 pp. Reprinted 1996 by The Lawbook Exchange, Ltd. ISBN 1-886363-07-2. Cloth. $40.

Davis, C.K. *The Law in Shakespeare.* Washington, D.C.: Washington Law Book Co., [1883]. 303 pp. Reprinted 1999 by The Lawbook Exchange, Ltd. ISBN 1-886363-75-7. Cloth. $60.

Gest, John Marshall. *The Lawyer in Literature.* London: Sweet & Maxwell, Limited, 1913. xii, 249 pp. Reprint available November 1999 by The Lawbook Exchange, Ltd. LCCN99-18365. ISBN 1-886363-90-0. Cloth. $60.

Holdsworth, William S. *Charles Dickens as a Legal Historian.* New Haven: Yale University Press, 1929. 157 pp. Reprinted 1995 by The Lawbook Exchange, Ltd. ISBN 1-886363-06-4. Cloth. $40.

☙ Legal Biography ☙

Foss, Edward. *A Biographical Dictionary of the Judges of England From the Conquest to the Present Time 1066-1870.* London: John Murray, 1870. xv, 792 pp. Reprint available December 1999 by The Lawbook Exchange, Ltd. LCCN 99-12577. ISBN 10886363-86-2. Cloth. $100.

Richards, John T. *Abraham Lincoln The Lawyer-Statesman.* Boston: Houghton Mifflin, 1916. Frontis. Illustrated. xii, 260 pp. Reprint available October 1999 by The Lawbook Exchange, Ltd. LCCN 99-20587. ISBN 1-886363-94-3. Cloth. $60.

☙ Legal Codes ☙

[Field Codes]. [New York 1850-1865]. New York Field Codes. 1850-1865.
Vol. I. *The Code of Civil Procedure of the State of New-York, Reported Complete by the Commissioners on Practice and Pleadings. 1850.*
Vol. II. *The Code of Criminal Procedure of the State of New York, Reported Complete by the Commissioners on Practice and Pleadings. 1850.*
Vol. III. *The Civil Code of the State of New York, Reported Complete by the Commissioners of the Code. 1865.*
Vol. IV. *The Penal Code of the State of New York, Reported Complete by the Commissioners of the Code. 1865.*
Vol. V. *The Political Code of the State of New York. 1860.*
With a new introduction by Michael Weber. Reprinted 1998 by The Lawbook Exchange, Ltd. Five volume series. [8], xcvi, 791; liii, [1], 486; cxii, 776; lxiv, 406, clxvii; xlvii, 607 pp. ISBN 1-886363-40-4 (set). Cloth. $495.

Livingston, Edward. *A System of Penal Law, for the State of Louisiana: Consisting of A Code of Crimes and Punishments, A Code of Procedure, A Code of Evidence, A Code of Reform and Prison Discipline, A Book of Definitions. Prepared Under the Authority of a Law of the Said State. To Which are Prefixed a Preliminary Report on the Plan of a Penal Code, and Introductory Reports to the Several Codes*

Embraced in the System of Penal Law. Philadelphia: James Kay, Jun. & Brother, 1833.v, 745 pp. Reprint available November 1999 by The Lawbook Exchange, Ltd. LCCN 99-11403. ISBN 1-886363-83-8. Cloth. $95.

☙ Legal Dictionaries ☙

Anderson, William C. *A Dictionary of Law, Consisting of Judicial Definitions and Explanations of Words, Phrases, and Maxims, and an Exposition of the Principles of Law: Comprising a Dictionary and Compendium of American and English Jurisprudence*. Chicago: T.H. Flood and Company, 1889. viii, 1140pp. Reprinted 1996 by The Lawbook Exchange, Ltd. ISBN 1-886363-23-4. Cloth. $125.

Black, Henry Campbell. *A Law Dictionary. Containing Definitions of the Terms and Phrases of American and English Jurisprudence, Ancient and Modern. And Including the Principal Terms of International, Constitutional, Ecclesiastical and Commercial Law, and Medical Jurisprudence, with a Collection of Legal Maxims, Numerous Select Titles from the Roman, Modern Civil, Scotch, French, Spanish, and Mexican Law, and Other Foreign Systems, and a Table of Abbreviations*. St. Paul, Minn.: West Publishing, 1910. 1314 pp. Reprinted 1995 by The Lawbook Exchange, Ltd. ISBN 1-886363-10-2. Cloth. $125.

Black, Henry Campbell. *A Dictionary of Law. Containing Definitions of the Terms and Phrases of American and English Jurisprudence, Ancient and Modern. Including the Principal Terms of International, Constitutional, and Commercial Law; with a Collection of Legal Maxims and Numerous Select Titles from the Civil Law and Other Foreign Systems*. St. Paul, Minn.: West Publishing, 1891. x, 1253 pp. Reprinted 1991 by The Lawbook Exchange, Ltd. ISBN 0-9630106-0-3. $125.

Bouvier, John. *A Law Dictionary Adapted to the Constitution and Laws of the United States of America, and of the Several States of the American Union; with References to the Civil and Other Systems of Foreign Law*. Philadelphia: T. & J.W. Johnson, 1839. Two volumes. 559; 28 pp. Reprinted 1993 by The Lawbook Exchange, Ltd. ISBN 0-9630106-7-0. Cloth. $130.

Burrill, Alexander M. *A New Law Dictionary and Glossary: Containing Full Definitions of the Principal Terms of the Common and Civil Law, Together with Translations and Explanations of the Various Technical Phrases in Different Languages, Occurring in the Ancient and Modern Reports, and Standard Treatises; Embracing Also All the Principal Common and Civil Law Maxims. Compiled on the Basis of Spelman's Glossary, and Adapted to the Jurisprudence of the United States; with Copious Illustrations, Critical and Historical*. New York: John S. Voorhies,

1850. Two volumes. xviii, 1099 pp. Reprinted 1998 by The Lawbook Exchange, Ltd. LC 97-38481. ISBN 1-886363-32-3. Cloth. $175.

Holthouse, Henry James. *A New Law Dictionary, Containing Explanations of Such Technical Terms and Phrases As Defined in the Works of Legal Authors, in the Practice of the Courts, and in the Parliamentary Proceedings of the Houses of Lords and Commons, To Which Is Added An Outline of An Action at Law and of A Suit in Equity. Edited, from the Second and Enlarged London Edition, With Numerous Additions, by Henry Penington.* Philadelphia: Lea and Blanchard, 1847. viii, [17]-495 pp. Reprinted 1999 by The Lawbook Exchange, Ltd. ISBN 1-886363-67-6. Cloth. $75.

Jacob, Giles. [1686-1744]. *The Law-Dictionary: Explaining the Rise, Progress, and Present State of the English Law; Defining and Interpreting the Terms or Words of Art; and Comprising Copious Information on the Subjects of Law, Trade, and Government. Corrected and Greatly Enlarged by T[homas] E[dlyne] Tomlins.* New York: Printed for, and Published by I. Riley, 1811. Originally six volumes, viii, 531; [2], 543; [2],618; [2], 472; [2], 553; [2], 471pp. Reprint available December 1999 by The Lawbook Exchange, Ltd. ISBN 1-886363-68-4. Cloth. $495.

Rapalje, Stewart and Lawrence, Robert L. *A Dictionary of American and English Law with Definitions of the Technical terms of the Canon and Civil Laws. Also, Containing a Full Collection of Latin Maxims, and Citations of Upwards of Forty Thousand Reported Cases, in which Words and Phrases Have Been Judicially Defined or Construed.* Jersey City: Frederick C. Linn & Co., 1888. Two volumes. xxxviii, 1380 pp. Reprinted 1997 by The Lawbook Exchange, Ltd. LC 97-38484. ISBN 1-886363-33-1. Cloth. $195.

Stimson, Frederic Jesup. *Glossary of Technical Terms, Phrases, and Maxims of the Common Law.* Boston: Little, Brown, and Company, 1881. iv, 305pp. Reprinted 1999 by The Lawbook Exchange, Ltd. ISBN 1-886363-70-6. Cloth. $60.

Tayler, Thomas. *The Law Glossary: Being a Selection of the Greek, Latin, Saxon, French, Norman and Italian Sentences, Phrases, and Maxims, Found in the Leading English and American reports, and Elementary Works.* New York: Lewis & Blood, 1856. 580 pp. Reprinted 1995 by The Lawbook Exchange, Ltd. ISBN 1-886363-12-9. Cloth. $65.

☙ Legal History ☙

Bar, Carl Ludwig von. *A History of Continental Criminal Law.* Boston: Little, Brown, and Company, 1916. lvi, 561 pp. Reprint available September 1999 by The Lawbook Exchange, Ltd. LCCN 99-32341. ISBN 1-58477-013-9. Cloth. $90.

[Brandeis, Louis D.]. *Brandeis on Zionism. A Collection of Addresses and Statements by Louis D. Brandeis with a Foreword by Mr. Justice Felix Frankfurter.* Washington, D.C.: Zionist Organization of America, [1942]. viii, 156 pp. Reprinted 1999 by The Lawbook Exchange, Ltd. ISBN 1-886363-60-9. Cloth. $65.

Calhoun, George M. *The Growth of Criminal Law in Ancient Greece.* Berkeley: University of California Press, 1927. x, 149 pp. LC 99-43192. ISBN 1-58477-037-6. Reprint available December 1999 by The Lawbook Exchange, Ltd. Cloth. New. $50.

Corwin, Edward. *The Doctrine of Judicial Review: Its Legal and Historical Basis and Other Essays.* Princeton: Princeton University Press, 1914. ix, 178 pp. Reprint available December 1999 by The Lawbook Exchange, Ltd. LCCN 99-32362. ISBN 1-58477-011-2. Cloth. $60.

Darrow, Clarence and William J. Bryan. The *World's Most Famous Court Trial. Tennessee Evolution Case. A Complete Stenographic Report of the Famous Court Test of the Anti-Evolution Act, at Dayton July 10 to 21, 1925, Including Speeches and Arguments of Attorneys.* Cincinnati: National Book Company, [1925]. [4], 339 pp. Reprinted 1997 by The Lawbook Exchange, Ltd. LC 97-38485. ISBN 1-886363-31-5. Cloth. $65.

Dawson, John P. *A History of Lay Judges.* Cambridge, Mass.: Harvard University Press, 1960. viii, [2], 310 pp. Reprinted 1999 by The Lawbook Exchange, Ltd. ISBN 1-886363-69-2. Cloth. $75.

Evans, E.P. *The Criminal Prosecution and Capital Punishment of Animals.* New York: E.P. Dutton, 1906. x, 384pp. Reprinted 1998 by The Lawbook Exchange, Ltd. LC 98-12801. ISBN 1-886363-52-8. Cloth. $65.

Forsyth, William. *History of Trial by Jury [Second edition].* Jersey City: Frederick D. Linn, [1875]. x, 388 pp. Reprinted 1994 by The Lawbook Exchange, Ltd. ISBN 0-9630106-8-9. Cloth. $65.

Forsyth, William. *The History of Lawyers. Ancient and Modern.* Boston: Estes & Lauriat, 1875. Illustrated. xvii, 404 pp. Reprinted 1996 by the Lawbook Exchange, Ltd. ISBN 1-886363-14-5. Cloth. $60.

Fortescue, Sir John. [?1394-1476?]. *The Governance of England: Otherwise Called The Difference between an Absolute and a Limited Monarchy. A Revised Text edited with Introduction, Notes, and Appendices by Charles Plummer.* London:

Oxford University Press, 1885. xxiii, 387pp. Reprinted 1999 by The Lawbook Exchange, Ltd. ISBN 1-886363-79-X. Cloth. $65.

Futrell, William H. *The History of American Customs Jurisprudence.* New York: Published privately, 1941. 314pp. Reprinted 1998 by The Lawbook Exchange, Ltd. LC 98-11342. ISBN 1-886363-51-X. Cloth. $60.

Greenidge, A.H.J. *The Legal Procedure of Cicero's Time.* Oxford: The Clarendon Press, 1901. xiii, 599 pp. Reprint available December 1999 by The Lawbook Exchange, Ltd. LCCN 99-26771. ISBN 1-886363-99-4. Cloth. $85.

Harper, Robert Francis. *The Code of Hammurabi King of Babylon. About 2250 B.C. Autographed Text transliteration...* Chicago: The University of Chicago Press, 1904. xxviii, 194, ciii (plates) pp. London: John Murray, 1832. xx, 392, lxxvi pp. Illus. LC 99-23953. ISBN 1-58477-003-1. Reprint available December 1999 by The Lawbook Exchange, Ltd. Cloth. New. $75.

Harris, Virgil M. *Ancient, Curious, and Famous Wills.* Boston: Little, Brown, and Company, 1911. xiv, 472 pp. Reprinted 1999 by The Lawbook Exchange, Ltd. LCCN 99-20588. ISBN 1-886363-93-5. Cloth. $75.

Henderson, Gerard Carl. *The Position of Foreign Corporations in American Constitutional Law. A Contribution to the History and Theory of Juristic Persons in Anglo-American Law.* Cambridge: Harvard University Press, 1918. xix, 199 pp. Reprint available November 1999 by The Lawbook Exchange, Ltd. LCCN 99-18233. ISBN 1-886363-89-7. Cloth. $50.

Holdsworth, William S. *Essays in Law and History.* Edited by A.L. Goodhart and H.G. Hanbury. Oxford: At the Clarendon Press, 1946. xv, 302 pp. Reprinted 1995 by The Lawbook Exchange, Ltd. ISBN 1-886363-13-7. Cloth. $50.

Holdsworth, W.S. *The Historians of Anglo-American Law.* New York: Columbia University Press, 1928. 175 pp. Reprinted 1994 by The Lawbook Exchange, Ltd. ISBN 0-9630106-9-7. Cloth. $50.

Johns, C.H.W. *Babylonian and Assyrian Laws, Contracts and Letters.* dinburgh: T. & T. Clark, 1904. xxii, 424 pp. LC 99-32862. ISBN 1-58477-022-8. Reprint available December 1999 by The Lawbook Exchange, Ltd. Cloth. New. $75.

Langdell, C.C. [1826-1906]. *A Selection of Cases on the Law of Contracts. with References and Citations. Prepared for Use as a Text-book in Harvard Law School.* Boston: Little, Brown & Co., 1871. xvi, 1022 pp. Reprint available

September 1999 by The Lawbook Exchange, Ltd. LCCN 99-28293. ISBN 1-58477-001-5. Cloth. $120.

[MacDonell, Sir John and Edward Manson]. *Great Jurists of the World.* Edited by Sir John MacDonell and Edward Manson. With an Introduction by Van Vechten Veeder. Boston: Little, Brown, and Company, 1914. Illustrated. xxxii, 607 pp. Reprinted 1997 by The Lawbook Exchange, Ltd. ISBN 1-886363-28-5. Cloth. $95.

Maitland, Frederick W., et.al. *A General Survey of Events, Sources, Persons & Movements in Continental Legal History. By Various European Authors.* With an introduction by Albert Kocourek. Boston: Little, Brown, 1912. liii, 754pp. Reprinted 1998 by The Lawbook Exchange, Ltd. LC 98-11159. ISBN 1-886363-47-1. Cloth. $110.

Maitland, Frederic William. *Roman Canon Law in the Church of England: Six Essays.* London: Methuen & Co., 1898. vii, 184 pp. Reprinted 1998 by The Lawbook Exchange, Ltd. LC 98-22357. ISBN 1-886363-57-9. Cloth. $65.

Maitland, Frederick W., et.al. *Select Essays in Anglo-American Legal History. By Maitland, Pollock, Holmes, Beale, Holdsworth and Others.* Boston: Little, Brown, and Company, 1907. Three volumes. 847; 823; 862 pp. Reprinted 1992 by The Lawbook Exchange, Ltd. LCCN 91-77977. ISBN 0-9630106-0-1. Cloth. $195.

Maitland, Frederick W., Montague, Francis C., *A Sketch of English Legal History.* Edited with Notes and Appendices by James F. Colby. New York: G.P. Putnam's Sons, 1915. x, 234pp. LCCN 98-11337. ISBN 1-886363-50-1. Reprinted 1998 by The Lawbook Exchange, Ltd. Cloth. $50.

Merriam, C.E., Jr. *History of the Theory of Sovereignty Since Rousseau.* New York: Columbia University Press, [1900]. x, [11]-233 pp. Reprinted 1999 by The Lawbook Exchange, Ltd. LCCN 98-32385. ISBN 1-886363-76-5. Cloth. $65.

[Nichols, J.]. *A Collection of all the Wills, Now Known to Be Extant, of the Kings and Queens of England, Princes and Princesses of Wales, and every Branch of the Blood Royal, from the Reign of William the Conqueror, to that of Henry the Seventh Exclusive: With Explanatory Notes and a Glossary.* London: J. Nichols, 1780. x, 434 pp. Reprinted 1999 by The Lawbook Exchange, Ltd. LCCN 99-17114. ISBN 1-886363-87-0. Cloth. $75.

Pollock, Frederick and Frederic William Maitland. *The History of English Law before the Time of Edward I.* Cambridge: Cambridge University Press, 1898. Two volumes. xxxviii, 688; xiv, 691 pp. Reprinted 1996 by The Lawbook Exchange, Ltd. ISBN 1-886363-22-6. Cloth. $165.

Reeve, Tapping. [1744-1823]. *The Law of Baron and Femme, of Parent and Child, Guardian and Ward, Master and Servant, and of the Powers of the Courts of Chancery; with an Essay on the Terms Heir, Heirs, Heirs of the Body. Third Edition, With Notes and References to English and American Cases by Amasa J. Parker and Charles E. Baldwin, Counselors-At-Law.* Albany: William Gould, 1862. xlvi, 677pp. LCCN 98-36057. ISBN 1-886363-58-7. Reprinted 1998 by The Lawbook Exchange, Ltd. Cloth. $75.

Sandys, Sir John Edwin. *Aristotle's Constitution of Athens. A Revised Text with an Introduction Critical and Explanatory Notes Testimonia and Indices. Second edition, Revised and Enlarged.* London: Macmillan & Co., Limited, 1902. xcii, 331 pp. Frontis. Illus. LC 99-23952. ISBN 1-58477-004-X. Reprint available March 2000 by The Lawbook Exchange, Ltd. Cloth. New. $75.

Schechter, Frank I. *The Historical Foundations of the Law Relating to Trade-Marks.* New York: Columbia University Press, 1925. xxviii, 211 pp. LC 99-41673. ISBN 1-58477-035-X. Reprint available December 1999 by The Lawbook Exchange, Ltd. Cloth. New. $60.

Schwartz, Bernard, editor. *The Code Napoleon and the Common-Law World. The Sesquicentennial Lectures Delivered at The Law Center of New York University December 13-15, 1954.* New York: New York University Press, 1956. x, 438pp. LCCN 98-34100. ISBN 1-886363-59-5. Reprinted 1998 by The Lawbook Exchange, Ltd. Cloth. $65.

Schwarz, Philip J. *Twice Condemned: Slaves and the Criminal Laws of Virginia, 1705-1865.* [Baton Rouge: Louisiana State University Press]. [1988]. xvi, 354pp. Reprinted 1998 by The Lawbook Exchange, Ltd. LCCN 98-4424 ISBN 1-886363-54-4. Cloth. $75.

Tucker, Henry St. George. *Commentaries on the Laws of Virginia. Comprising the Substance of a Course of Lectures Delivered to the Winchester Law School. With an Introduction by David Cobin and Paul Finkelman.* Richmond: Shepherd and Colin, 1846. Two volumes. 34, 468; 24, 512 pp. Reprinted 1998 by The Lawbook Exchange, Ltd. LCCN 97-10313. ISBN 1-886363-26-9. Cloth. $175.

Vinogradoff, Sir Paul. *Outlines of Historical Jurisprudence.* London: Oxford University Press, 1920. Two volumes. 428; x, 315 pp. Reprinted 1999 by The Lawbook Exchange, Ltd. LCCN 98-42298. ISBN 1-886363-64-1. Cloth. $150.

Walker, James. *The Theory of the Common Law.* Boston: Little, Brown and Co., 1852. xxiv, 130pp. Reprinted 1998 by The Lawbook Exchange, Ltd. LCCN 98-9522. ISBN 1-886363-45-5. Cloth. $65.

Warren, Charles. *History of the Harvard Law School and of Early Legal Conditions in America.* New York: Lewis Publishing Company, 1908. Three volumes. xiv, 543; iv, 560; 397 pp. Illustrated. Reprint available September 1999 by The Lawbook Exchange, Ltd. LCCN 99-29193. ISBN 1-58477-006-6. Cloth. $275.

Wiener, Leo. *Commentary to the Germanic Laws and Mediaeval Documents.* Cambridge: Harvard University Press, 1915. lxi, 224 pp. Reprint available October 1999 by The Lawbook Exchange, Ltd. LCCN 99-23969. ISBN 1-58477-005-8. Cloth. $60.

☙ Legal Reference and Bibliography ☙

Benedict, Russell. *Acts and Laws of the Thirteen Original Colonies and States: Constituting the extraordinary collection of Hon. Russell Benedict.* New York: American Art Association, 1922. [272]pp. Reprinted 1998 The Lawbook Exchange, Ltd. LCCN 98-20196 ISBN 1-886363-56-0. Cloth. $85.

Eller, Catherine Spicer. *The William Blackstone Collection in the Yale Law Library. A Bibliographical Catalogue.* New Haven: Yale University Press, 1938. Reprinted 1993 by the Lawbook Exchange, Ltd. xvii, 113 pp. Cloth. LCCN 99-38826. ISBN 0-9630106-5-4. $40.

Finkelman, Paul. *Slavery in the Courtroom. An Annotated Bibliography of American Cases.* Washington:Library of Congress, 1985. Illustrated. xxvii, 312pp. Reprinted 1998 by The Lawbook Exchange, Ltd. LCCN 98-11284. ISBN 1-886363-48-X. Cloth. $85.

Friend, William L. *Anglo-American Legal Bibliographies. An Annotated Guide.* Washington, D.C.: United States Government Printing Office, 1944. xii, 166 pp. Reprinted 1996 by The Lawbook Exchange, Ltd. ISBN 1-886363-21-8. Cloth. $65.

Hicks, Frederick. *Men and Books Famous in the Law. With an introduction by Harlan F. Stone.* Rochester, New York: Lawyers Co-operative Publishing, 1921. 259 pp. Reprinted 1992 by The Lawbook Exchange, Ltd. LCCN 92-070809. ISBN 0-9630106-2-X. Cloth.$50.

Jackson, E. Hilton. *Latin for Lawyers. Containing I: A Course in Latin, with Legal Maxims and Phrases As a Basis of Instruction. II. A Collection of Over One Thousand Latin Maxims, with English Translations, Explanatory Notes, and Cross-References. III. A Vocabulary of Latin Words.* London: Sweet & Maxwell, 1915. viii, 300 pp. Reprinted 1992 by The Lawbook Exchange, Ltd. LCCN 92-074408. ISBN 0-9630106-4-6. Cloth. $50.

McNamara, M. Frances. *Ragbag of Legal Quotations.* Albany: Matthew Bender & Company, 1960. xi, 334 pp. Reprinted 1992 by The Lawbook Exchange, Ltd. LC 92-074141. ISBN 0-9630106-3-8. Cloth. $50.

Maxwell, W. Harold and C.R. Brown. *A Complete List of British and Colonial Law Reports and Legal Periodicals. Arranged in Alphabetical and in Chronological Order with Bibliographical Notes.* **[With]:** *Check List of Canadian and Newfoundland Statutes.*[Third Edition]. Toronto: The Carswell Company, Limited, 1937. viii, 141, 49 pp. Reprinted 1995 by The Lawbook Exchange, Ltd. ISBN 1-886363-11-0. Cloth. $70.

[Worrall, John and Edward Brooke]. *Bibliotheca Legum Angliae. Or, a Catalogue of the Common and Statute Law Books of This Realm, and Some Others Relating Thereto: Giving an Account of Their Several Editions, Ancient Printers, Dates, and Prices, and Wherein They Differ. [With a Supplement to 1800]. Part I Compiled by John Worrall, Part II and Supplement Compiled by Edward Brooke. Parts I, II and Supplement bound in one volume.* London: Printed for Edward Brooke, 1788-1800. 316; 264; 48 pp. 1788-1800. Reprinted 1997 by The Lawbook Exchange, Ltd. ISBN 1-886363-29-3. Cloth. $110.

☙ Legal Sources ☙

Bouvier, John. [1787-1851]. *Institutes of American Law. New Edition by Daniel A. Gleason. In Two Volumes.* Boston:Little, Brown, & Company, 1880. Two volumes. lxviii, 651; iv, 798pp. Reprint available December 1999 by The Lawbook Exchange, Ltd. LCCN 98-54288. ISBN 1-886363-80-3. Cloth. $265.

[Cardozo, Benjamin]. *Law is Justice. Notable Opinions of Mr. Justice Cardozo.* Foreword by Robert F. Wagner. Edited by A.L. Sainer. New York: Ad Press Ltd., [1938]. xvii, 441 pp. Frontis. Reprint available September 1999 by The Lawbook Exchange, Ltd. LCCN 99-34154. ISBN 1-58477-010-4. Cloth. $75.

[Cherokee Laws]. *Compiled Laws of the Cherokee Nation.* Tahlequah, I.T.:National Advocate Print, 1881. 370pp. LC 98-12741. ISBN 1-886363-42-0. Reprinted 1998 by The Lawbook Exchange, Ltd. With a new introduction by Michael Weber. Cloth. $60.

Coke, Edward, Sir. *The First Part of the Institutes of the Laws of England, or, A commentary upon Littleton...* London, J. & W.T. Clarke, 1823. Two volumes. ccxvi,[606]; iv, [772] pp. LC 99-41675. ISBN 1-58477-033-3. Reprint available December 1999 by The Lawbook Exchange, Ltd. Cloth. New. $195.

Fortescue, John. *DeLaudibus Legum Angliae. A Treatise in Commendation of the Laws of England.* With Translation by Francis Gregor. Notes by Andrew Amos and a Life of the Author by Thomas (Fortescue) Lord Clermont. Cincinnati: Robert Clarke & Co., 1874. Reprint available September 1999 by The Lawbook Exchange, Ltd. LCCN 99-16485. ISBN 1-58477-019-8. Cloth. $65.

[St. Germain, Christopher]. [1460-1540]. *The Doctor and Student or Dialogues Between a Doctor of Divinity and a Student in the Laws of England Containing the Grounds of Those Laws Together with Questions and Cases Concerning the Equity Thereof Revised and Corrected by William Muchall, Gent. to which are added two pieces concerning Suits in Chancery by Subpoena.* Cincinnati:Robert Clarke & Co., 1874. xiv, 401pp. Reprinted 1998 by The Lawbook Exchange, Ltd. LCCN 98-11338. ISBN 1-886363-49-8. Cloth. $65.

Woodbine, George E. *Four Thirteenth Century Law Tracts. A Thesis Presented to the Faculty of the Graduate Schol of Yale University in Candidacy for the Degree of Doctor of Philosophy.* New Haven: Yale University Press, 1910. vi, 183 pp. Reprint available October 1999 by The Lawbook Exchange, Ltd. LCCN 99-29294. ISBN 1-58477-007-4. Cloth. $50.

☙ *Legal Treatises* ☙

Beck, Theodric Romeyn. *Elements of Medical Jurisprudence.* Albany: Websters and Skinners, 1823. Two volumes. xxxiv, 418; viii, [9]-471 pp. Reprinted 1997 by The Lawbook Exchange, Ltd. ISBN 1-886363-24-2. Cloth. $125.

Calabresi, Guido. *A Common Law for the Age of Statutes.* Cambridge: Harvard University Press, 1982. xi, 319 pp. LC 99-44889. ISBN 1-58477-040-6. Reprint available December 1999 by The Lawbook Exchange, Ltd. Cloth. New. $85.

Freeman, A.C. *A Treatise of the Law of Judgments. Including All Final Determinations of the Rights of Parties in Actions or Proceedings at Law or in Equity. Revised, and Greatly Enlarged by Edward W. Tuttle.* San Francisco: Bancroft-Whitney, 1925. Three volumes. 1216; 1280; 1264 pp. Reprinted 1993 by The Lawbook Exchange, Ltd. ISBN 0-9630106-6-2. Cloth. $295.

Gilmore, Grant. *Security Interests in Personal Property.* Boston: Little, Brown & Company, 1965. Two volumes. xxxiv, 651; xiii, 653-1508 pp. Reprinted

1999 by The Lawbook Exchange, Ltd. LCCN 99-10258. ISBN 1-886363-81-1. Cloth. $195.

Pomeroy, John N. *A Treatise on Equity Jurisprudence As Administered in the United States of America. Adapted for All the States and to the Union of Legal and Equitable Remedies under the Reformed Procedure.* San Francisco and New York: Bancroft-Whitney and Lawyers Cooperative, 1941. Five volumes. 914; 1134; 1063; 1104; 716 pp. Reprinted 1995 by The Lawbook Exchange, Ltd. ISBN 1-886363-05-6. Cloth. $450.

Pothier, Robert Joseph [1699-1772]. *A Treatise on Obligations, Considered in a Moral and Legal View. Translated from the French of Pothier. Translated by Francois-Xavier Martin.* Newburn, N.C.: Martin & Ogden, 1802. Reprint available December 1999 by The Lawbook Exchange, Ltd. With a new introduction by Warren M. Billings. LC 98-38360. ISBN 1-886363-62-5. Cloth. $75.

Pothier,R.J. *Treatise on the Contract of Sale.* Translated from the French by L.S. Cushing. Boston: Charles C. Little and James Brown, 1889. xvi, 406 pp. LC 99-10260. ISBN 1-886363-82-X. Reprint available December 1999 by The Lawbook Exchange, Ltd. Cloth. New. $70.

[Ricardo, David]. McCulloch, J.R. *The Works of David Ricardo, Esq., M.P. with a Notice of the Life and Writings of the Author.* London: John Murray, 1846. xxxiii, 584 pp. LC 99-39612. ISBN 1-58477-028-7. Reprint available March 2000 by The Lawbook Exchange, Ltd. Cloth. New. $90.

Sears, John H. *Trust Estates as Business Companies. [Second Edition].* Kansas City, Mo.:Vernon Law Book Company, 1921. xx, 782 pp. [1921]. Reprinted June 1998 by The Lawbook Exchange, Ltd. LCCN 97-32423 ISBN 1-886363-41-2. Cloth. $95.

Philosophy of Law

Austin, John. *The Province of Jurisprudence Determined.* London: John Murray, 1832. xx, 392, lxxvi pp. LC 99-33457. ISBN 1-58477-023-6. Reprint available December 1999 by The Lawbook Exchange, Ltd. Cloth. New. $75.

Fuller, Lon L. *The Law in Quest of Itself.* Boston: Beacon Press, 1966. [vi], 150 pp. Reprint available October 1999 by The Lawbook Exchange, Ltd. LCCN 99-32863. ISBN 1-58477-016-3. Cloth. $45.

Jhering, Rudolf Von. *Law as a Means to an End.* Translated from the German by Isaac Husik with an Editorial Preface by Joseph H. Drake and with Introductions by Henry Lamm and W.M. Geldart. Boston: The Boston Book Company, 1913. lxi, 483 pp. Reprint available September 1999 by The Lawbook Exchange, Ltd. LCCN 99-23754. ISBN 1-58477-009-0. Cloth. $80.

Jhering, Rudolph von. *The Struggle for Law. Translated from the Fifth German Edition by John J. Lalor. Second Edition, with an Introduction by Albert Kocourek.* Chicago: Callaghan and Company, 1915. lii, 138 pp. Reprinted 1997 by The Lawbook Exchange, Ltd. ISBN 1-886363-25-0. Cloth. $60.

Kelsen, Hans. [1881-1973]. *General Theory of Law and State.* Translated by Anders Wedberg. Cambridge: Harvard University Press, 1945. xxxiii, 516pp. LCCN 98-32334. ISBN 1-886363-74-9. Reprinted 1999 by The Lawbook Exchange, Ltd. Cloth. $75.

Vinogradoff, Paul. *Custom and Right.* Oslo: H. Aschehoug, 1925. 110 pp. LC 99-0474851. ISBN 1-58477-048-1. Reprint available March 2000 by The Lawbook Exchange, Ltd. Cloth. New. $45.

☙ Special Editions☙

Stokes, I.N. Phelps. *The Iconography of Manhattan Island 1498-1909.* New York: Robert H. Dodd, 1915. Six volumes. Reprinted 1998 by The Lawbook Exchange, Ltd. LCCN 97-30604. ISBN 1-886363-30-7. Cloth. $750.

☙ U.S. Constitutional History ☙

Bauer, Elizabeth Kelley. *Commentaries on the Constitution 1790-1860.* New York: Columbia University Press, 1952. 400 pp. Reprinted 1999 by The Lawbook Exchange, Ltd. LCCN 98-45409. ISBN 1-886363-66-8. Cloth. $75.

Beard, Charles A. *The Supreme Court and the Constitution.* New York: The Macmillan Company, 1912. vii, 127 pp. Reprinted 1999 by The Lawbook Exchange, Ltd. LCCN 98-50368. ISBN 1-886363-78-1. Cloth. $45.

Bondy, William. *Separation of Governmental Powers in History, in Theory, and in the Constitutions.* New York: Columbia College, 1896. Reprinted 1999 by The Lawbook Exchange, Ltd. vi,[7]-185, [1] pp. LCCN 98-44994. ISBN 1-886363-65-X. Cloth. $65.

Cohn, Morris M. *An Introduction to the Study of the Constitution; A Study showing the play of Physical and Social Factors in the Creation of Institutional Law.* Baltimore: The Johns Hopkins Press, 1892. xi, 235 pp. LC 99-38730. ISBN 1-58477-032-5. Reprint available March 2000 by The Lawbook Exchange, Ltd. Cloth. New. $50.

Cooley, Thomas McIntyre. *A Treatise on the Constitutional Limitations Which Rest Upon the Legislative Power of the States of the American Union. [1st edition].* Boston: Little, Brown, and Co., 1868. xlvii, 720pp. Reprinted 1999 by The Lawbook Exchange, Ltd. LCCN 99-20589. ISBN 1-886363-92-7. Cloth. $95.

Cooley, Thomas M. *A Treatise on the Constitutional Limitations which Rest Upon the Legislative Power of the States of the American Union. Fifth edition.* Boston: Little, Brown, and Co., 1883. lxxxi, 886pp. Reprinted October 1998 by The Lawbook Exchange, Ltd. LCCN 98-12730. ISBN 1-886363-53-6. Cloth. $120.

Dodd, Walter Fairleigh. *The Revision and Amendment of State Constitutions.* Baltimore: The Johns Hopkins Press, 1910. xvii, 350 pp. Reprinted 1999 by The Lawbook Exchange, Ltd. ISBN 1-886363-73-0. Cloth. $65.

Duer, William Alexander. *A Course of Lectures on the Constitutional Jurisprudence of the United States; Delivered Annually in Columbia College, New York. The Second Edition, Revised, Enlarged, and Adapted to Professional as well as General Use.* Boston: Little, Brown & Co., 1856. xxiv, 545 pp. LC 99-16385. ISBN 1-58477-020-1. Reprint available December 1999 by The Lawbook Exchange, Ltd. Cloth. New. $85.

Fisher, Sydney George. *The Evolution of the Constitution of the United States. Showing That It Is a Development of Progressive History and Not an Isolated Document Struck Off at a Given Time or an Imitation of English or Dutch Forms of Government.* Philadelphia: J.B. Lippincott, 1897. 398 pp. Reprinted 1996 by The Lawbook Exchange, Ltd. LCCN 97-41054. ISBN 1-886363-08-0. Cloth. $65.

Flanders, Henry. *An Exposition of the Constitution of the United States. Designed as a Manual of Instruction.* Philadelphia: E.H. Butler & Co., 1860. xii, 311 pp. Reprint available October 1999 by The Lawbook Exchange, Ltd. LCCN 99-31594. ISBN 1-58477-014-7. Cloth. $60.

Ford, Paul Leicester. *Pamphlets on the Constitution of the United States, Published During Its Discussion by the People 1787-1788.* Brooklyn, N.Y., 1888. viii, 451 pp. LC 99-25089. ISBN 1-886363-95-1. Reprint available March 2000 by The Lawbook Exchange, Ltd. Cloth. New. $75.

[Madison, James]. Hunt, Gaillard, Scott, James Brown. *The Debates in The Federal Convention of 1787 Which Framed the Constitution of the United States of America.* New York: Oxford University Press, 1920. xcvii, [1], 731 pp. Reprinted 1999 by The Lawbook Exchange, Ltd. LCCN 98-51911. ISBN 1-886363-77-3. Cloth. $110.

Minor, Raleigh C. *Notes on the Science of Government and the Relations of the States to the United States.* [Charlottesville]: University of Virginia, 1913. x, 171 pp. Reprinted 1995 by The Lawbook Exchange,Ltd. ISBN 1-886363-09-9. Cloth. $40.

Story, Joseph. [1779-1845]. *A Familiar Exposition of the Constitution of the United States: Containing a Brief Commentary on Every Clause, Explaining the True Nature, reasons, and Objects Thereof; Designed for the Use of School, Libraries and General Readers. With an Appendix, Containing Important Public Documents, Illustrative of the Constitution.* New York: Harper & Brothers: 1865. 372 pp. Reprinted 1999 by The Lawbook Exchange, Ltd. ISBN 1-886363-71-4. Cloth. $60.

[Taylor, John]. [1753-1824]. *A Defence of the Measures of the Administration of Thomas Jefferson. By Curtius.* Washington: Samuel H. Smith, 1804. 136 pp. Reprinted 1999 by The Lawbook Exchange, Ltd. LCCN 99-24139. ISBN 1-886363-97-8. Cloth. $60.

Taylor, John. *Construction Construed and Constitutions Vindicated.* Richmond:printed by Shepherd & Pollard, 1820. iv, 344pp. Reprinted 1998 by The Lawbook Exchange, Ltd. LCCN 97-49411. ISBN 1-886363-43-9. Cloth. $65.

Taylor, John. *An Inquiry into the Principles and Policy of the Government of the United States.* Fredericksburg:Green and Cady, 1814. With an introduction by Roy Franklin Nichols, Yale University Press, 1950. 562pp. Reprinted 1998 by The Lawbook Exchange, Ltd. LCCN 98-11147. ISBN 1-886363-46-3. Cloth. $75.

Tucker, St. George. *Blackstone's Commentaries. With Notes of Reference to the Constitution and Laws, of the Federal Government of the United States, and of the Commonwealth of Virginia. In Five Volumes, with an Appendix to Each volume, Containing Short Tracts upon Such Subjects As Appeared Necessary to Form a Connected View of the Laws of Virginia As a Member of the Federal Union.* Philadelphia: William Young Birch and Abraham Small, 1803. Five volumes. Reprinted 1996 by The Lawbook Exchange, Ltd. ISBN 1-886363-15-3. Cloth. $450.

[Upshur, Abel Parker]. *A Brief Enquiry Into the True Nature and Character of Our Federal Government, being a review of Judge Story's Commentaries on the Constitution of the United States. By a Virginian.* Petersburg: Printed by Edmund and Julian C. Ruffin, 1840. 132pp. Reprinted 1998 by The Lawbook Exchange, Ltd. LCCN 97-11151. ISBN 1-886363-44-7. Cloth. $45.

Wright, John S. *Citizenship Sovereignty.* Chicago: Published for American Citizens, the True Maintainers of State Sovereignty, 1864. Reprinted 1998 by The Lawbook Exchange, Ltd. LCCN 98-15940 ISBN 1-886363-55-2. Cloth. $65.